PILGRIMS' LONDON

Discover London's rich Christian heritage with the help of this thoroughly practical book, packed full of interesting sites to visit: historic churches, statues, monuments, gravestones, portraits . . .

London has been home to many great Christian personalities, and here some of the worldwide confessions — Baptists, Methodists, Salvationists — were born. The city is full of reminders of lives and events. Piece the story together with the help of this book. Easy-to-follow maps locate the sites. A-Z pen portraits introduce the movements and personalities. Each historical period has its own introduction. All sorts of things are explained, from styles of church architecture to when the museums are open.

ROBERT BAYLIS is a Californian with a lifetime love for British history and literature. He has visited London repeatedly over many years, and conducted tours of London's history.

Pilgrims' London

Robert H. Baylis

A LION BOOK

Oxford · Batavia · Sydney

Copyright © 1990 Robert H. Baylis

Published by
Lion Publishing plc
Sandy Lane West, Littlemore, Oxford, England
ISBN 0 7459 1645 7
Albatross Books Pty Ltd
PO Box 320, Sutherland, NSW 2232, Australia
ISBN 0 7324 0215 8

First edition 1990

British Library Cataloguing in Publication Data
Baylis, Robert H.
Pilgrim's London.
1. London. Places with Christian associations – Visitors'
guides
1. Title
914.21'04858

ISBN 0-7459-1645-7

Printed and bound in Great Britain
by Cox & Wyman Ltd, Reading

Contents

Introduction

There are three cities in the world which are the supreme objects of Christian pilgrimage: Jerusalem, Rome and London.

Pilgrimage to Jerusalem began very early. The first recorded pilgrim was Alexander, a friend of the famous theologian Origen, who went in 212 'for the sake of prayer and the investigation of the places'. Origen himself visited twice, first in AD216 and again in 231. Pilgrimage to Palestine became very popular after the Edict of Milan in 413. The most celebrated of these intrepid Western visitors was Helena, the mother of the Emperor Constantine. She founded the Church of the Holy Sepulchre built over the empty tomb of our Lord. It is still one of the Holy City's most revered shrines. The Muslim conquest of the seventh century put a stop to western visits for a while, and the twelfth and thirteenth centuries saw numerous bloody battles fought over the City of Peace. In the 1840s Thomas Cook took the first party of modern tourists to view the biblical sites, and today Jerusalem is an object of pilgrimage for millions of Christians from around the world.

Rome became the capital of the Roman Catholic Church in 451. But long before this pilgrims had made their way there to visit the places where the bones of the apostles and martyrs were laid. The two great pilgrimage sites were exactly as today—the tombs, or memorials, of St Peter upon the Vatican Hill and the tomb of St Paul off the Ostian Way. The early pilgrim would lower a cloth down the shaft leading to Peter's tomb below, on the site where now is Bernini's magnificent baldacchino and above the mighty dome built by Michelangelo. In the Middle Ages as today, too, the pilgrim made a round of seven churches: St Peter's, St Paul's Outside the Walls, St Mary Major, St John Lateran, Holy Cross in Jerusalem, St Lawrence-Outside-the-Walls and St Sebastian on the Appian Way. He or she could also visit the Holy Staircase, the steps brought from the palace of Pilate by St Helena.

London enshrines an historical and physical record of Christianity altogether different from either Jerusalem or Rome, yet equally important. Almost certainly the Christian faith reached here almost as early as Rome. Here one may visit churches founded during the so-called Dark Ages and walk the aisles of medieval structures as fine as any in Europe. But more importantly, London is the city of the English Reformation, where the earliest Bibles in English were circulated (and burned) and where martyrs paid the extreme penalty to remain true to the Word of God. Here, too, the Church of England was born, and at least four Protestant denominations came into being as underground 'conventicles'. Here Wren and his contemporaries raised from among the ashes nearly three score of the most unique Renaissance church buildings in the world. And most important of all, this great city of London has been the scene of periodic spiritual awakenings based on the gospel of Jesus, a tradition still very much alive today.

So this book is an invitation to discover 'Pilgrims' London' for yourself. If you have a spare morning or afternoon, or day, or week — or lifetime — you won't begin to see it all.

Robert H. Baylis

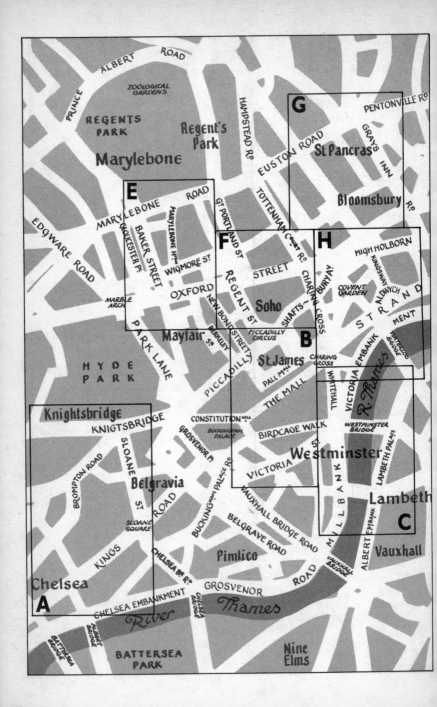

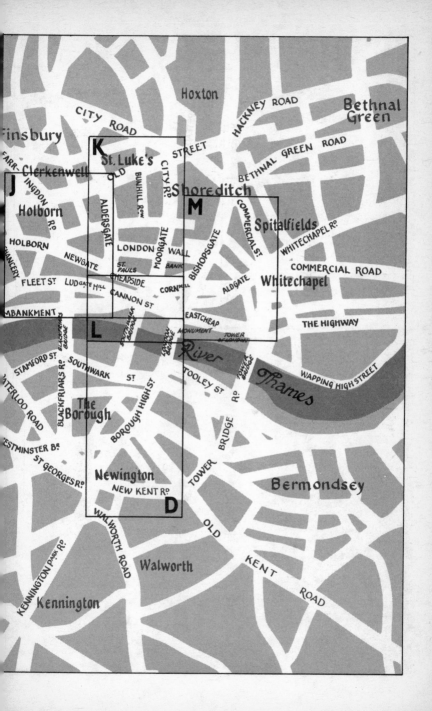

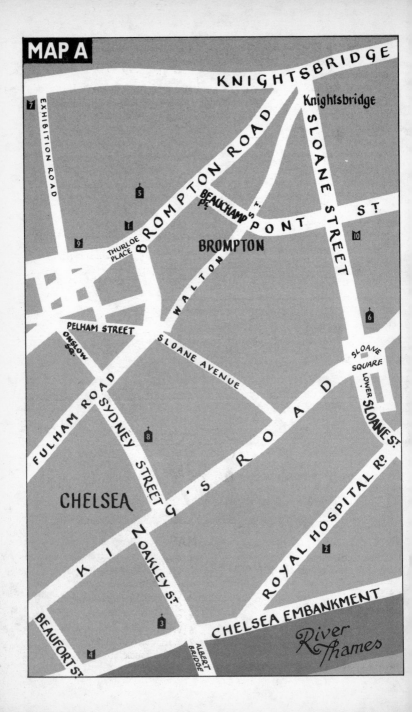

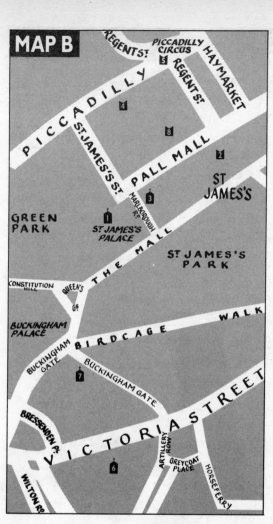

MAP B

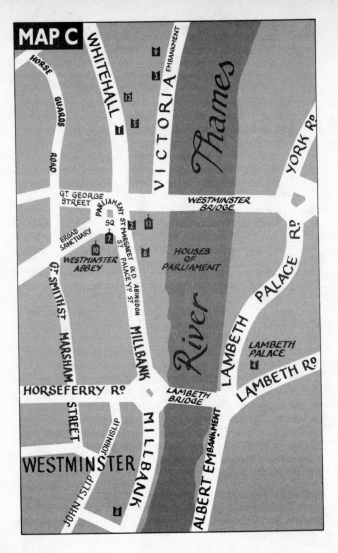

MAP C

1 Cenotaph
2 Cromwell, Oliver, statue (outside Westminster Hall)
3 Gordon, General, statue
4 Lambeth Palace
5 Raleigh, Walter, statue
6 Richard I, statue, Old Palace Yard

7 St Margaret, Westminster
8 Tate Gallery
9 Tyndale, William, statue
10 Westminster Abbey
11 Westminster Hall with St Mary Undercroft
12 Whitehall Banqueting House

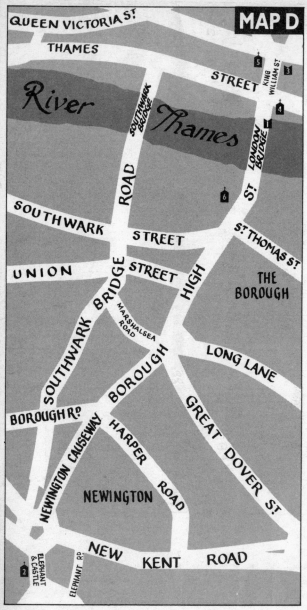

MAP D

1 London Bridge
2 Metropolitan Tabernacle, Elephant & Castle
3 Monument, The
4 St Magnus, London Bridge
5 St Martin Orgar, Martin Lane (tower only)
6 Southwark Cathedral

13

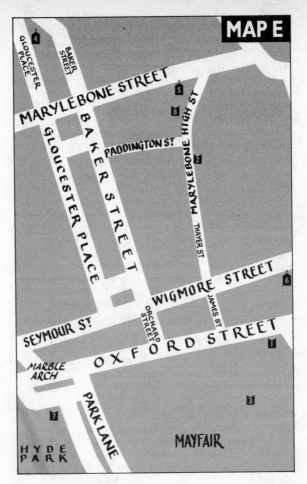

MAP E

1 Blake's Residence, 17 South Moulton Street
2 Dickens' Residence, Marylebone High Street
3 Handel's Residence, 25 Brook Street
4 St Cyprian, Clarence Gate
5 St Marylebone Parish Church
6 St Peter, Vere Street
7 Speaker's Corner, Marble Arch
8 Wesley, Charles, monument, Old Marylebone Churchyard

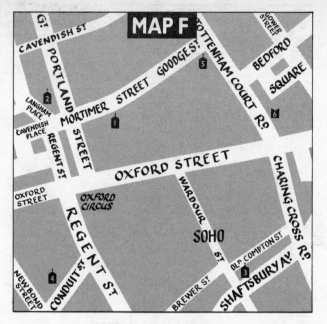

MAP F

1 All Saints, Margaret Street
2 All Souls, Langham Place
3 St Anne, Soho (Dorothy Sayers' grave)
4 St George, Hanover Square
5 Whitefield Memorial Church (site of old Tabernacle)
6 YMCA (Chas. Williams' portrait)

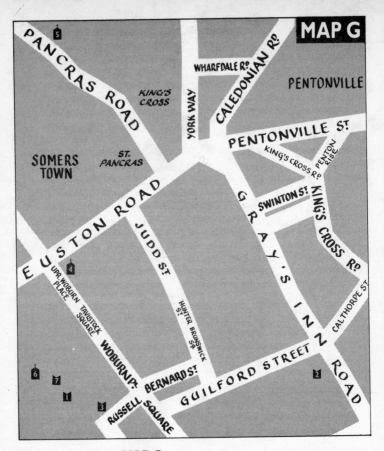

MAP G

1 Courtauld Galleries
2 Dickens, Charles, house & library,
  48 Doughty Street
3 T.S. Eliot plaque
4 St Pancras, New Church
5 St Pancras, Old Church
6 University Church of Christ the King
7 Williams, Dr, Theological Library

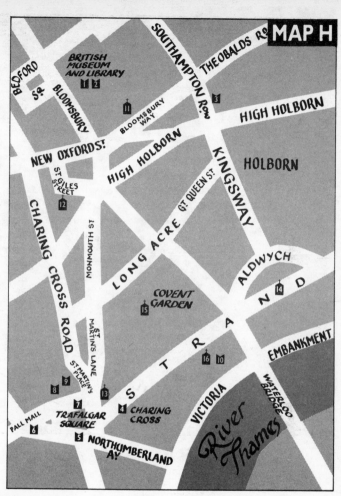

MAP H

1 British Library
2 British Museum
3 Bunyan, John, statue, Baptist Church House, Southampton Row
4 Charing Cross
5 Charles I on Horseback, statue (site of old Charing Cross)
6 George III on horseback, statue
7 James II statue
8 National Gallery
9 National Portrait Gallery
10 Raikes, Robert, statue, Victoria Embankment
11 St George, Bloomsbury
12 St Giles-in-the-Fields
13 St Martin-in-the-Fields
14 St Mary-le-Strand
15 St Paul's, Covent Garden
16 Savoy Chapel

17

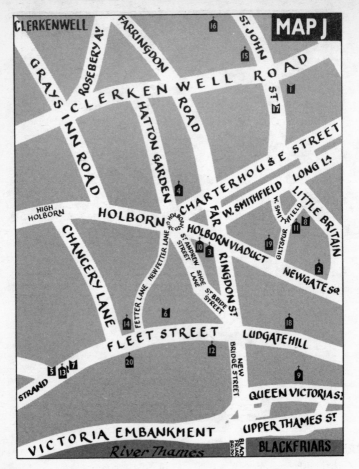

MAP J

1 The Charterhouse
2 Christ Church, Newgate Street (tower & ruins)
3 City Temple
4 Ely Chapel (St Etheldreda Catholic Chapel)
5 Gladstone Monument
6 Samuel Johnston's house
7 Samuel Johnson, statue
8 Martyrs' Memorial, Smithfield
9 St Andrew by-the-Wardrobe
10 St Andrew, Holborn
11 St Bartholomew-the-Less
12 St Bride, Fleet Street
13 St Clement Danes
14 St Dunstan's-in-the-West, Fleet Street
15 St James, Clerkenwell
16 St John, Clerkenwell
17 St John's Gate
18 St Martin-within-Ludgate
19 St Sepulchre
20 Temple Church

MAP K

1. Bunhill Fields Burying Ground
2. Dutch Church, Austin Friars
3. Fox, George, grave
4. Museum of London, Barbican
5. Old Jewry
6. St Alban, Wood Street (tower only)
7. St Alphage, London Wall (tower only)
8. St Anne & St Agnes, the Lutheran Church
9. St Bartholomew-the-Great, Smithfield
10. St Botolph, Aldersgate
11. St Giles, Cripplegate
12. St Lawrence, Jewry
13. St Margaret, Lothbury
14. St Mary, Aldermanbury (garden site only)
15. St Olave, Jewry (tower incorporated into new buildings)
16. St Vedast, Foster Lane
17. Wesley's Chapel, house, statue and monument, City Road

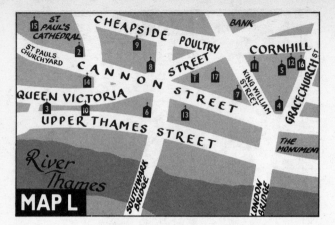

MAP L

1 Mithraic Temple
2 St Augustine with St Faith (tower incorporated into new building)
3 St Benet, the Welsh Church
4 St Clement, Eastcheap
5 St Edmund, King & Martyr
6 St James Garlickhythe
7 St Mary Abchurch
8 St Mary Aldermary
9 St Mary-le-Bow
10 St Mary Somerset (tower only)
11 St Mary Woolnoth
12 St Michael, Cornhill
13 St Michael, Paternoster Royal
14 St Nicholas, Cole Abbey
15 St Paul's Cathedral
16 St Peter, Cornhill
17 St Stephen, Walbrook

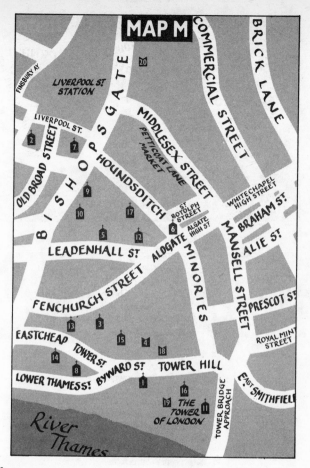

MAP M

1	All Hallows, Barking	12	St Katharine Cree
2	All Hallows, London Wall	13	St Margaret Pattens
3	All Hallows, Staining (tower only)	14	St Mary-at-Hill
4	Pepys, Samuel, bronze bust	15	St Olave's, Hart St
5	St Andrew Undershaft	16	St Peter-ad-Vincula, Tower
6	St Botolph, Aldgate	17	Spanish & Portuguese Synagogue, Bevis Marks
7	St Botolph, Bishopsgate	18	Tower Hill Memorial, Trinity Square Gardens
8	St Dunstan-in-the-East (tower & ruins only)	19	Tower of London
9	St Ethelburga-the-Virgin	20	Wesley, Susanna, birth house, end of Spital Yard off Spital Square
10	St Helen, Bishopsgate		
11	St John the Evangelist, White Tower		

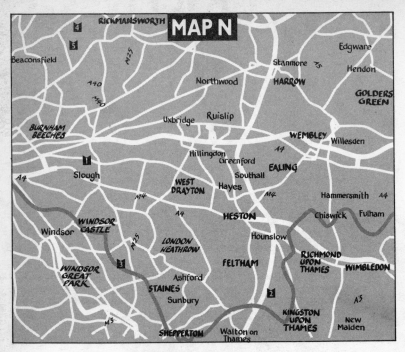

MAP N

1. Gray, Thomas, monument. Stoke Poges Church & Churchyard
2. Hampton Court Palace, including Chapel Royal
3. Magna Carta Memorial, Runnymede Meadow
4. Milton's Cottage, Chalfont St Giles
5. Quaker Meeting House & Mayflower Barn, Jordans

PART

1

A TO Z

OF

PILGRIMS' LONDON

Actes and Monuments   The original name of *Foxe's Book of Martyrs*.
▶ Elizabethan London

Addison, Joseph (1672-1719)   Addison is chiefly remembered as a man
of letters, possibly the most brilliant essayist in the history of English
literature, and the creator of the lovable country squire, Sir Roger de
Coverley. He is generally associated with Sir Richard Steele, with
whom he collaborated in two London periodicals, *The Tatler* and *The
Spectator*. In these publications and their successor, the *Guardian*,
appeared the essays which were later published as *Evidences of the
Christian Religion*.

Besides his literary achievements, Addison was successful in
politics. He was a member of Parliament for a number of years, and
was twice appointed as Secretary of State. But despite these honours
and the fame that accompanied them, he exhibited a truly Christian
character, a genial serenity in his outlook on life and a wholesome
morality. His famous hymn *The Spacious Firmament on High* strikes a
balance between the new scientific discoveries of an ordered universe
and faith in the Creator God of the Bible:

> The spacious firmament on high,
> With all the blue etherial sky,
> And spangled heavens, a shining frame,
> Their great Original proclaim:
> Th' unwearied sun, from day to day,
> Does his Creator's power display;
> And publishes to every land
> The work of an almighty hand.
>
> What though, in solemn silence, all
> Move round this round terrestrial ball?
> What though no real voice nor sound
> Amid their radiant orbs be found?
> In reason's ear they all rejoice,
> And utter forth a glorious voice,
> Forever singing as they shine,
> 'The hand that made us is divine!'

It is said that when Addison lay dying, he reflected on his life and,
having thought that he had wronged a friend, called the man to his
bedside to ask forgiveness. Toward the end he sent for his stepson,
Lord Warwick, whose rather careless life worried Addison. At first he
was so weak that he could not say anything, but finally he uttered his
last words, 'See in what peace a Christian can die!'   ▶ Restoration
London   **M** Monument in 'Poet's Corner,' Westminster Abbey, C-10
Three portraits in National Portrait Gallery, H-9

Alban   St Alban is celebrated as Britain's first known Christian martyr.
The traditional site of his death, in the late third-century, is located

in the large town of St Albans just northwest of London. ▶ Roman London

Albert Memorial Chapel, Windsor This ancient chapel at Windsor Castle was rebuilt by Henry VII as a burial place for Henry VI, but was not completed until the time of Cardinal Wolsey. Wolsey's magnificent tomb, unoccupied, was broken up during the Civil War. Queen Victoria had the chapel made into a splendid memorial for her husband, who died in 1861 (however, only Prince Albert's cenotaph is here; he is buried next to Queen Victoria in the mausoleum at Frogmore House). It contains the tombs of the Duke of Clarence (d. 1892), the elder son of Edward VII, and the Duke of Albany (d. 1884), Queen Victoria's youngest son. Beneath the chapel are buried George III, Queen Charlotte and six of their sons (including George IV and William IV). **M** Map location N-6

Alfred the Great (849-99) Alfred, the greatest of the Saxon monarchs, was king of the West Saxons from 871. He was responsible for restoring the church in Britain after Danish raids had laid waste much of the eastern half of the land. He was also instrumental in translating some of the great Christian classics into Anglo-Saxon (Old English), including Bede's *History of the English Church*. He built up the defences of the City of London to prevent further attacks. ▶ Saxon London

All Hallows, Barking (or All Hallows-By-the-Tower) All Hallows is one of London's earliest churches, founded by the famous Erkenwald, Bishop of London, before AD675. It is one of a very few City churches to have physical evidence of its Saxon beginnings. After the bombing a discovery was made of a Saxon door arch, and also the stone shaft and part of the wheel-head of a cross inscribed in Anglo-Saxon. The name 'Barking' also takes us back to early Saxon times. Originally a nunnery at Barking, a few miles down river, was supported by rents from the property around the church.

A Norman church replaced the Saxon one in 1088, ten years after the construction of the Tower of London. During medieval times various changes and additions were made, including a chapel across the road to the north. This later had a royal chantry attached to it by Edward IV in 1465. Both chapel and chantry were removed during the Reformation.

Because of All Hallows' proximity to the Tower, the headless bodies of several notable persons executed on Tower Hill were brought here first before burial elsewhere. These included Bishop John Fisher; Thomas Howard, the Earl of Surrey; Lady Jane Grey's father, Lord Thomas Grey; and, later, Archbishop William Laud. Buried here (though his monument has disappeared) is the body of draper and sheriff Humphrey Monmouth, who protected and encouraged William Tyndale in his translation of the New

Testament. Monmouth was punished by Thomas More with imprisonment in the Tower.

On 4 January 1649, the year of the execution of King Charles I, a ship's chandler whose shop was close to All Hallows was busy barrelling gunpowder when it somehow ignited. The explosion destroyed fifty or sixty houses in the vicinity and badly damaged the church tower, which was replaced in 1659 (a rare event in the Cromwellian period). The disaster took place at 7 p.m. when a parish dinner was under way at the Rose Tavern just two houses away. Everyone in the crowded pub was killed, some blown to bits and others found perfectly intact but dead by concussion. Amazingly, an infant in a cradle was discovered alive and unharmed on the roof of the church. The parents were never found, and the little girl was raised by one of the parishioners.

All Hallows narrowly escaped major damage in the Great Fire of September 1666, primarily because it was east of Pudding Lane and thus upwind from the source. Samuel Pepys says in his famous *Diary* for 5 September:

> About two in the morning my wife calls me up and tells me of new cryes of fire, it being come to Barking Church, which is at the bottom of our lane (Seething Lane).

He again refers to All Hallows on the afternoon of the 5th:

> But going to the fire, I find by the blowing up of houses, and the great helpe given by the workmen out of the King's yards, sent up by Sir W. Pen, there is a good stop given to it, as well at Markelane end as ours; it having only burned the dyall of Barking Church, and part of the porch, and was there quenched. I to the top of Barking steeple, and there saw the saddest sight of desolation that I ever saw…

The 'Sir W. Pen' who played such an important part in stopping the spread of the fire was Sir William Penn, father of William Penn, the founder of Pennsylvania. Young William was baptized in All Hallows. Another notable person associated with America, John Quincy Adams, was married here in 1797 to Louisa Catherine Johnson, daughter of the American consul.

In December 1940, All Hallows, which had stood intact for nearly 900 years, was reduced to a ruin by hits from two air raids. The red brick tower of 1759 survived, however, and is now topped by a spire sheathed in copper. The rest of the building was admirably restored by Lord Mottistone and Paul Paget, and many of the original furnishings, monuments and brasses may still be seen. A museum below the nave houses the Saxon finds mentioned earlier as well as Roman artifacts and other items of historical interest.   **M** Map location M-1

All Hallows, London Wall   The name of this church was originally 'In-the-Wall', as the site was a narrow strip of land adjoining the old wall and partly resting on one of the bastions. It is now at the east end of the street called London Wall, where it crosses Old Broad Street. It survived the Great Fire, but was pulled down and rebuilt in 1765-67 by George Dance the Younger. Badly damaged in World War II, it was abandoned for some twenty years, but was restored by David Nye and reconsecrated in 1962. It presently is the headquarters of the Council for Places of Worship, which concerns itself with the preservation of churches throughout England. The former parish is served by St. Botolph's, Bishopsgate. ▶ Classical London ▬ Map location M-2

All Hallows, Staining. See *Towers.*

All Saints, Margaret Street This church is the first and finest example in London of the lavishness of decoration and furnishings advocated by the Tractarians. A descripton from 1888 says, 'Its interior is more richly decorated than any other church of the Anglican communion in London'. It was built between 1849 and 1859 on the site of the Margaret Chapel, once a nonconformist chapel of Lady Huntingdon's Connexion, and the first stone was laid by Dr Edward Pusey himself. Here, in the 1830s, Frederick Oakeley began to adopt the principles of the Oxford Movement already alluded to.

All Saints, Margaret Street, was designed by William Butterfield, Anglican architect of nearly 100 Gothic Revival churches. The building has a very tall steeple, 230 feet high, atop a brick tower. The entrance to the church is through a courtyard entered from the street. Inside one finds much rich wood carving, marble Corinthian columns and stained glass. Ceiling frescoes depict the birth and crucifixion of Christ and the court of heaven, showing the saints with Our Lord in the centre. The west window, illustrating the Tree of Jesse, is of particular interest. In the Victorian age this church was attended by large upper-class congregations, predominantly ladies. This gave rise to the following from the pen of a clerical wit:

> In a church that is furnished with mullion and gable,
> With altar and reredos, with gargoyle and groin,
> The penitents' dresses are seal-skin and sable,
> The odour of sanctity's Eau de Cologne.
>
> But if only could Lucifer flying from Hades
> Gaze down on this crowd with its panniers and paints,
> He could say, as he looked at the lords and the ladies,
> Oh! where is 'All Sinners', if this is 'All Saints'?

▶ Victorian London ▬ Map location F-1

All Souls, Langham Place All Souls occupies a prominent site at the top of Regent Street, where Langham Place curves to meet Portland

Place. From Regent Street the old BBC Broadcasting House forms a somewhat unusual backdrop. A curious feature is the semi-detached porch and steeple, built out from the nave so as to appear at the centre of Regent Street. The rounded porch supports a unique conical steeple.

This church was built in 1822-24 during the reign of George IV. It is the only church left in London designed by the famous John Nash, the person responsible for the architecture of Regent Street. His bust on the porch looks down the street that he created.

The interior of All Souls has been beautifully restored. Underneath is a church hall constructed in the early 1970s at a cost of over £655,000, paid before completion with contributions from around the world. The church was reconsecrated on All Souls Day (2 November) 1976. It is a parish church with one of the largest congregations in London and is well known in America and throughout the English-speaking world due to the international ministry of John Stott, now rector emeritus. Attendance of 1,000 or more is not unusual. ▶ Classical London **M** Map location F-2

Andrewes, Launcelot (1555-1626) Launcelot Andrewes was the favorite court preacher of King James I. He epitomizes the learned churchman of his age. He was not only a theologian and a brilliant speaker, but a linguist, translator of the Scriptures, statesman and man of letters as well. Andrewes came to the royal court first as chaplain to Queen Elizabeth. He was present at the Hampton Court Conference as one of the Episcopalian prelates, and later became one of the translators of the Authorized Version of the Bible.

Early in his career Andrewes was vicar of St. Giles, Cripplegate, in London, but eventually he became Bishop of Chichester, Bishop of Ely, Bishop of Winchester, and then a privy councillor and dean of the king's chapel. Among his best known writings are a series of seventeen sermons on the Nativity preached before James I from 1605 to 1624. He played a primary role in formulating the intellec- tual and historical position of the Church of England. ▶ Stuart and Commonwealth London **M** Monument over grave with reclining effigy, Southwark Cathedral, D-6

Anglican Church, Anglicans 'Angle' or 'Anglo' refers to the Angles, a tribe that invaded the British Isles along with the Saxons in the fifth century, and is the root of the word 'English'. The Angli- can Church is the Church of England, and members are Anglicans.

Askew, Anne (1521-46) Probably the most celebrated of all the Smithfield martyrs was Anne Askew, who suffered during the last days of Henry VIII. She was a bright and pretty young woman from a well-to-do Midlands family who, early in her teens, became a keen student of the Bible, now available in English. Her father married her off to a country gentleman in Lincolnshire who had no sympathy for Anne's spiritual convictions, and the young wife soon got into trouble for being a 'gospeller'—a person who competed with the clergy by expounding the Bible to neighbours and friends, sometimes even at church. She boldly courted a confrontation with the religious hierarchy by going to London, attending Protestant meetings in the city, and proclaiming the Gospel of Christ from the Scriptures wherever she went.

Eventually she was brought to trial in the Guildhall. When asked if she denied that Christ was in the sacrament, she answered, 'I believe faithfully the eternal Son of God not to dwell there', and quoted from memory texts from Daniel 3, Acts 7 and 17 and Matthew 24. Her conclusion was, 'I neither wish death nor yet fear his might; God have the praise thereof, with thanks'. She was put to the most excruciating torture in the Tower, but refused to deny her Lord. An enormous number of Londoners witnessed her death in July 1546, many of them sympathetic. Even today she is somewhat of a legend in the grim history of the Smithfield fires. ▶ Reformation London

Anne Boleyn (1507-36)   Second wife of Henry VIII and the mother of Queen Elizabeth I. ▶ Reformation London **M** Portrait in National Portrait Gallery, H-9

Anne of Cleves   Fifth wife of Henry VIII (marriage annulled). ▶ Reformation London

Archbishop of Canterbury   The highest ranking prelate in the Church of England, who resides at Lambeth Palace, London.   **M** Map location of Lambeth Palace, C-4

Augustine of Canterbury (d.604?)   Sent as a missionary to England by Pope Gregory I, he founded a church (St. Martin's) in Canterbury in 596. One of his band of priests, Mellitus, became first bishop of the East Saxons, including London. ▶ Saxon London

Baptists   Baptists, with their many modern denominations and local churches around the world, were born out of a study of the Bible made by an English Separatist congregation in Amsterdam (though some historians see them as an extension of the Anabaptists of Reformation times). Under the leadership of their pastor, John Smyth, the group in 1609 came to the conclusion that the Scriptures did not support the practice of infant baptism. Instead, they felt that baptism as taught in the New Testament was for those who had made a responsible decision to be identified with the death, burial and resurrection of Christ.

As a result of this conclusion, the group decided to disband and reorganize, with 'believer's' baptism as the basis of fellowship. In 1615 they joined with the Mennonites, but meanwhile, in 1612, a smaller segment returned to London under the leadership of Thomas Helwys. This became the first Baptist church on English soil, meeting in the area of the present Spitalfields Market. Helwys was a powerful preacher and the group grew. Later Helwys, who had been educated in law at Gray's Inn, wrote a paper pleading for liberty of conscience, which came to the notice of King James and incurred his displeasure. Helwys was imprisoned in Newgate, and his fate is unknown. However, the Baptists continued to flourish, and by 1660 there were between 200 and 300 congregations in Britain, many of them in and around London.　**M** Stuart & Commonwealth London

Barker, Christopher (?1529-89) & Barker, Robert (d.1645)　London father and son printers who, as royal stationers and printers to Queen Elizabeth and King James I, produced both the first English edition of the Geneva Bible (1575) and the first edition of the King James Version (1611). Christopher obtained the exclusive patent for all state printing including religious books. He and his agents produced some seventy-two editions of the Bible between 1575 and 1599. Robert obtained his father's royal patent at the latter's death and continued to print Bibles, prayer-books, statutes and proclamations, as well as all books in Latin, Greek and Hebrew, and all charts and maps. In addition to the first edition of the King James Bible he was responsible for the so-called wicked Bible of 1631 which rendered the seventh commandment, 'Thou shalt commit adultery' (probably the most famous omission in history). The Barker company (now Barker & Howard) still produces navigational books and is one of London's oldest firms, said to have started before 1490. An evangelical family are part owners.

Barnardo, John Thomas (1845-1905)　One of the best known of British orphanage founders, Barnardo began his career as a medical student in London with the intent of going to China as a missionary. While still in training, he assisted in medical work in the East London slums during an 1865 cholera epidemic. This experience convinced him to work toward the rescue of street waifs. He opened the East End Juvenile Mission in Stepney Causeway, London, in 1867, and this became the headquarters for the institution still familiarly known as the 'Dr Barnardo Homes'.

Homeless children taken off the streets were fed, clothed and given training so that they could later seek employment. Care was taken that they also received Christian education. The motto of the homes was, 'No destitute child ever refused admission'. Barnardo believed, contrary to popular opinion, that environment was more important than heredity in bringing up children.

John Thomas Barnardo was a practising Christian, a born leader, and a man who devoted his life to alleviating suffering. By the time of his death in 1905 he had founded 112 district 'homes', and some 60,000 children had been rescued from the streets by his organization. While orphanages are a thing of the past today, the work of caring for orphaned children still goes on in his name.　▶ Victorian London

Baxter, Richard (1615-91) Richard Baxter, whose life spanned nearly the entire Stuart dynasty, was the leading Nonconformist minister at the time of the Restoration and one of the greatest of the Puritan divines. His early life was associated with the west of England and Kidderminster in particular, where from 1641 to 1660 he preached to and shepherded a congregation that grew to one fifth of the town. For eighteen months during the Civil War he also moved about preaching to various units of the Parliamentarian army.

In April 1660, just prior to the arrival of King Charles II, Baxter left Kidderminster for London, and was associated with the city much of the remainder of his life. He was for a time one of the king's chaplains and played a leading role in the attempt by the Nonconformists to reach a peaceful settlement with the Anglicans. He was the Nonconformist spokesman at the Savoy Conference of April 1661, and he prepared a list of proposed additions to the prayer-book, which unfortunately were rejected. In 1662 he was deprived of his living as a preacher by the Act of Uniformity.

Baxter had preached at St. Dunstan's-in-the-West, St. Bride's and other London churches, but after 1662, though he continued to preach on occasion, he was under great restraint, often watched, and was imprisoned several times. He married in 1662, and in 1669 his wife Margaret kept house for him in prison at Clerkenwell for six months. She died in 1681. In 1685, ill and barely able to stand, he was abused and sentenced to yet another prison term by the vicious Judge Jeffries. Yet his mental and spiritual output during all these years of hardship was phenomenal—countless sermons and 168 books, some of them large volumes. Two of his books, *The Saints' Everlasting Rest* and *The Reformed Pastor*, are among the greatest Christian classics. One of his last statements was a prayer for London: 'Lord, pity, pity, pity the ignorance of this poor city!' ▶ Restoration London **M** Portrait and miniature in National Portrait Gallery, H-9

Becket, Thomas (1118-70) During the Middle Ages it was considered a very worthy act of Christian devotion to make a pilgrimage to the tomb of a saint. Not only could the saint, from his or her privileged position in heaven, pray for an individual Christian more effectively, but numerous pilgrims had evidence to show that at this or that shrine they had been healed of bodily infirmities. The most popular place of pilgrimage in all England was the shrine of St Thomas in Canterbury Cathedral. Thomas was looked upon by Londoners (along with Erkenwald) as their very own saint. The son of Gilbert Becket, a wealthy, devout London merchant, Thomas was a brilliant and handsome young churchman with an Oxford education behind him when Henry II came to the throne in 1154. The king was intent on restoring order in England after the disastrous reign of Stephen, his predecessor. Recognizing young Thomas's potential, the king appointed him to the high office of chancellor.

After eight years Henry wanted to make Thomas archbishop, thinking that he would thus be able to control the growing power of the church. Thomas at first refused, but then accepted under the king's insistence. However, he also resigned the chancellorship and soon became the champion of the church against the king. When Thomas left England under pressure from Henry, the king seized his properties. Returning, Thomas excommunicated several of his enemies, including the bishop of London, without permission from Henry.

When the king heard this news he was in Normandy, and is said to have cried out in a rage, 'Will no one avenge me of this turbulent priest?' Four knights took Henry literally and, crossing the Channel, slew Thomas in the transept of Canterbury Cathedral as he was saying the evening office. Thomas's murder fired the imagination of the faithful all over Europe, and the magnificent shrine that was built was visited by untold thousands until it was destroyed by Henry VIII. As Chaucer illustrates by his wide cross-section of pilgrims in the *Canterbury Tales*, it would have been difficult to find any devout Londoner in medieval times who had not made the fifty-mile pilgrimage to Canterbury. ▶ Medieval London

Bede, the Venerable (or Baeda) (c.673-735) Bede is well known to historians as the author of *A History of the English Church and People*, and is our primary source for such important early events as the martyrdom of St Alban, the founding of the church at Canterbury by Augustine, the establishment of the monastery at Iona by St Columba and the proceedings of the Synod of Whitby. His references to London unfortunately are few, mainly citing the appointment of bishops. ▶ Saxon London

Bells of London Churches Such a familiar part of everyday life in London were the bells of its churches that they acquired individual personalities in the minds of the populace. Anyone who has read Dickens's *A Christmas Carol* may well remember the description of such a bell in the opening chapter:

> The ancient tower of a church, whose gruff old bell was always peeping slily down at Scrooge out of a gothic window in the wall, became invisible, and struck the hours and quarters in the clouds, with tremulous vibrations afterwards, as if its teeth were chattering in its frozen head up there.

And of course there was young Richard Whittington, who while climbing Highgate Hill heard the bells of St. Mary-le-Bow saying,

> Turn again Dick Whittington,
> Lord Mayor of London!

What the bells of London said eventually became a series of nursery rhymes, as follows:

Gay go up and gay go down,
To ring the bells of London Town.

Bulls eyes and targets,
Say the bells of St. Margaret's.

Brickbats and tiles,
Say the bells of St Giles'.

Halfpence and farthings,
Say the bells of St Martin's.

Oranges and lemons,
Say the bells of St Clemen's.

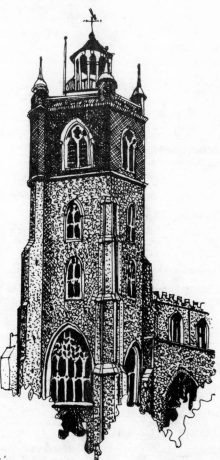

St Giles, Cripplegate:
'Brickbats and tiles,
Say the bells of St Giles.'

Pancakes and fritters,
Say the bells of St Peter's.

Two sticks and an apple,
Say the bells of Whitechapel.

Old Father Baldpate,
Say the slow bells at Aldgate.

Pokers and tongs,
Say the bells of St John's.

Kettles and pans,
Say the bells of St Anne's.

You owe me ten shillings,
Say the bells of St Helen's.

When will you pay me?
Say the bells at Old Bailey.

When I grow rich,
Say the bells at Shoreditch.

Pray when will that be?
Say the bells of Stepney.

I'm sure I don't know,
Says the great bell at Bow.

Here comes a candle to light you to bed,
And here comes a chopper to chop off your head!

Berkeley, George (1685-1753)   Berkeley was the most brilliant
Christian philosopher of the 'Age of Reason', and bishop of Cloyne in
Ireland. His major work, *Alciphron*, shows that ideas rather than
things have true existence and that the existence of ideas stems from
God. He is buried in St Clement Danes (H-1).   ▶ Classical London

Bible Translation in Sixteenth-century London   Three other pioneer
Bible translators followed William Tyndale during the reign of Henry
VIII, and of these three, two preached for a time in surviving London
churches. Miles Coverdale was the rector of St Magnus, Martyr
(D-5), from 1563 to 1566. When he died in 1568 he was interred in
this church and later, in 1837, a memorial extolling his translation
work was placed by the parishioners against the east wall. It says in
part, '...he spent many years of his life in preparing a translation of the
Scriptures. On the 4th of October, 1535, the first complete printed
English version of the Bible was published under his direction'.

Like Tyndale, Coverdale started his translation work in secret and
went to the Continent where the danger attached to such a project
was less. But unlike Tyndale, he had a friend at the royal court,
Thomas Cromwell, Henry VIII's principal advisor. Coverdale

actually served his apprenticeship assisting Tyndale in the work on the first five books of the Bible. He then completed the Old Testament using German and Latin texts. In 1535 he published the whole Bible combining his and Tyndale's work. Because of Coverdale's connection with Cromwell and the fact that Henry VIII was favourable to an English Bible that he could approve of, Coverdale's Bible circulated freely in England and was reprinted on home soil with the royal licence in 1537. Tyndale's prayer had been answered before he uttered it!

Yet another English Bible appeared in 1537 bearing the royal licence of Henry VIII. This was the so-called Matthew Bible done by a priest named John Rogers who had become a Protestant through Tyndale's influence and who used the Bibles of Tyndale and Coverdale for his sources. The licence had been obtained by Archbishop Cranmer, and the king ordered that a copy should be placed in every parish church, to be read by the people. With Cromwell's encouragement, Coverdale revised the Matthew Bible, and this was then officially published in 1539 in a large size known as the 'Great Bible'. Rogers was pastor to an English congregation at Antwerp during his translation work, but returned to London after its publication. He became rector of St Margaret Moses, vicar of St Sepulchre's (J-19) and a lecturer at St Paul's (J-14). He became the first martyr of Mary Tudor's reign.

The same year that the Great Bible appeared, a Greek scholar named Richard Taverner came out with his own revision of the Matthew Bible, which we now call the 'Taverner Version'. The notes in this Bible tone down those of John Rogers, which tend to be violently Protestant in places, and the New Testament shows Taverner's skill in Greek. While at Oxford Taverner had undergone persecution for his circulation of Tyndale's New Testament in 1528, but as a friend of Thomas Cromwell he was by 1539 Clerk of the Signet. The Taverner Bible was printed first in folio and quarto versions, and reprinted once before being superseded by the Great Bible.

Three more English translations of the Bible were published during the reign of Elizabeth I. The first to appear was the Geneva Version, which for a century was the Bible of the Reformed Church, of the Puritans and of the Pilgrim Fathers. Geneva was the birthplace of the Reformed Church under the leadership of John Calvin and the Greek scholar Theodore Beza. It was natural that the English exiles who fled to that city would want a Bible with notes reflecting the Reformed doctrines. The Geneva Bible was the result. The New Testament came first, in 1557, a revision of Tyndale's version by William Wittingham. The whole Bible was published in 1560. It was smaller in size than its predecessors and was the first to use Roman type, verse divisions and italics. It was first printed in London in 1575.

The Bishops Bible was so called because it was a version entrusted to Elizabeth's bishops under the leadership of Archbishop Matthew Parker. The queen was intimidated by the growing Puritan influence in England, and she intended the Bishops Bible to be an answer to the Geneva Version and to replace the Great Bible. It was published in 1568, but proved too stiff and formal to gain wide usage.

The Douai-Rheims Bible, like the Bishops Bible, was a reaction to the popularity of the Geneva version, but by Roman Catholics. It was also similar to the Geneva Bible in that it was the work of English exiles on the Continent. The project was begun at Douai in France where there was a Roman Catholic training college for English-speaking priests. The main translator was Gregory Martin, an Oxford scholar in Greek and Hebrew. The New Testament was published in Rheims, where the college had moved, in 1582. The college later moved back to Douai, and here the Old Testament was published in 1609-10. This version was actually a translation of a translation, that is, from Hebrew and Greek into Latin by Jerome and from Latin into English by Martin and others. While possessing the long-standing credibility of Jerome's Latin Vulgate version, it lacked the readability in English achieved by Tyndale and those who followed him.

▶ Reformation London   Elizabethan London

Blake, William (1757-1827)

Blake occupies a place in the Christian history of London through his now-famous illustrations dealing with religious and Christian subjects, and for his own mystical poetry. His drawings were reproduced by means of etched plates and later coloured. Blake's best-known works include *Songs of Innocence*, *Marriage of Heaven and Hell*, *Visions of the Daughters of Albion*, *Songs of Experience* and *Inventions from the Book of Job*. Illustrations for Dante's *Divine Comedy*, Bunyan's *Pilgrim's Progress* and Thomas Gray's poems were unfinished when he died.

In 1782 Blake was married, and his wife assisted him with his work. They lived at various addresses in London and Hampstead Heath, one of which survives today (20 Molton Street). His religious experience consisted of a series of visions in which he claimed to have talked face to face with figures such as Moses, Milton and Shakespeare. His was, therefore, no orthodox faith, but a highly romanticized individualism in which, for example, he accepted the Christian doctrine of the forgiveness of sins but rejected the atonement of Christ.

In the period immediately after his death he was neglected and almost forgotten. Today he is considered one of the greatest creative spirits of the late eighteenth century. A monument was placed on his grave in Bunhill Burying Ground in 1927, one hundred years after his death.

Some of Blake's short poetry is still very well known, including 'Tiger, Tiger, Burning Bright', 'Little Lamb, Who Made Thee?' and the following which alludes to the myth that Jesus visited England:

And did those feet in ancient time

Walk upon England's mountains green?
And was the holy Lamb of God
On England's pleasant pastures seen?

And did the countenance divine
Shine forth upon our clouded hills?
And was Jerusalem builded here
Among these dark Satanic mills?

▶ Classical London   **M** Major collection of works, Tate Gallery, C-8
Other works, Victoria & Albert, A-9   Bust in Poet's Corner, Westminster
Abbey, C-10   Two portraits, two castings of head, National Portrait Gallery,
H-9   House, 17 South Molton Street, E-1

'Bloody Mary'   An epithet for Queen Mary Tudor, referring to the
numerous burnings for heresy at Smithfield and elsewhere during her
reign.   ▶ Reformation London

Boniface of Savoy (d.1270)   Boniface was Archbishop of Canterbury
under Henry III, to whom he was related by marriage. His property
near the Strand on the banks of the Thames later became the site of
the famous Savoy Palace. The Savoy Chapel is now located on this
site.   ▶ Medieval London   **M** Map location of Savoy Chapel, H-16

Bonner, Edmund (c.1500-69)   Bonner was bishop of London, first under
Henry VIII and later under Mary. As the chief agent of the royal
persecution, he was intensely hated by many of the people of
London.   ▶ Reformation London

Book of Common Prayer   This is the worship-book of the Church of
England, consisting of prayers and readings for various services of the
church throughout the year. Initially the work of Thomas Cranmer,
it was adopted by Parliament in 1549, revised in 1552. During the
17th century it was the center of controversy between the Anglicans
and the Puritans, which was resolved by the Act of Uniformity of
1662. The 1662 version remains the official order of worship for the
Church of England, despite periodic attempts to introduce revisions.
▶ Reformation London

Booth, William (1829-1912)   William Booth, first general of the
Salvation Army, was early in life a minister and evangelist in the
Methodist 'New Connexion' Church, but resigned in 1865 to devote
himself to missionary work among the poor in East London. In this he
was aided by his wife, Catherine, herself a gifted speaker. At first the
work was called the 'East London Christian Revival Society', and
included social work such as running cheap food shops alongside
evangelistic preaching. Booth and his co-workers suffered a great deal
of abuse and were sometimes physically assaulted, but many lives were
transformed and the work spread to other centres.

In 1878 Booth's growing organization was formed into a Christian 'army' with military ranks, units and 'Orders and Regulations'. With Booth as general of this 'Salvation Army', there were by 1879 eighty-one mission stations manned by 127 full-time evangelists, and the first Salvation Army band. Eventually the Salvation Army was to be found in fifty-five different countries.

Booth's great book, *In Darkest England and the Way Out*, was published in 1890. By his death in 1912 he had travelled five million miles, preached nearly 60,000 sermons and appointed some 16,000 officers. Over 40,000 people attended his funeral. At the centenary of the Salvation Army in London in 1965, 10,000 delegates from around the world were addressed in Albert Hall by Queen Elizabeth II.

General William Booth Enters into Heaven, by the American poet Vachel Lindsey, captures something of the spirit of Booth's amazing ministry among the wretched outcasts of East London. Here is the first stanza:

> Booth led boldly with his big bass drum –
> (Are you washed in the blood of the Lamb?)
> The Saints smiled gravely and they said: 'He's come.'
> (Are you washed in the blood of the Lamb?)

William Booth, founder of the Salvation Army. When he died, 40,000 people marched through London behind his co

Walking lepers followed, rank on rank,
Lurching bravos from the ditches dank,
Drabs from the alleyways and drug fiends pale –
Minds still passion-ridden, soul-powers frail:
Vermin-eaten saints with moldy breath,
Unwashed legions with the ways of Death –
(Are you washed in the blood of the Lamb?)

▶ Victorian London   M Several portraits and sketches in National Portrait Gallery, H-9   Bronze bust on left at beginning of Mile End Road, East London   Buried in Abney Park Cemetery   Memorabilia in Salvation Army Museum, Kings Cross

Bradford, John (1510-55)   Famous Protestant martyr burned at Smithfield during the reign of Mary.   ▶ Reformation London
M Martyr's Memorial, Smithfield, J-8

Brethren, The   The Christian Brethren movement originated in Dublin, Ireland, in the 1820s. It became known as the 'Plymouth Brethren' because the first large church developed in that city under the leadership of J.N. Darby, B.W. Newton and others. At about the same time another large congregation recognizing similar principles grew up in Bristol under Henry Craik and George Muller of orphanage fame. The movement expanded to about half the size of the Baptist denomination by the 1860s. Its impact in evangelistic outreach was significant in that many of its evangelists were laymen who preached on street corners, at race tracks and wherever crowds of people gathered.

Essentially, the brethren (they prefer a small 'b') were opposed to sectarianism, believing that Christians should gather together 'as unto the Lord' without any other name. They put great stress on the communion or Lord's Supper as the focal point of worship, in which any brother could participate audibly. They also believed strongly in the urgency of preaching the gospel, and from the beginning of the movement they were well represented in worldwide missions. In modern times the more 'open' assemblies are often active in local inter-faith evangelistic campaigns, open-air meetings, beach missions and the like. Finally, they were keen on the biblical concept of every believer being a priest, which led to an extraordinary knowledge of the Bible in the rank and file.

The exact beginnings of the Christian Brethren in London are obscure. But according to Roy Coad, a modern historian of the movement, 'it is known that a church was started in the early 1830s, largely on the initiative of G.V. Wigram' (an associate of Darby's). In 1839 a group led by Robert and John Eliot Howard of the chemical manufacturing firm of Howard & Sons opened a chapel in Brook Street off Tottenham High Road. This is still in use, and it is the earliest of the Christian Brethren chapels in London. It was here that

39

J. Hudson Taylor attended for a time before leaving for China. Other notable figures associated with this movement in London include Sir John Vesey Parnell; Second Baron Congleton; Philip Gosse, the eminent zoologist; and Lt Gen. Sir William Dobbie, the defender of Malta during World War II. ▶ Victorian London **M** Portrait of John Nelson Darby, National Portrait Gallery, H-9

British & Foreign Bible Society An organization whose purpose is 'to encourage the wider circulation of the Holy Scriptures without note or comment', the BFBS was founded in London in 1804 by members of the Clapham Sect and other evangelicals. Today, known simply as The Bible Society, it prints and circulates Bibles in hundreds of world languages. ▶ Classical London British Library from galley 9

British Library The British Library once was part of the British Museum, having begun with the library of Sir Hans Soane. Several other valuable collections were added over the years, including the Royal Library begun by Edward IV in the 1470s, and George III's extensive library. The great domed reading room was opened in 1857. (Among the nineteenth-century readers who spent much time there was Karl Marx.) In 1973 a separate British Library was created by act of Parliament, though the Reference Division with its book displays is still physically part of the British Museum. Eventually it will move to new quarters on Euston Road.

Like the British Museum, the British Library has many exhibits of great interest to Christian visitors. Some of the most important are:

The Codex Sinaiaticus, earliest Bible in existence (fourth-century), together with the fifth-century Codex Alexandrinus;

The Lindisfarne Gospels, one of the greatest masterpieces of medieval book illumination, produced in AD698;

The Harley Golden Gospels, produced around AD800 at the court of Charlemagne;

The Bedford Hours, a masterpiece of French book painting of the fifteenth century;

A copy of the 42-line Gutenberg Bible, the world's first printed book;

A Wycliffe Bible (very few escaped the flames);

A Tyndale Bible which belonged to Anne Boleyn;

A first edition of the King James Bible of 1611;

A manual of prayers carried to the scaffold by Lady Jane Grey;

Two of the four existing copies of the Magna Carta.

M Map location H-1

British Museum The British Museum on Great Russell Street in Bloomsbury is England's national museum of archaeology and ethnography. This may not sound very exciting, but for Christians this is one of the most significant collections of artifacts in the world. For over 200 years British archaeologists have been digging in the sites of ancient cities throughout the eastern Mediterranean, and many discoveries have been made confirming the people and events which appear in the biblical record. For visitors interested in the Bible, the museum shop sells a book called *Illustrations of Old Testament History* by R.D. Barnett that describes many of the findings on display and their significance. Here are four samples:

Pottery from Hazor, the chief city of the Canaanites which was destroyed by Joshua (Joshua 11:10-11);
Finely carved fragments from Ahab's House of Ivory, condemned by the Prophet Amos (Amos 3:15);
A picture of Jehu on an obelisk of Shalmaneser III, king of Assyria, earliest surviving depiction of an Israelite. Jehu slew Joram, Ahab's second son and ordered the death of Jezebel (2 Kings 19);
An extensive reference to Hezekiah and the siege of Jerusalem on a six-sided prism (the 'Taylor Prism') relating the annals of Sennacherib, king of Assyria (2 Kings 18).

All of these items and a great many others of biblical significance are to be found in the exhibits of the Department of Western Asiatic Antiquities (Assyrian, Babylonian civilizations, and so on). There are also a few in the Department of Egyptian Antiquities.

The British Museum also possesses some articles from New Testament times, including coins mentioned in the Bible. The Romano-British section (reached by taking the stairs at the left of the lobby) has exhibits which, while not dating from Bible times, are very early. Most significant is the Lullingstone Pavement, a mosaic floor taken from a fourth-century Roman villa near Lullingstone, Kent. A portrait of a young man together with a chi-rho symbol is believed to be one of the earliest portraits of Christ in existence.

The British Museum originated in 1753 when the library, natural-history collection, antiquities and works of art of Sir Hans Soane were bequeathed to the nation. The Museum (and also the British Library) are entered from Great Russell Street by way of the magnificent colonnaded portico designed by Sir Robert Smirke and opened in 1852. There is a fine shop offering numerous books, posters, slides, replicas of art objects, postcards and so on. The building also has a self-service restaurant.　**M** Map location H-2

Brompton Oratory This is the London home of an association of secular priests founded in Rome by St Philip Neri (1515-95). The church popularly known as the 'Brompton Oratory' is, officially, the church of the London Oratory, the church house being next door on the west. The oratory is unique in the Roman Catholic church in that it emphasizes the aesthetic and artistic in the practice of devotional exercises. Hence in the church of the London Oratory may be seen a beautiful Italian Renaissance building, furnished with statuary and paintings of the highest quality, and featuring an Oratory Choir who sing, at vespers and solemn Mass, the greatest music of the Christian tradition.

The Italian Oratory was discovered by two leaders of the Oxford Movement who had become Roman Catholic converts, John Henry Newman and Frederick William Faber. Faber, who had studied the life of Philip Neri, founded a brotherhood in the Midlands, while Newman and his companions sought instruction in the traditions of the Oratory in Rome. Upon returning to England as Oratorians, they were joined by Faber and his group, the latter remaining in London. It was Faber who was responsible for the church now known as the Brompton Oratory, and his remains rest beneath a stone before the Altar of St Wilfred. A statue of Newman faces Brompton Road on the west of the church.

The Oratory church was designed by Herbert Gribble, a twenty-nine-year-old architect recently converted to Roman Catholicism. It was consecrated in 1884, and the south facade completed in 1893. The interior features a very wide nave with seven chapels on the sides. The great dome surrounded by circular windows sheds rays of light down into the centre before the sanctuary with its ornate high altar. Perhaps the most noteworthy feature of the church is St Wilfrid's Chapel at the right of the sanctuary. Outstanding among its many splendours is the Altar of St Wilfred, a fine example of Flemish Baroque from the eighteenth century, and the Altar of the English Martyrs. Above the latter is a triptych (three painted wooden panels, which form a backdrop to the altar) by American painter Rex Whistler, showing St Thomas More on the left, St John Fisher on the right, and a scene of the executions at Tyburn in the centre.
▶ Victorian London   **M** Map location A-1

Browning, Robert (1812-89) & Elizabeth Barrett (1806-61)   The famous husband and wife poets, whose courtship was dramatized in the play *The Barretts of Wimpole Street*, were secretly married in the parish church of St Marylebone in 1846 and are commemorated there by a memorial chapel (left side of entry hall).   ▶ Victorian London
M Map location E-5

Bunhill Fields Burial Ground   Bunhill Fields Burial Ground is on City Road just north of the Artillery Ground, and directly opposite Wesley's Chapel. A public walkway leads through the grounds from City Road to Bunhill Row, affording a pleasant tree-shaded escape from the street. The property was set apart and consecrated in 1665 as a burial place for plague victims outside the city. However, according to historian William Maitland writing in 1739, the actual ground where a huge pit was dug to bury the victims was elsewhere, and this land was simply held by the city until the Restoration.

After 1660 rents were demanded, and the city then let the property out for a cemetery. Somehow, perhaps because it was outside the city and not attached to a church, it became the customary burial ground for Dissenters. Among the more famous buried here are Dr Goodwin, Cromwell's favourite minister; John Owen, the Puritan divine; General Fleetwood, the Civil War commander; John Bunyan; Daniel Defoe; William Blake; Isaac Watts; and Susanna Wesley, mother of John and Charles.

Eventually Bunhill Fields was closed as a cemetery, but an act for the preservation of the grounds was passed in 1867. In 1869 the Lord Mayor opened the grounds to the public. The name is thought to be derived from 'bone hill', though nobody knows for sure. The poet Robert Southey called it the 'Campo Santo (sacred ground) of Dissenters.' ▶ Restoration London　**M** Map location K-1

Bunhill Fields Burial Ground, where many famous Dissenters are buried.

Bunyan, John (1628-88)　John Bunyan is perhaps the most famous of the Nonconformist ministers of the mid-seventeenth century to suffer imprisonment because of his preaching (although this actually occurred before the Act of Uniformity was passed). Bunyan, a brazier or mender of pots and pans by trade, had served in the Parliamentarian army during the Civil War and had then returned to his home at Elstow near Bedford. He was converted in 1651 and joined the Bedford congregation of John Gifford in 1653. Two years later he began to preach. For five years he developed this gift while still plying his trade. In 1660, the year of the Restoration, he was

43

arrested and ultimately committed to jail for twelve years.

Bunyan's imprisonment came to an end in May 1672, and the January before this the Bedford congregation had decided to appoint him as their pastor. His long confinement had strengthened his faith, and his writings had proven his maturity. Indeed, his *Pilgrim's Progress* ranks with *Foxe's Book of Martyrs* among the greatest of the Christian classics (other famous books include another allegory, *The Holy War*, and his autobiography, *Grace Abounding*). He was licensed on 9 May, and a barn belonging to one of his people was licensed as a place of worship, 'for the use of such as doe not conforme to the church of England who are of the Perswasion commonly called Congregationall'.

John Bunyan's popularity as a preacher was such that the first time he appeared at his barn-chapel the crowds were so great he had to speak to them outside. Before long he was being called 'Bishop Bunyan', for he commenced to organize congregations from Bedford to the outskirts of London, and applied for licences for some twenty-four other preachers. On numerous occasions he went to London to preach before great crowds in the various Nonconformist chapels. Often there would be more people than the meeting house could hold, even at seven on a working-day morning. In 1688, on one of his visits to London on horseback, he was drenched with rain and became very ill. He died at the house of a friend on Snowhill and was interred in Bunhill Burying Ground. ▶ Restoration London **M** Monument with reclining effigy and scenes from *Pilgrim's Progress* on the base, Bunhill Fields, K-1 Statue on Baptist Church House, East side of Southampton Row, H-3

Carlile, Wilson (1847-1942) Carlile's business was ruined by an economic depression in 1873, which led to his spiritual conversion. He began to minister to the down-and-outers of London, showing great skill in presenting the Gospel, and eventually was ordained. As a London pastor, he continued his evangelistic efforts among the poor, using his musical talent with effect in open-air meetings, and in 1882 founded the Church Army, which he led for many years.
▶ Victorian London **M** Medallion above tomb (ashes only)in the crypt of St Paul's, L-15 Carlile's trombone is on view in a case at St Mary At Hill, M-14

Catherine Howard (died 1542) The fifth wife of Henry VIII, whom he had arrested and executed for treason, she is said to haunt one of the galleries at Hampton Court. ▶ Reformation London **M** Named at site of the block, Tower of London, M-19 Buried in St Peter ad Vincula, M-16

Catherine of Aragon The first wife of Henry VIII, she was the daughter of Ferdinand and Isabella of Spain and was married first to Prince Arthur. Her failure to produce a son and heir to the English throne became a catalyst for events leading to the establishment of the Church of England. ▶ Reformation London **M** Portraits, National Portrait Gallery, H-9 Depicted in the east window of St Margaret's, Westminster, C-10

Catholic Apostolic Church This was an early nineteenth-century movement that emphasized the work of the Holy Spirit in healing, speaking in tongues and so on, with a very great emphasis on prophecy concerning the last days before the return of Christ. It is generally associated with Edward Irving and the church that he founded in London after his break with the London Presbytery. In 1832 twelve apostles were recognized by the community (not including Irving). It was thought that these would join the original twelve in occupying the twenty-four thrones of Revelation 4.

In time the group developed an ultra-formal ritual which included the Real Presence, holy water, and a sacrament of sealing, meaning that members became part of the 144,000 mentioned in Revelation 7. The impact of the Catholic Apostolic Church upon British Christianity was slight in comparison with the Oxford Movement which in some ways it came to resemble. The community is now almost non-existent, but the impressive University Church of Christ the King on Gordon Square, built in 1853, is associated with it.

▶ Victorian London **M** University Church of Christ the King, G-6

Caxton, William (?1422-91), and London's First Printed Books The Christian history of London, particularly in Reformation times, is so closely associated with the publication of Bibles that we cannot ignore the introduction of printing into England by William Caxton. Caxton began his career as an apprentice to a cloth dealer in London and was sent to Bruges by his employer. In 1446 he set up his own business and became a leader in the English business community in Bruges. He travelled widely, developed a literary interest and began translating books into English. During this period, in 1456, the first printed book, the 42 line Bible, was produced in Mainz by Johann Gutenberg. Soon printing presses were springing up all over Europe.

Caxton finished his first translation in 1471 and decided to learn the new skill of printing in order to produce his own books. He set up a press in Bruges and in 1476 returned to Britain and set up the same press at the almonry (head of Tothill Street) near the Abbey at Westminster. His first printed book was the *Sayings Of the Philosophers*, followed by Chaucer's *Canterbury Tales* and Malory's *King Arthur* (1485). In fourteen years he printed 18,000 folio pages, making up eighty separate books in English.

Because of the law against heresy passed by Parliament in 1401 and the so-called 'constitutions of Clarendon' adopted by a synod in 1408 declaring it heresy for anyone to 'translate on his own authority any text of holy scripture in the English tongue', no Bible in English (except a few Wyclifite versions that had escaped the flames) was available in Caxton's time. However, in 1483 he published the *Golden Legend* which contains fourteen lives of Old Testament characters translated by himself. Certain other of his books also contain Scripture or paraphrases of the Bible from Latin and European languages. Caxton, therefore, is technically the first person to print the Bible in English. Ironically, perhaps, the first *complete* English translation of the New Testament, William Tyndale's version, was printed abroad—in Cologne, Germany (in 1525). ▶ Medieval London   ◼ Examples of Caxton's printing in British Library, H-1

Cenotaph, The   This is a simple stone obelisk in the centre of Whitehall near Parliament Square which commemorates the members of the British armed forces who fell in the two World Wars. It was designed by Sir Edwin Lutyens and first erected in plaster in 1919 as a saluting point for the Allied 'victory march'. The stone monument was unveiled on 11 November 1920, and the inscription referring to World War II unveiled in 1946. Here on 'Remembrance Sunday' (nearest Sunday to Armistice Day) an outdoor service is held, attended by the sovereign, the prime minister and other dignitaries, who lay wreaths of red poppies at its base. The Lord's Prayer is recited, prayers offered and hymns sung, participated in by huge throngs. The service is followed by a 'march-past' of war veterans, some among them in wheelchairs or otherwise bearing marks of wounds sustained in the war.   ◼ Map location C-1

Chapel Royal, St James Palace   St James Palace on Pall Mall was built by Henry VIII in 1531 on the site of a former lepers' hospital. While the official home of the sovereign is now Buckingham Palace, the royal court is still known as the Court of St James. The Chapel Royal dates partly to the sixteenth century when the palace was built; its beautiful ceiling is said to have been designed by Holbein in 1540. It has a tradition of fine music, which today is provided by the private choir of the sovereign, composed of six men and ten boys. Famous organists have included Orlando Gibbons and Purcell. At Epiphany (6 January) the service is conducted by the bishop of London, and an offering of gold, frankincense and myrrh is made on behalf of the sovereign. This has been the site of several royal marriages, including those of William III and Mary II (1677), Queen Anne (1683), George IV (1795), Queen Victoria (1840) and George V (1893). Visitors may attend services in the Chapel Royal if there is no service in the Queen's Chapel nearby.   ◼ Map location B-1

Charing Cross (and Cheapside Cross)   One of London's most famous landmarks, whose name is almost synonymous with London itself, is Charing Cross. This is a medieval-appearing stone monument in the forecourt of the Charing Cross Railway Station at the western end of the Strand. As many of the troop trains bound for France left from here during both World Wars, it had a particularly sentimental connotation during those periods. The monument seen today is a reproduction done in the nineteenth century. But behind it is a story that has very much to do with Christian London.

In medieval times there were in Cheapside (the main

commercial or market street of old London) and at the hamlet of Charing, about half way along the road between London and Westminster, beautiful crosses of stone set atop carved monuments. These were originally erected by the great warrior-king Edward I as memorials to his beloved queen, Eleanor, who died in 1290. A series of these crosses, thirteen in all, were placed along the way from Nottingham to Westminster, wherever Eleanor's bier rested. In London the crosses (which were reconstructed several times over the years) became familiar landmarks. Like all market crosses, which still may be seen today in many English towns and in the ancient parts of European cities, they were symbols of the centrality of the Christian faith in the medieval community.

During the Reformation, however, London's crosses became the targets of the more extreme Puritans, who wanted to do away with all Catholic 'objects of superstition and idolatry'. Cheapside Cross was first attacked and mutilated as early as 1581. Eventually it was rebuilt, but in 1641 the new cross was defaced, and this attack was followed by a series of pamphlets denouncing it. Finally in 1643 Parliament authorized its destruction, which was accomplished by 'a troop of horse and two companies of foot'. We are told that 'at the fall of the top cross drums beat, trumpets blew, and multitudes of caps were thrown into the air, and a great shout of people with joy'.

Charing Cross, which was said 'to have been more elegant than any of the other crosses erected to Queen Eleanor's memory', was also sentenced by Parliament to be taken down in 1643, but the order was not carried out until 1647. Some of the stones were then used for paving in front of Whitehall. In 1679 an equestrian statue of Charles I, that had been hidden during the Commonwealth period, was set up on the site of the old cross. It still stands at the top of Whitehall, and is recognized as one of London's finest outdoor sculptures.

The area never ceased to be known as Charing Cross, however, and in the nineteenth century the Charing Cross Railway Station and Hotel were built just east of the original site, replacing the old Hungerford Market. In 1863 a new Charing Cross was built and set up outside the station facing the Strand. It is seventy feet high in the decorated Gothic style of the thirteenth and fourteenth centuries, reproducing as near as possible the old one. In its upper storey are eight crowned statues of Queen Eleanor, four representing her as queen with the royal insignia, and the other four with the attributes of a Christian woman. Its presence beside the bustling traffic of the Strand is a pleasant reminder of piety and devotion of a bygone age.
▶ Medieval London   M Map location H-4

Charles I (reigned 1625-49)

Charles I, though more handsome, courteous and manly than his father James I, was unfortunately no more wise. He plunged recklessly into wars with Spain and France and in both cases met with disastrous defeats. The continued tension with

Parliament, now led by three capable men named Wentworth, Eliot and Pym, culminated in the formulation of a 'Petition of Rights' in 1528 which Charles was forced to sign because of his need for funds. This has been compared with the Magna Carta which King John reluctantly signed in 1215.

In religious affairs, Parliament tried to surpress non-Protestant sermons and books while Charles encouraged such views. The situation exploded in 1629 when the king refused to allow the appearance of certain offending clergymen and others who had been summoned to appear before Parliament. He sent instead a message that Parliament should postpone its sitting. Certain members held the speaker down in his chair while Eliot read a series of resolutions against the king's actions. For this, Charles suspended Parliament for eleven years, and during this period got his revenge by charging Eliot and Pym with rioting. The former died in the Tower of London.

Eventually, in 1640, Charles became embroiled in a bitter controversy with the Scots by attempting to force on them a prayer book and the rule of bishops, as in England. A great number of prominent Scots signed a 'National Covenant' to resist the king, and formed an army which proved to be stronger than that sent by Charles. He was obliged to call Parliament in hopes of raising money, and from this point on Parliament gained the upper hand. Pym became its most influential leader, new constitutional powers were voted in, and in time a long document called the 'Grand Remonstrance' enumerated all of the crimes and wrongdoing that could be charged to Charles.

In 1641 the king, taking advantage of some disunity among Parliament members over a rebellion in Ireland, marched with 500 armed men to the Parliament House and attempted personally to arrest Pym and some other leaders (who escaped into the City of London). The entire Parliament then moved from Westminster to London for a few days, with the welcome and support of its citizens. Charles, seeing that the only route open to him was armed conflict, rode with his followers to the north of England where the people generally were royalist, and on 22 August 1642, called on all loyal citizens to support him. The Civil War was on! ▶ Stuart & Commonwealth London **M** Seventeenth-century equestrian statue, head of Whitehall (where old Charing Cross once stood), H-5 Bust over entrance to Whitehall Banqueting House, C-12 Portraits, National Portrait Gallery, H-9

Charles II (reigned 1660-85) The son of Charles I, he spent many years in exile before being invited by Parliament to return to the English throne. Prior to coming to England Charles sent a message to Parliament, called the 'Declaration of Breda', indicating among other things that he was willing to support any law in favour of liberty of conscience. He also made it clear that in a conflict of interests he would not challenge the will of Parliament. Therefore it seems obvious that, though he hoped existing laws restricting freedom of worship would not be enforced or new laws passed, he was not in a position to exercise very much influence.

In the early years of Charles II's reign Parliament feared that the very large numbers of Nonconformists and former soldiers from Cromwell's army now in England might once again pose a threat of Civil War. Consequently, a number of very harsh laws were passed against Nonconformists or 'Dissenters'. By 1669 the king had made it known to some of his intimates that he was a Roman Catholic, and in 1672 he attempted to pass a 'Declaration of Indulgence'. This would have suspended enforcement of religious laws, but once again his good intentions were overridden. When Titus Oates revealed his so-called Popish Plot it seemed that indeed there was danger of an uprising. But after this was exposed, public feeling ran against those who persecuted the Catholics, and Charles's popularity increased.

Charles II was, in fact, a popular monarch for most of his reign. He was handsome, witty and full of charm, and became known as the 'Merry Monarch'. Morally he was a rake and profligate (which probably added to his charm in the popular mind); two of his paramours, Nell Gwynne and Louise de Keroualle, the Duchess of Portsmouth, were known to all the world. Even on his deathbed his wit never failed him; he asked pardon for taking such a very long time to die. At the last he made confession to a Catholic priest and received the final rites of the Catholic church. ▶ Restoration London **M** Portraits, National Portrait Gallery, H-9   Statue, South Court, Chelsea Royal Hospital, A-2

Charterhouse, The   The Charterhouse includes some of the last bits of Elizabethan architecture in London (along with the Staple Inn, Middle Temple Hall and parts of the Tower). The property faces a wooded green (Charterhouse Square) just off Charterhouse Street and only a few steps from Aldersgate Street. The name is a corruption of 'Chartreuse', the place in France where the Carthusian order was founded.

This lovely and quaint bit of Old London traces its history back to a terrible plague which occurred in 1348. People died so rapidly that the bodies were simply thrown into pits outside the city walls. The bishop of London, Ralph Stratford, grieved that these burials were in unsanctified ground, consecrated three acres of land not far from the Smithfield for a burying ground and erected a chapel where masses could be said for the souls of the victims. The place was called Pardon Churchyard (later New Church Hawe), and Stow says that some 50,000 persons were interred here.

A few years later, in 1361, another bishop of London named Michael de Northburgh left in his will a large sum of money to endow a Carthusian monastery at Pardon Churchyard. The Carthusian order had been founded in 1080 by Bruno, a German priest, and was known for its severe discipline. An additional thirteen acres were added to the original three in 1371 by the famous knight, Sir Walter de Manny. At this time the first prior, John Lustote, was nominated.

The Order apparently gained a good reputation for maintaining the discipline and holy life prescribed by Bruno, and Thomas More himself lived under the rigorous rule of the monastery for four years toward the end of the fifteenth century, but without taking vows. When the Carthusians were suppressed in 1535 the prior and some of the brothers suffered most cruelly. As they were being led from the Tower of London More observed to his daughter Margaret Roper, 'Seest thou that these blessed Fathers be now as cheerful in going to their deaths as bridegrooms to their marriages'.

For the next seventy-six years this immense and valuable property was tossed about like a royal bauble. In the process, of course, it was considerably altered, though fragments of the original monastery including the gate still remain. First Henry VIII gave it to two of the caretakers, then to Sir Thomas Audley, speaker of the House of Commons, then to Sir Edward North, one of the king's privy councillors. The Duke of Northumberland had it for a time before his execution, then Lord North took it back again and was nearly bankrupted by entertaining Queen Elizabeth several times. His son sold it to the Duke of Norfolk, but it reverted to the crown when this unfortunate gentleman was beheaded for conspiring to marry Mary, Queen of Scots. Later it was given to the Duke's son, Lord Thomas Howard. King James (who of course was Mary's son) was a guest of Howard for several days and made him Earl of Suffolk. Eventually Howard sold it to the remarkable philanthropist, Thomas Sutton.

With Sutton begins the period of the Charterhouse's greatest fame. Sutton was nearing the end of his adventurous life and had no heir to whom he could leave his vast fortune. All sorts of people, including King James, were after his money, but what decided the issue for the old man was a letter from the Bishop of Exeter which began as follows:

> The very basest element yields gold. The savage Indian gets it, the servile apprentice works it, the very Midianitish camel may wear it, the miserable worldling admires it, the covetous Jew swallows it, the unthrifty ruffian spends it. What are all these better for it? Only good use gives praise to earthly possessions... To be a friend to this Mammon is to be an enemy to God; but to make friends with it is royal and Christian.

Accordingly, Sutton bought the Charterhouse for the purpose of founding a charity hospital for aged pensioners and a school for boys of poor parents. It was called 'the greatest gift in England, either in Protestant or Catholic times, ever bestowed by any individual'. Letters patent for the hospital were issued in June 1611. Sutton died the following December.

From this notable act of Christian charity grew one of the most famous public schools in England. By the early nineteenth century it numbered over 600 boys, and the list of old Carthusians who attained national and even international fame is extensive. While most of these names of lord chancellors, chief justices, generals, judges, bishops and scholars may now be unfamiliar, lasting fame has been achieved by John Wesley, the founder of the Methodist Church; William M. Thackeray the novelist, Joseph Addison, essayist, poet and statesman; Sir Richard Steele, author and politician; Richard Lovelace and Richard Crashaw, poets; Rodger Williams, the founder of Rhode Island; Max Beerbohm, author and friend of G.K. Chesterton; and Lord Baden-Powell, founder of the Boy Scouts.

In 1935 most of the old Charterhouse School property with its playing fields was purchased by St Bartholomew's Hospital and soon disappeared forever. The pensioner's hostel, however, still remains. This includes the medieval stone arch that is the entryway from the street and Charterhouse Square, the lovely Elizabethan Great Hall with the date 1611 over the doorway, the Chapel containing the elaborate tomb of the founder and other parts such as the Chapel Cloisters, the Master's Court, the Great Chamber and the Wash-House Court. Due to decreased revenue the present number of brethren is about forty. They must be bachelors or widowers over sixty, members of the Church of England, and either retired military, clergy, doctors, lawyers, artists or professional men. While Charterhouse Square is public, permission must be obtained to visit the Hostel. ▶ Elizabethan London   Stuart & Commonwealth London
M Map location J-1

Chaucer, Geoffrey (?1340-1400), and *The Canterbury Tales*

Chaucer is the most famous English poet of the medieval period, and one of the greatest story-tellers of all time. A courtier and civil servant most of his life, he wrote many poems, some modelled after the French and Italian literature of the Renaissance. But he is known primarily for his *Canterbury Tales*, written around 1387 in the 'Middle English' spoken at the time. This long narrative poem describes a merry group of thirty pilgrims who start out from the Tabard Inn in Southwark to visit the shrine of the 'holy blisful martir' Thomas Becket. The pilgrims agree to tell two tales each, and between Chaucer's descriptions of the participants and the kinds of stories they tell we get a very vivid picture of a cross-section of fourteenth-century English society.

Not surprisingly, seven of the pilgrims are related in one way or another to the church, and they are in the main as worldly as the rest and hypocritical to boot. This portrait corresponds dramatically with the protests of the Lollards and the complaints of the peasants at that time. In fact, the most obnoxious individual of the whole party is the Pardoner, who sells fake relics. 150 years later the Reformation was triggered by Martin Luther's reaction to a Pardoner named Tetzel.

Significantly, however, Chaucer demonstrates in the description of the country parson and his brother the ploughman that he had a deep understanding of the part that true, Christlike religion played in medieval life. Of the parson, Chaucer says (Neville Coghill's translation):

> This noble example to his sheep he gave,
> First following the word before he taught it,
> And it was from the gospel he had caught it...
> His business was to show a fair behavior
> And draw men thus to Heaven and their Saviour.

Chaucer was the first great English literary figure to be buried in Westminster Abbey (C-10). Around his grave in the south transept are the tombs and monuments of many famous writers, and this section of the Abbey is now widely known as 'Poet's Corner'.

▶ Medieval London   **M** Monument in Poet's Corner, Westminster Abbey, C-10   Portrait in National Portrait Gallery, H-9   Copy of *Canterbury Tales* printed by Caxton in British Library, H-1

Chelsea Old Church   Chelsea Old Church (officially, All Saints, Chelsea) has been since medieval times the parish church of the riverside village of Chelsea, a mile or so up the Thames from Westminster. Its primary claim to fame is its association with the great Sir Thomas More, whose modern statue faces the river outside the church. During the 1520s and early 30s More lived at Beaufort House, a stately home surrounded by spacious gardens just a short distance from the church. In fact, the public gardens across Old Church Street are on the site of More's apple orchard. Beaufort House itself stood just beyond the orchard, and today the site is occupied by Crosby Hall, another of More's residences moved from Bishopsgate Street. The Beaufort Stairs down to the Thames once were at the back of his garden.

Thomas More, though a lawyer and politician by profession, practised his Christian faith with remarkable consistency. According to one historian, 'More rose early, and assembled his family morning and evening in the chapel, when certain prayers and Psalms were recited. He heard mass daily himself, and expected all his household to do so on Sundays and festivals'. His friend, Erasmus of Rotterdam, wrote of his domestic life: 'I should rather call his house a school, or university of Christian religion... there is no quarrelling or intemperate words heard; none seem idle; that worthy gentleman doth not govern with proud and lofty words, but with well-timed and courteous benevolence; everybody performeth his duty, yet is there always alacrity; neither is sober mirth anything wanting'.

More took considerable interest in the ancient parish church, and expended large sums of his own money for its improvement. He provided the communion plate, remarking prophetically, 'Good men give these things, and bad men will soon take them away'. The More Chapel, entered from the south aisle, was rebuilt at his expense in 1528 (the date is visible on one of the pillar capitals). On the south wall is a memorial to More and his first wife—it was originally placed by More for his first wife in 1532. He also wrote his own epitaph, which was engraved on a tablet of black marble and placed in the south wall of the chancel in 1532 (the present one is a copy of 1833).

A number of other interesting monuments are to be found in Chelsea Old Church, seven of which date from the sixteenth century. However, the fact that the memory of Thomas More (and possibly his severed head) is enshrined here is its outstanding feature. The whole building was blasted by two land mines in 1941, but because the More Chapel was redeemable the church was rebuilt along original lines.

▶ Reformation London   **M** Map location A-3

Chesterton, G.K. (1874-1936)   G.K. Chesterton was born in London and was associated with the journalistic and literary scene there all of his life, using its streets, traditions, people and legends as an integral part of his material. Probably best known today for his Father Brown stories, in which a witty Catholic priest pursues his sideline of solving murder mysteries, he wrote with humour and dexterity a wide range of poetry, essays, biography, novels, literary criticism and plays. 'His pages abound in epigrams, sleights, witty word play, allusion and almost farcical polemic, but his seriousness in social and moral questions, and the flowing abundance of his imaginative energies, generated a zeal that make his best writings remarkably distinctive of their kind.'

Chesterton became a Roman Catholic in 1922, but had progressed toward this step through years of speculation and study. Several of his novels—*The Napoleon of Notting Hill*, *The Man Who Was Thursday*, *Manalive*, *The Return of Don Quixote*—are allegories revolving around the Christian gospel. Some of his essays, notably *Orthodoxy* and *The Everlasting Man*, are original and imaginative defences of the biblical Christian world view. The famous Christian apologist C.S. Lewis later acknowledged a great debt to G.K. Chesterton.   ▶ Twentieth-century London   **M** Portrait in National Portrait Gallery, H-9   Marker on former residence, No. 1 Earl's Terrace, Holland Park

China Inland Mission   Founded by pioneer missionary J. Hudson Taylor in 1865, the C.I.M. (now Overseas Missionary Fellowship) was the leading faith mission in China up to the Communist takeover in the late 1940s. The former mission headquarters at Golders Green has some of the original buildings, including an arch facing the street surmounted with the words, 'Trust In God'.   ▶ Victorian London

Christ Church, Newgate Street. See *Towers.*

Church Missionary Society   One of the two great missionary arms of the

Anglican Church and Britain's largest missionary society, it was founded in London in 1799 by members of the Clapham Sect.
▶ Classical London

City Temple This famous Congregational church building on the south side of Holborn Viaduct was opened in 1874 under Dr Joseph Parker, though the congregation was first formed in 1640. The facade is original, but most of the building was rebuilt after the bombing.
M Map location J-3

The Civil War and the Execution of the King The Civil War between the royalist forces of King Charles I and the Parliamentarian troops (the so-called Roundheads) began in August, 1642. The kings's forces were at the first victorious in a number of engagements, but then the tide turned as a result of intervention from Scotland. The Scots and English parliaments entered into a 'Solemn League and Covenant' to adopt a uniform religion in the British Isles 'according to the Word of God and the example of the best reformed churches'. A Scottish army was soon on its way south and, joining the English Parliamentarians in the Battle of Marston Moor, comprehensively defeated the Royalists on 2 July 1644. In the meanwhile, Parliament declared that church government in England would be Presbyterian henceforth, did away with bishops and the prayer-book, and adopted the Westminster Confession as the rule of faith. In London and throughout England the 'purification' of churches and cathedrals took the severest turn yet, and all forms of Christian art and church decoration were ruthlessly destroyed.

The next phase of this amazing and terrifying religious drama was characterized by even further splintering of religious factions, as the Presbyterians and Parliament began to seek for peace while the 'Independents', represented by the army, determined to carry the war to a finish. A 'New Model' army was organized under Sir Thomas Fairfax and Oliver Cromwell, and the king was utterly defeated and forced to surrender in May 1646. For three years, while being held prisoner, he negotiated with the Presbyterians, the Scots, the Irish, the French, but no satisfactory plan for his restoration could be arrived at. At last the army took Charles under its own custody, a trial of sorts was held and the death sentence pronounced. On 30 January 1649, he stepped out of a window onto a platform outside the Banqueting House of Whitehall Palace and was beheaded in the sight of all the people. ▶ Stuart & Commonwealth London **M** Whitehall Banqueting House, C-1/2

Clapham Sect In the early 1780s a group of Christians of wealth and influence began to meet for Bible study and prayer in the London suburb of Clapham. Eventually they included a number of extraordinarily gifted individuals such as the great parliamentarian William Wilberforce; Henry Thonton, the banker; Charles Grant, a director of the East India Company; James Steven, a leading barrister; Lord Teignmouth, a governor-general of India; Zachary Macaulay, the first governor of Sierra Leone and the editor of the *Christian Observer*; and certain prominent non-residents such as Hannah More, the writer and pioneer educator, and Charles Simeon, the outstanding Anglican evangelical of his day.

The accomplishments of this body in proportion to their limited numbers is nothing short of astounding. They include anti-slavery laws, the founding of the colony of Sierra Leone for ex-slaves, the founding of schools and the betterment of education, the founding of the Religious Tract Society, the development of churches and missions in India, and the founding of the British and Foreign Bible Society and the Church Missionary Society. ▶ Classical London
M Memorial plaque on Clapham Parish Church, Clapham Commons

Classical Churches in London's West End Here and there in the midst of the bustling and fashionable West End are eight famous classical-style (or 'neo-classical') churches. All of them boast the familiar colonaded porch, but beyond that they are different both in design and in the parts they have played in London's history. Any one of them is well worth a visit, however brief. They are:

M All Souls, Langham Place, F-2   St George, Bloomsbury, H-11
St George, Hanover Square, F-4   St Martin-in-the-Fields, H-13   St Mary-le-Strand, H-14   St Marylebone Parish Church, E-5   St Pancras, New Church, G-4   St Peter's, Vere Street, E-6

Colet, John (c.1466-1519) Colet shares with Thomas More the distinction of being one of England's two greatest Christian Humanists and theologians. He was born into a wealthy family—his father was several times Lord Mayor of London—and while studying in Italy was influenced by the reformer Savonarola. Upon his return to England he proved his great knowledge of biblical Greek by lecturing at Oxford on the Epistles of Paul. He was an intimate friend of Thomas More and Erasmus. He became dean of St Paul's in 1505 and anticipated the Reformation by his scriptural preaching and emphasis on clerical reform. He was the founder of the famous St Paul's School. ▶ Renaissance London   **M** Bust, National Portrait Gallery, H-9

Congregationalists (or Separatists) During the Elizabethan period the Christians who objected to what they considered Roman Catholic elements in the Church of England form of worship seem to have been generally classed as 'Puritans', though in fact not all were followers of the Reformed doctrines of Calvin. Another group, which became known as 'Separatists', felt that the idea of a state church was foreign to the New Testament and was introduced by the Emperor Constantine over 300 years after Christ. In their view, the first churches consisted of groups of Christians who separated themselves from the world, or in a sense were 'gathered out' from the world by the Spirit of Christ. They contended that the church as defined in the New Testament was made up only of committed Christians who met together for 'the apostles' teaching and fellowship... breaking of bread and prayers' (Acts 2:42).

Another name applied to some of the Separatists was 'Brownists', referring to Robert Browne whose treatise, *Reformation without Tarrying for Any* (1582) gave birth to Congregational principles of church organization. Browne taught that the church is under the authority and law of God and Jesus Christ by a willing covenant. It should not, therefore, be required to answer to bishops or magistrates. Ordination, he taught, is not vested in elders but should be in the hands of the whole church. Many of the Separatists eventually left England under pressure from the state church, and large numbers settled in Holland. A group from John Robinson's congregation in Leyden, now known as the 'Pilgrim Fathers', sailed from Plymouth in 1620 to settle in Massachusetts, thus establishing Congregationalism (or Separatism) as the earliest form of church government in the New England colonies. But the Congregationalists also became one of the major Nonconformist bodies in England from the seventeenth century onward. ▶ Elizabethan and Stuart London

Coram, Thomas (died 1791) Thomas Coram was an eighteenth-century sea captain who, seeing the plight of infants born to prostitutes and other women unable to care for their offspring, established the famous Foundling Hospital in Bloomsbury. The Hospital received considerable support from George F. Handel, William Hogarth and other artists. He is buried in St. Andrew's, Holborn. ▶ Classical London **M** Tomb, St. Andrew's, Holborn, J- 10 Portrait, National Portrait Gallery, H-9 The Foundling Hospital Art Treasures at 40 Brunswick Square, WC1, has about 150 paintings and prints on display, plus other mementoes from the Foundling Hospital.

Courtauld Institute Galleries A very fine small museum of art attached to the University of London. The galleries, open every day, are located facing Woburn Square on the west. Rooms I-A, I-B and II consist of old masters and early Italian paintings including some by Fra Angelica, Botticelli, Giorgione, Rubens and other familiar names. Many are of biblical subjects. The museum also includes a collection of French Impressionist paintings. **M** Map location G-1

Coverdale, Miles (1488-1568) He was a priest who left the Augustinian monastery at Cambridge in 1528 to become an evangelical preacher and Bible translator. He spent seven years on the Continent, finishing in 1535 the first complete English translation of the Scriptures, the noble work that William Tyndale had begun. During the short reign of Edward VI, Coverdale was royal chaplain. However, he was imprisoned for two years under Mary, escaping through the intercession of the king of Denmark. From 1564 to 1566 he was rector of St. Magnus, London Bridge. ▶ Reformation London **M** Memorial, St. Magnus, London Bridge, D-4

Cranmer, Thomas (1489-1556) Cranmer played the most important clerical role in the progress of the Reformation in England through the reigns of both Henry VIII and Edward VI. He was university preacher at Oxford when Henry was seeking a reason to separate from Catherine, and he suggested that the matter be referred to the theologians of the universities. The king acted upon this proposal, and Cranmer was rewarded with advancement. He became archbishop of Canterbury in 1533 and, following this, declared Henry's marriage to Catherine null and void from the beginning.

As archbishop, Cranmer was able to retain the favour of the king and also bring about genuine reform to the church. He was particularly responsible for securing an official English translation of the Bible. Under Henry VIII he began to modify the liturgy of the church to bring it in line with the Bible rather than tradition, finishing this work under Edward VI. (He was also tutor to the young king.) But his greatest contribution to the Reformation was the *Book of Common Prayer*, first published in 1549 and revised in 1552. Most of the work on this was done in his study at Lambeth Palace.

Shortly after Mary succeeded to the throne Cranmer was sentenced to death for treason. Execution of the sentence was delayed for a time, but in 1555 he was tried and convicted at Oxford. Under great pressure, he recanted. But on the eve of his execution in March 1566, he renounced his recantation. At the stake he courageously extended over the flames the hand that had signed the compromising document. ▶ Reformation London **M** Portrait in Lambeth Palace, C-4 Portrait, National Portrait Gallery, H-9

Cromwell, Oliver (1599-1658) Following the execution of Charles I in the years between 1649 and 1660, England was at first governed as a republic or commonwealth under a Council of State appointed by Parliament. The power behind this new government was the army, led by Thomas Fairfax and Oliver Cromwell. When Ireland declared for Charles II, the heir to the English throne, Cromwell led his troops in a thorough and brutal defeat of that nation. Later, in 1650, Scotland also acknowledged Prince Charles, and when Fairfax refused to act against them, Cromwell was made supreme commander.

Oliver Cromwell was a brilliant commander, a man of culture and refinement and, in his own eyes, a humble servant of God. Personally, he was a man of prayer, and he was thoroughly familiar with the Bible. He chose as chaplains some of the most godly Puritan divines in the land, Richard Baxter for example. But first and foremost he was a military man, and in combat or in a punitive campaign as against the Irish he was utterly ruthless.

In two actions Cromwell also smashed the Scottish armies, and by

September 1651, armed resistance anywhere in the British Isles was no longer possible. In 1653 Cromwell, now the most powerful man in Britain, dissolved Parliament. A small 'nominated Parliament' met for a while, but this assembly put all their authority into the hands of Cromwell in December 1653, giving him the title of Lord Protector.

It was a time of strange extremes—brilliant military campaigns and treaties abroad and a general breakdown of all the old religious traditions at home, with radical movements starting off in all directions. Opposition to the military government and to the ascetic religious practices of the ruling powers grew apace, and when Oliver Cromwell suddenly died in 1658 London and most of the rest of the country was as ready for a change as it had been when it rose against Charles I.

The final two years of the Commonwealth were an anticlimax. The office of Lord Protector fell to Oliver Cromwell's son Richard, who soon proved inadequate for this high position. The army invited the former members of Parliament to meet again, but before long this body was dissolved and a new Parliament freely elected in its place. Everyone knew that the monarchy would soon be restored. ▶ Stuart & Commonwealth London **M** Statue outside Westminster Hall, C-11 Painting in National Portrait Gallery, H-9

Crosby, John (died 1475) One of London's famous lord mayors, Crosby was a wealthy grocer who was also a diplomat, ambassador and a great benefactor to the church. Sir John Crosby and his wife are buried under a fine monument in St. Helen's, Bishopsgate. ▶ Medieval London **M** St. Helen, Bishopsgate, M-10

Crosby Hall Crosby Hall is the only surviving example in London of a wealthy merchant's mansion from before the Reformation. Sir John Crosby, grocer and wool merchant, was a generous benefactor of St. Helen's, a member of Parliament for London and a Knight of the Garter. He built Crosby Hall in 1470 near St. Helen's on Bishopsgate Street, which Stow says was 'very large and beautiful, and the highest at that time in London'. Later in the fifteenth century it was rented by Sir John's widow to Richard, Duke of Gloucester (later Richard III). Shakespeare, who was himself familiar with Crosby Hall, uses the old mansion as a backdrop for Richard's intrigues to take over the crown in his historical play *Richard the Third*.

In 1501 a lord mayor, Sir Bartholomew Reed, entertained Princess Catherine of Aragon at Crosby Hall two days before her marriage to Prince Arthur. Between 1516 and 1523 the Hall was inhabited by the great Sir Thomas More when Under Treasurer, and here he was host to Erasmus of Rotterdam. He was followed by a good friend, the merchant Antonio Bonvici, to whom More wrote a farewell letter with a piece of charcoal in the Tower the night before his execution. In Elizabethan days Crosby Hall was owned by Sir John Spencer, who while lord mayor put on an entertainment here for the queen herself.

For a while the Dowager Countess of Pembroke was a tenant, at whose table Shakespeare was probably a frequent guest.

During the Civil War Crosby Hall was used as a temporary prison; then from 1672 until 1769 it became a Presbyterian chapel which was served by a number of eminent ministers. By the early nineteenth century this fine Gothic residence in the perpendicular style had fallen into decay, but it was ultimately restored through public subscription. It became a literary and scientific institute, then a restaurant, and was finally purchased by the University and City Association of London and moved to Chelsea in 1910. It is now a college hall of the British Federation of University Women, and open for view upon application at the door (enter from Cheyne Walk).

▶ Medieval London   **M** Map location, A-4

Crusades and London   Between the years 1095 and 1291 seven major military campaigns were waged by English and European knights against the Islamic forces which had occupied Jerusalem and much of Palestine. The First Crusade, proclaimed by Pope Urban II in 1095, resulted in the reconquest of Antioch and Jerusalem. The Second Crusade, initiated by Bernard of Clairvaux in 1147, ended in defeat at Damascus. The Islamic armies under Saladin then succeeded in re-taking Jerusalem in 1187. The answer of the church in Europe was the famous Third Crusade, led by Frederick Barbarossa of Germany, Philip II of France and Richard I of England, who was nicknamed 'the Lionheart'. (His heroic statue may be seen in Old Palace Yard outside the Houses of Parliament.) During this campaign the English knights played a particularly important role as Frederick was drowned and Philip returned to France, leaving Richard in command. After much fierce fighting a three-year truce was arranged and Christian pilgrims were granted free access to Jerusalem. The last battle of the Crusaders was their loss of Acre in 1291.

During the two-hundred-year era of the Crusades, various strategic parts of the Middle East were held by the Christians as Crusade States; ruins of their fortresses may still be seen in Jordan, Israel and other places. The purpose of these was partly military, to provide protection for pilgrims, and partly monastic, to create Christian communities in the lands of the Bible. To man these Crusader outposts two semi-monastic orders were created, the Knights Templar and the Knights Hospitaller. In reality, the system did not work—the forces of the Crusader States were not strong enough to establish permanent control over the holy sites—but the Templars and Hospitallers distinguished themselves in many a battle, and in medieval London they grew to be among the most powerful of the City's many religious houses.

The legendary courage, discipline and Christian demeanor of the knights of the Crusader orders have been celebrated in innumerable romantic tales, and it is partly from these that Western civilization

has derived the ideal of chivalry. Chaucer is thought to have had a
Crusader in mind in the following description from the Prologue to
the *Canterbury Tales*:

> A Knight was with us, and an excellent man,
> Who from the earliest moment he began
> To follow his career loved chivalry,
> Truth, openhandedness and courtesy…
> He had never spoken ignobly all his days
> To any man by even a rude inflection,
> He was a knight in all things to perfection.

The Order of Knights Templar was established in 1118 by Baldwin,
King of Jerusalem, to protect Christian pilgrims on the road to the
Holy City. Ten years later the first master of the Order, Hugh de
Payens, established a home for the Templars in London on the south
side of Holborn. Later, when the Order had increased in wealth, a
property was purchased between Fleet Street and the river and a vast
monastery was set up, consisting of a council chamber, refectory,
barracks, cloisters and a river terrace. Their beautiful round church,
dedicated to the Virgin Mary, was consecrated in 1185 by Heraclius,
the Patriarch of Jerusalem, who had come to seek help from Henry II
against the victorious Saladin.

The Knights Hospitaller of St. John of Jerusalem began as a hospital
for pilgrims near the Church of the Holy Sepulchre in Jerusalem and
became military when the Crusades got under way. Their priory in
London was founded during the reign of Henry I (1100-35). It
occupied an extensive property at Clerkenwell north of Smithfield
with a number of grand buildings. St. John's Gate, to be seen today on
St. John's Lane just off Clerkenwell Road, was the south entrance.
Their church, similar to that of the Templars with a round chancel in
imitation of the Church of the Holy Sepulchre, was also dedicated by
Heraclius in 1185.

Both the Templars and the Hospitallers became immensely rich
and powerful, and ultimately corrupt. The Templars were abolished
by Pope Clement in 1312, and the property, still called the Temple,
became a resort of the legal profession. Temple Church is the only one
of the original buildings remaining. The order of St. John of
Jerusalem, on the other hand, lasted until the Dissolution under
Henry VIII, when the property and buildings were sold off or given
away. After changing hands many times the Church of St. John and
St. John's Gate and Gatehouse were taken over in 1831 by the revived
Order of St. John of Jerusalem. This organization, which operates a
voluntary ambulance corps, is in charge of the property today.

▶ Medieval London

Danes in London During the Saxon period (407-1066) London did not
remain permanently under the control of the East Saxons (though

they were the first to occupy it, and the famous Cockney accent is said to have been derived from their language), but became a prize in wars among various Saxon tribes—the Northumbrians, the Mercians, the West Saxons. Then early in the ninth century a new enemy appeared at the gates—the Vikings from Denmark. London was sacked and burned and, for a time, was under Danish subjugation. Eventually certain of the pagan invaders settled down in the City and became Christians. Three of their churches remain today: St Olave's, Hart Street; St Magnus the Martyr; and St Clement Danes. Danish control of London was ended by the great West Saxon King Alfred, and never again has the City fallen to a foreign enemy. ▶ Saxon London

Dickens, Charles (1812-70) Charles Dickens was by far the most popular of Victorian novelists, and he is one of the widest-read English authors of all time. Scenes from many of his stories were set in London, and a number of the City's historic churches are mentioned by characters or described by the author. During the Dickens Centenary in 1970 the London Transport published a guide to the remaining Dickens landmarks, and twenty-six churches were included.

Wherever Dickens gives any detail of London's churches he tends to show us scenes of gloom and dreariness, of stuffy pews, mouldering gravestones and uninspiring clergymen droning sermons over the heads of small audiences of unimportant people. One of the sketches in *The Uncommercial Traveller* is entitled 'City of London Churches'. In this essay the Traveller (Dickens himself) indicates that his childhood memories of churchgoing disposed him to an 'unwholesome hatred' of preachers of a certain sort but that, being unacquainted with the churches in the City, he is determined to make the rounds for a year. Predictably, he finds them universally dull and uninviting, subjects merely for satire. His conclusion: 'They remain like the tombs of the old citizens who lie beneath them and around them, monuments of another age'.

Paradoxically, Dickens holds at the same time a very high view of Christianity and Jesus Christ. He speaks frequently in his novels of the loving Saviour and the hope of Heaven, though in sentimental rather than orthodox terms. Who will ever forget Sydney Carton in *A Tale of Two Cities* walking the streets of Revolutionary Paris while the immortal words from the Church of England burial service echo through his mind: 'I am the Resurrection and the Life. He who believes in Me, though he were dead, yet shall he live'?

A book written in manuscript form for his children and not published until 1934, the *Life of Our Lord*, bears out the earnestness of Dickens's convictions, as does his genuine concern in his novels for the forgotten poor of London's streets: the waifs, the widows, the disenfranchised prisoners languishing in debtors' prisons. These lines from *Domby and Son*, where Harriet reads the Bible to the dying

Alice, illustrate his consistent view of Jesus Christ as the hope of the world:

> Harriet… read the eternal book for all the weary and the heavy-laden, for all the wretched, fallen, and neglected of this earth… read the ministry of Him who, through the round of human life and all its hopes and griefs, from birth to death, from infancy to age, had sweet compassion for, and interest in, its every scene and stage, its every suffering and sorrow.

▶ Victorian London   **M** House/museum and library at 48 Doughty Street, G-2   Portrait, National Portrait Gallery, H-9   Monument, Poet's Corner, Westminster Abbey, C-10   Sculptural frieze on former residence, Ferguson House, Marylebone High Street, E-2

Dissenters   Another term for Nonconformists, Dissenters were Protestants who refused to conform to the established church.

The Dissolution (of the Monasteries)   In 1536 Henry VIII, with the aid of his advisor Thomas Cromwell, induced Parliament to pass a law doing away with one hundred of the smaller monasteries. This was followed in 1540 by a general dissolution of all monastic houses. Considering the concentration of these monastic buildings in London, the effect, according to Walter Besant, was 'Ruins everywhere! Ruins of cloisters, halls, dormitories, courts, and chapels, and churches. Ruins of carved altar-pieces, canopies, statues, painted windows, and graven fonts'.

What actually happened was that the properties were sold off by the crown for whatever could be got for them, and the buildings themselves were either demolished or stripped to the walls and used for other purposes. In a very few cases, notably that of the Nunnery of St Helen's and the Priory of St Bartholomew's, part of the original structures became parish churches and thus retained something of their medieval appearance.

What became of the sites where once could be seen the splendours of medieval Christendom—noble monuments of lords and ladies, rich tapestries, splendid carvings, brilliant stained glass, walls covered with paintings and frescoes—has been partly explained elsewhere. Here are a few more instances:

> The church of the Holy Trinity Priory was sold in its entirety for sixpence a cartload.
> The Crutched Friar's church was made into a carpenter's shop and tennis court.
> The hall of the abbey of the Blackfriars was made into a storehouse for 'properties' of pageants. A playhouse, the famous Blackfriars Theatre, was erected among the ruins by Shakespeare and his friends.
> Charterhouse, of the Carthusian Order, became a private

residence and eventually a pensioners' home and charity school. The church of the Knights Hospitaller was blown up with gunpowder and left a ruin. It was reconstructed and used for a while as a Presbyterian church, later attacked by a mob and burned. The original crypt, however, remains today.

▶ Reformation London

Donne, John (1573-1631)   John Donne is the first—some say the greatest—of several famous poets of the early seventeenth century who make up what scholars call the 'Metaphysical School' of poetry. This name suggests that Donne, the acknowledged leader of the school, followed by Richard Crashaw, Abraham Cowley, George Herbert, Henry Vaughan and others, applied to poetry themes relating to human sin and guilt, Christ's atoning death on the cross, the brevity of mortal life, the joys of heaven, and so on. Donne's poetry is particularly interesting in that it reflects a progression from an early preoccupation with sexual passion to the deeply spiritual insights of his later years.

Donne was born in London of wealthy parents, and was raised a Catholic (his mother was descended from the family of Thomas More). He started his career as a lawyer, but took holy orders in the

St Dunstan-in-the-West. On the east side of the entry arch is a likeness of John Donne, the famous poet who became dean of St Paul's.

Anglican Church in 1615 and became dean of St Paul's Cathedral six years later (a statue of him in his shroud may be seen in St Paul's today, on the south aisle). His poetry and sonnets abound with complex imagery, tending to express the spiritual in unusual, almost bizarre 'conceits' or analogies. Here in these excerpts are two famous examples:

> Death be not proud, though some have called thee
> Mighty and dreadful, for thou art not so;
> For those whom thou think'st thou dost overthrow
> Die not, poor Death, nor yet canst thou kill me.

> At the round earth's imagin'd corners, blow
> Your trumpets, Angells, and arise, arise
> From death, you numberlesse infinities
> Of soules, and to your scattred bodies goe.

However, Donne is perhaps best known for these lines from his prose work *Devotions upon Emergent Occasions*:

> No man is an Iland, intire of it selfe; every man is a peece of the Continent, a part of the maine; if a Clod bee washed away by the Sea, Europe is the lesse, as well as if a Promontorie were, as well as if a Mannor of thy friends or of thine owne were; any man's death diminishes me, because I am involved in Mankinde; And therefore never send to know for whom the bell tolls; It tolls for thee.

▶ Stuart & Commonwealth London   **M** Effigy in the south aisle of the choir, St Paul's, L-15   Face in stone at the entrance to St Dunstans-In-The-West, J-14   Portrait in National Portrait Gallery, H-9

Dutch Church of the Austin Friars   One of the old London monasteries that was closed by Henry VIII has had a colourful history related to the Reformation and has survived in various forms down to the present day. This is the Dutch Church of the Austin Friars, originally built in 1253, enlarged in 1354, and reconsecrated by Dutch and Flemish immigrants in 1550. It was described by Stow as a handsome building with 'a most fine spired steeple, small, high, and straight. I have not seen the like'.

After the Dissolution the friars were turned out, and Henry gave the choir and transepts of their church to William Paulet, First Marquess of Winchester, who apparently used the space for storage until these parts were pulled down in 1611. However, the nave was given by Edward VI to Dutch and Flemish Protestants. Thousands of these Christians had come to England fleeing religious persecution (as later the English Separatists would go to Holland), and this place of worship was given them partly in gratitude for the aid received by Archbishop Cranmer from Protestant theologians on the Continent.

Though briefly interrupted by the reign of Mary, the Dutch

congregation continued to use this building until 1940. They called it 'Jesus Temple'. A fire in 1862 destroyed the roof and most of the old fittings; the floor with its memorial slabs and the fourteenth-century arcades were the only remaining parts of the original interior. This was all swept away by a direct bomb hit in October 1940.

The foundation stone of a completely new church was laid by the Dutch Princess Irene on 23 July 1950, the 400th anniversary of its consecration by the Dutch refugees. The new building, less than half the size of the old church, has an unusual design with rooms on different levels. A large pulpit with canopy is at the front of the sanctuary together with a communion table that can be extended for commnunicants to sit around it. There is some striking stained glass and a beautiful tapestry, all modern. The outside of the building, located on a narrow lane off Austin Friars, is of massed concrete rectangles.   **M** Map location K-2

Edward VI (reigned 1547-53)

Edward VI, Henry VIII's only son, was a boy of ten when his father died in 1547. His reign of six years was controlled by two uncles, first the duke of Somerset and then the duke of Northumberland. Both of these men were ardent Protestants, and as a result a number of bishoprics were turned over to clergymen who favoured the Reformation. Tyndale's Bible and many Protestant books were printed during this period, and it was also during this time that churches in many cases were stripped of images, stained glass was destroyed, pictures were plastered or whitewashed over and clergymen abandoned the use of coloured robes. Priests were also allowed to marry. The Book of Common Prayer brought simpler services with the use of Scripture in English.

The duke of Somerset, the young king's uncle, who took the title of Protector, realized enormous personal gain from his position and built a magnificent palace on the riverbank, midway along the Strand, which came to be known as Somerset House. An eighteenth-century building still called by this name occupies the site today. Somerset made himself unpopular by insisting on conformity to Reformation doctrine and practices by both clergy and laity. Many longstanding practices such as chantries—endowments for the saying of prayers for dead benefactors— were abolished, creating widespread unemployment. Somerset fell from power in 1549, was imprisoned in the Tower and eventually beheaded for treason.

Another of Edward VI's uncles, John Dudley, the Earl of Warwick who was also the duke of Northumberland and Somerset's successor, was equally ambitious and extreme in his Protestant views. During this period young Edward showed himself to be precocious, but his sickly nature gave way to consumption and he died in 1553 at the age of sixteen. Northumberland, realizing that if Mary, the daughter of Catherine of Aragon, came to the throne it would mean the end of a Protestant monarchy and of his power, made a bold but tragic move.

He arranged a marriage between his son and Lady Jane, the daughter of one of Henry VIII's sisters, and got the dying king to set aside Henry VIII's will and appoint Jane to the throne. The plan failed and Lady Jane Grey, a sweet affectionate girl of seventeen and innocent of any political ambition, eventually paid with her life, as did her husband and Northumberland himself. ▶ Reformation London ■ Portrait, National Portrait Gallery, H-9

Eleanor   The queen of Edward I, who died in 1290, she was greatly beloved by her husband and by the people. Eleanor is memorialized by the figures on Charing Cross. ▶ Medieval London

Elizabeth I (reigned 1558-1603)   Elizabeth is considered one of England's outstanding monarchs, in that she was able to unify the nation both politically and religiously. Her courageous navy defeated the great Spanish invasion fleet, and some of the greatest poets of all time, including William Shakespeare, flourished during her later years. However, she alienated the growing numbers of Bible-believing Protestants, which led in time to the tragedy of civil war. ▶ Elizabethan London ■ Statue outside St Dunstan's-In-the-West, J-14 Portraits, National Portrait Gallery, H-9   Effigy on tomb, Royal Chapels, Westminster Abbey, C-10

Episcopalians   Members of the Church of England, which is organized under the authority of bishops. 'Episcopos' is the Greek word for 'bishop'.

Erasmus, Desiderius, or Erasmus of Rotterdam (1466-1536)   Dutch Humanist and the most brilliant mind of his age. His Greek New Testament (the 'Textus Receptus') was a primary source for the translation work of both Martin Luther and William Tyndale. Though a Catholic, he is said to have 'laid the egg that Luther hatched'. Ironically, he was a great friend of Sir Thomas More, who was one of Tyndale's worst enemies. ▶ Reformation London

Eliot, T.S. (1888-1965)   Thomas Stearns Eliot is generally recognized as one of the twentieth-century's foremost poets and literary critics. Although born in America, Eliot was a resident of London from 1915 onward and became a British citizen in 1927. His often-quoted definition of himself is 'classicist in literature, royalist in politics, and Anglo-Catholic in religion'.

Eliot's first mature poems, 'The Love Song Of J. Alfred Prufrock' and 'Preludes', were published in 1915, followed by *Poems* in 1919. He founded his important literary and critical quarterly, *The Criterion*, in 1922, the same year that his poem *The Waste Land* appeared, now recognized as perhaps the most significant work of the twentieth century. '*The Waste Land* must, under any critical reservation, stand as a clue and summary of much of the spiritual and literary history of our time.' This was followed by a number of other

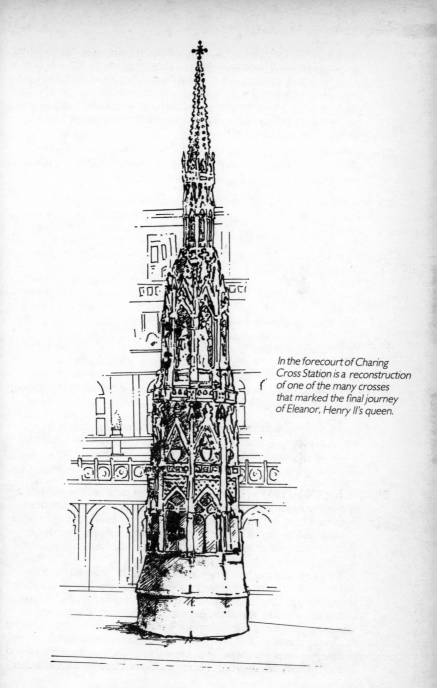

In the forecourt of Charing Cross Station is a reconstruction of one of the many crosses that marked the final journey of Eleanor, Henry II's queen.

67

now-famous poems and collections, 'The Hollow Men' (1925), *Ash Wednesday* (1930) and *Four Quartets* (1943), as well as two plays, *Murder in the Cathedral* (1935) and *The Cocktail Party* (1950), and a host of works dealing with literary criticism.

The heart of T.S. Eliot's literary affirmation is his perception of the spiritual desolation and sterility of mankind in the modern age compared with the 'heroic and sanctified glories of the past'. Modern man, so to speak, inhabits a spiritual wasteland. He is, so far as an awareness of the spiritual significance of life is concerned, empty:

> We are the hollow men.
> We are the stuffed men.
> Leaning together,
> Headpiece filled with straw. Alas!
> Our dried voices, when
> We whisper together,
> Are quiet and meaningless
> As wind in dry grass,
> Or rats' feet over broken glass
> In our dry cellar.

For Eliot, modern man tragically lacks the mystical support of the Christian doctrines of grace and redemption. He is in need of expressing his dependence upon God in prayer (*Four Quartets*), and of the acceptance of sacrifice in the specifically Christian sense (*Murder In the Cathedral*). ▶ Twentieth-century London **M** Portrait, National Portrait Gallery, H-9 Plaque, Northwest corner of Russell Square at Thornhaugh Street (ex Faber & Faber offices), G-3

Ely Chapel (St Etheldreda's Catholic Chapel)
Ely Chapel is the one remnant of a medieval bishop's palace remaining in London. Its story takes us back to very early times when the bishops of Ely had their town residence in the Temple, an arrangement which apparently was not very satisfactory. Thus when John de Kirkeby, bishop of Ely, died in 1290 he left a piece of property above Holborn to his successors for a town house. Over the next few generations this became Ely Place, one of the most magnificent mansions in London. The chapel, dedicated to St Etheldreda, was probably built by de Kirkeby's immediate successor, William de Luda, and was served by three chaplains.

By the end of the fourteenth century Ely Place was further beautified by an orchard, vineyard and kitchen garden, its entrance made stately by the addition of a handsome gatehouse graced by the arms of the famous archbishop Arundel. The chapel stood at the northwest corner of the cloisters, in a field planted with trees and surrounded by a wall. At about this time the celebrated John of Gaunt, Duke of Lancaster, patron of Geoffrey Chaucer and John Wyclif, somehow came to reside at Ely Place. Here the old nobleman died in 1399, and in *Richard II*, Act ii, scene 1, Shakespeare has him admonishing with his last breath his dissipated nephew, King Richard II:

> Landlord of England art thou, and not king!

Ely Place figures in another memorable scene from a Shakespearean play, *Richard III*, when Richard, the villainous Duke of Gloucester, to bide his time before denouncing Lord Hastings, says to the bishop of Ely:

> My lord of Ely, when I was last in Holborn,
> I saw good strawberries in your garden there;
> I do beseech you, send for some of them!

Richard's conqueror at Bosworth Field and the first of the Tudor monarchs, Henry VII, was present at a great banquet at Ely Place in 1495. Some thirty-six years later his more famous son, Henry VIII, was also a guest at a magnificent feast at Ely Place lasting five days. Henry's queen, Catherine of Aragon, also attended, but dined separately from her husband, a sign of the strained relationship which contributed eventually to a break with the Roman Catholic Church and the founding of the Church of England.

During Elizabeth I's reign a gentleman lawyer named Sir Christopher Hatton attracted the attention of her majesty, and eventually was elevated to the post of Lord Chancellor. In 1576 the bishop of Ely, wishing to oblige Elizabeth, granted to Hatton the gatehouse of Ely Place and fourteen acres on a twenty-one year lease. The rent was one red rose for the gatehouse and ten loads of hay and ten pounds sterling a year for the rest. Hatton spent a fortune improving the estate, with money mainly borrowed from the queen. When Elizabeth demanded the money back, the pressure of this unexpected debt brought on a heart attack, and Hatton died in Ely Place in 1591, a broken man.

Hatton's nephew succeeded to the property, and a couple of years later the bishops of Ely occupied part of Ely Place once again. In the tense days of Charles I's reign when theatres were under fire from the Puritans, Ely Place was the scene of a lavish masque, made up by the members of the inns of court to please Queen Henrietta Maria. Later, during the Civil War, the estate was made into a hospital and prison. Finally, in 1762, the last Lord Hatton died and the property reverted to the crown. The bishops of Ely at this time were granted a spacious house in Piccadilly.

Old Ely Chapel is now the lone survivor of Ely Place (and the only pre-Reformation Roman Catholic place of worship in London). Entrance from the street (Ely Place, which runs north off of Charterhouse Street) is via a passageway on the left of the chapel, and next to this is a small paved courtyard, the remnant of the garden where once roses and strawberries grew. Inside the chapel itself the most important item is the large east window with its delicate tracery (the stained glass, of course, is gone). The side windows also boast fine tracery. In between are arcaded niches now filled with statues of English Catholic martyrs done by Charles and May Blakeman, 1952-64. Beneath is a vaulted crypt which stands on Roman foundations. At one time it served as a tavern called The Mitre. The Chapel is open to visitors upon application at the door. ▶ Medieval London **M** Map location J-4

Erkenwald Of the several Saxon saints whose names have been given to London churches, none were Londoners. Probably the most famous Christian name associated with the City in the early Saxon period is Erkenwald, Bishop of London in the early seventh century, who was the son of King Ethelbert, a convert of Augustine. Erkenwald was the third successor to Mellitus, and under him St Paul's Cathedral rose to prominence. Not only was he a popular churchman and a good administrator, but he is said to have performed miracles. Once, on a preaching mission to the woodmen in the forests north of London, his cart lost a wheel but miraculously kept its balance. He died at the convent of his sister Ethelburga at Barking, and the waters of the River Lea subsided when the procession carrying his body came to its shores. Erkenwald's shrine in St Paul's was the old cathedral's most prominent attraction, and accounted for much of its wealth. ▶ Saxon London

Evangelicals *Evangel* means 'good news' in Greek, and refers to the message of the Bible which brings good news about salvation through Christ. The Evangelicals are those in any church who have a high view of the 'good news'.

Evangelical Library This is a lending library of over 50,000 volumes available both for resident research and for borrowing by post anywhere in the world. The works cover all aspects of evangelical thought from earliest times to the present. They range from deep theological tomes to devotionals. The library was founded by Geoffrey Williams in 1924 in his living-room at Beddington, Surrey. It came to the notice of Dr Martin Lloyd-Jones of Westminster Chapel in 1939, and through his efforts was transferred to London. Its present address is 78a Chiltern Street, W1.

Evelyn, John (1620-1706) It is a remarkable coincidence that one of the most eventful periods in the Christian history of London produced not just one but two of England's great diarists, Samuel Pepys and John Evelyn. Pepys and Evelyn both recorded the turbulent Restoration years following the return of Charles II in 1660. Both occupied important government posts and, in fact, were acquainted with and had some association with one another. But while Pepys covers just ten years, 1659 to 1669, Evelyn's *Diary* records incidents beginning with his birth and background and running up to just a short time before his death.

Of John Evelyn, the *Oxford Companion to English Literature* says: '... educated at Balliol College, Oxford, was a man of means, of unblemished character, and a dilettante, who helped to advance English civilization'. Another reference says, '... he remained a pious Christian, loyal Anglican and Royalist all his life'.

Evelyn was the author of over forty books on numerous learned subjects, such as the problem of smoke in London air, engraving, arboriculture, navigation, gardening, and so on. The *Diary* briefly deals with Evelyn's birth and early life, but in a sense it really begins with his vivid descriptions during a three years' sojourn on the Continent from 1643 to 1646.

In 1646 Evelyn settled at Deptford, southeast of London. He occupied numerous government posts, and was a co-founder of the Royal Society. Over the following six decades the *Diary* abounds with sketches of important persons in and around the capital, and descriptions of many of the great events of the times. Here is his entry for 29 May 1660, the day of Charles II's return to London:

> This day, his Majesty, Charles II, came to London, after a sad and long exile and calamitous suffering both of the King and Church, being seventeen years. This was also his birthday, and with a triumph of above 20,000 horse and foot, brandishing their swords, and shouting with inexpressible joy; the ways strewn with flowers, the bells ringing, the streets hung with tapestry, fountains running with wine; the Mayor, Aldermen, and all the companies, in their liveries, chains of gold, and banners; Lords and Nobles, clad in cloth of silver, gold and velvet; the windows and balconies, all set with ladies; trumpets, music, and myriads of people flocking, even so far as from Rochester, so as they were seven hours in passing the city, even from two in the afternoon till nine at night. I stood in the Strand and beheld it, and blessed God. And all this was done without one drop of blood shed, and by that very army which rebelled against him: but it was the Lord's doing, for such a restoration was never mentioned in any history, ancient or modern, since the return of the Jews from their Babylonish captivity...

Evelyn's *Diary*, only recently published in its entirety (1955), is unfortunately rarely read, in contrast to that of Pepys, which is known by every student of English literature and often referred to by travel guides and the like. It is true that Evelyn lacks the chatty style and intimate personal indiscretions that characterize Pepys. But his descriptive powers are every bit as keen, and his curiosity about the nature of things far more penetrating. And for the Christian reader his genuine godliness makes his vast cultural prowess even more exciting. ▶ Restoration London   M Portrait, National Portrait Gallery, H-9

Faber, Frederick William (1814-63)   Father Faber was the founder and first provost of the London Oratory, and a notable preacher, author and hymn writer. He is buried in Brompton Oratory and a monument in Latin marks the site. ▶ Victorian London   M Brompton Oratory, A-1

Farrar, F.W. (1831-1903)   Farrar was a schoolmaster, author, highly acclaimed religious lecturer, and honorary chaplain to Queen Victoria. In 1876 he was appointed by Prime Minister Disraeli as canon of Westminster Abbey and rector of St Margaret's, where his brilliant preaching drew great crowds. His numerous publications included commentaries for the *Expositor's Bible* and the *Cambridge Bible*, the *Life and Works of St Paul*, *The Bible: Its Meaning and Supremacy*, and many others. Farrar, a member of the Royal Society, preached at the funeral of Charles Darwin in 1882. ▶ Victorian London   M Portrait, National Portrait Gallery, H-9

Fawkes, Guy, and the Gunpowder Plot   Even though James I's mother and wife had both been Roman Catholics, and he had tried to marry his son to a Catholic princess, he enacted severe penalties against the Catholics in England and banished their priests from the country. In 1604 a plot was formed by a group of desperate Catholics to kill the king, ministers and members of Parliament. To accomplish this the plotters rented a cellar under the Parliament House, in which they stored barrels of gunpowder. The plan was to touch a match to this during the opening of Parliament when the king was present, and blow up the entire government at once.

One of the thirteen conspirators, Sir Guy Fawkes, was appointed to keep watch over the powder. Somehow word leaked out, the cellars were searched and Fawkes was arrested. Eventually all of the conspirators were tried and executed or died defending themselves. From that time on the fifth of November has been celebrated in England as 'Guy Fawkes Day', as per the nursery rhyme:

> Remember, remember the fifth of November,
> Gunpowder treason and plot;
> I see no reason why gunpowder treason
> Should ever be forgot.

The early prayerbooks after 1604 contained a special thanksgiving service on 5 November for deliverance of the king and Parliament. To this day children burn Guy Fawkes in effigy. ▶ Stuart & Commonwealth London   M Drawing of the conspirators, National Portrait Gallery, H-9

Fire, The Great (1666)   The year 1666 is of great importance in the history of London's Christian landmarks. In a few short days during early September medieval London, as represented by four-score parish churches and the largest cathedral in Europe, vanished forever.

The fire (often referred to as the Great Fire of London), which started in a bakery shop on Pudding Lane just a short distance north of London Bridge, got out of hand because of the particularly dry weather combined with a high wind. Such firefighting equipment as existed was crude. Until the king himself and his brother James, the duke of York, stepped in on the second day, the scene was one of almost total panic and confusion. At times the flames, whipped by the winds, amounted to what in World War II came to be called a 'fire storm'. In the end the centre of the old city as far north as Cripplegate and westward beyond the walls as far as Chancery Lane was totally destroyed. Because the winds were blowing out of the east, a small portion of the eastern and northeastern precincts was fortunately spared.

Before the fire there were 109 churches within the City of London. Of these, the fire destroyed eighty-nine, and thirty-five were not rebuilt. Most of the twenty that survived the fire were destroyed later in other ways; a few were rebuilt and towers of others were left standing. The precious handful that have come down to us relatively unchanged from before 1666 are described individually.

The Monument commemorating the Great Fire measures the exact distance from its base to its crown as from the base to the spot where the fire is thought to have started (on Pudding Lane). Originally the text on the base of the Monument blamed the Catholics for the disaster, but that has since been eliminated. ▶ Restoration London **M** Map location of the Monument, D-3

Fitz-Stephens, William (the Earliest Description of Christian London) Unfortunately there are no pictures or maps of the City in earliest times. The first picture of London landmarks appeared about 1500 in the frontispiece of a book of poems by Charles, duke of Orleans, during his imprisonment in the Tower. And the earliest map was that done by Ralph Aggas which was published early in Elizabeth's reign (1558-1603). But we do have a written description, by William Fitz-Stephens, a learned cleric formerly in the service of Thomas a Becket during the reign of Henry II (1154-89). It is from his description that we get our information about churches and the various monastic establishments in medieval London. ▶ Medieval London

Fisher, John (1469-1535) Fisher was bishop of Rochester under Henry VIII and a strong defender of traditional Roman Catholic doctrine. He protested against Henry's divorce from Catherine of Aragon and was imprisoned in the Tower for refusing to take the oath supporting the Act of Succession. He was beheaded on Tower Hill in June 1535. Along with Thomas More he was canonized by Pope Pius XI in 1936. ▶ Reformation London **M** Name on memorial plaque to execution victims, Tower Hill, K-14   Portrait on triptych behind the Altar of the English Martyrs, St Wilfred's Chapel, Brompton Oratory, A-1 Represented in the altarpiece in the Chapel of St George and the English Martyrs, Westminster Cathedral, B-6   Portrait, National Portrait Gallery, H-9

Five Mile Act   This was one of the parliamentary statutes intended to suppress Nonconformity after the restoration of King Charles II. Nonconformist ministers and teachers were subject to a severe fine if they came within five miles of any city, town or parliamentary borough.   ▶ Restoration London

Foundry Chapel, or Old Foundry Chapel   John Wesley's first London headquarters and chapel were located in a former foundry in the Moorfields, not far from the present chapel on City Road.   ▶ Classical London

Fox, George (1624-91)   Born in Leicestershire in 1624, Fox forsook church attendance and rejected established religious bodies at an early age. He preached that truth is to be found in God's voice speaking to the soul. His movement was called 'Friends of Truth', later abbreviated to 'Friends' (now the Society of Friends).

Fox felt impelled to interrupt church services with impassioned appeals from the Scriptures to the Holy Spirit as authority and guide, and this resulted in his languishing some six years in various prisons. His later years were spent in the London area, where he campaigned against social evils and for religious toleration. He worked until his death in 1691 helping others, promoting schools, and so on. He is buried under a simple marker in what used to be the Friends Burial Ground (now a garden of rest) on Bunhill Row near Bunhill Fields.
▶ Restoration London   **M** George Fox grave, K-3

Foxe's Book of Martyrs   Next to the Bible and the Book of Common Prayer, the work that most profoundly stirred the souls of Christians in Elizabeth's reign and for centuries thereafter (it is still in print) was a book called *Actes and Monuments* by John Foxe (1516-87). Foxe tells in a most interesting and convincing style the stories of men, women and children from apostolic times onward who had suffered and given up their lives for the sake of remaining true to Christ and his gospel. He describes vividly the persecutions of the Wyclifites or Lollards in the fifteenth century and the Reformers during the time of Henry VIII such as William Tyndale, Thomas Bilney and John Frith.

In particular he focuses on the martyrs of Mary's (and his own) time, both the famous, such as Hugh Latimer, Nicholas Ridley, Thomas Cranmer and John Hooper, and also a large number of unknown common people. In these stories the wickedness of such men as Bishop Bonner of London and Stephen Gardiner, bishop of Winchester and Lord Chancellor under Mary, is illustrated by numerous examples.

Foxe himself, in his early years a brilliant fellow of Magdalen College, Oxford, was both an historian of note and a Christian of exemplary reputation. He made a hair's breadth escape to the Continent in 1554 with Mary's officers in hot pursuit, but returned to London in Elizabeth's reign after the publication of his book in Latin in 1559. The first English edition came off the press of John Day, London, in 1563. Foxe was recognized by Elizabeth, who called him 'Our Father Foxe', and his immensely popular book became an instrument of religious tolerance. During his life he served for a time as vicar of St Giles, Cripplegate, and here he was buried following his death in 1587. ▶ Elizabethan London   **M** Portrait, National Portrait Gallery, H-9

Friends, or Society of Friends   The formal name for the religious body known more popularly as Quakers.

Fry, Elizabeth (1780-1845)   A Quaker, and a recognized minister in that body, Elizabeth Fry is still famed for her crusade against the then-prevailing inhumane treatment of female prisoners. She started welfare work among women inmates of Newgate Prison in 1813, and in 1817 began her campaign for the separation of the sexes in prison, classification of criminals, women warders to supervise women prisoners, and provision for secular and religious instruction. Later, in 1839, she formed a society for the care and rehabilitation of discharged prisoners. Throughout her life she was concerned to communicate the gospel of Jesus alongside her reforming work, in keeping with her maxim, 'Charity to the soul is the soul of charity'.
M Portrait and miniature in ivory, National Portrait Gallery, H-9

Gardiner, Stephen (1490-1555)   Private secretary to Cardinal Wolsey and later King Henry VIII, he was made bishop of Winchester in 1531. Gardiner was imprisoned in Edward VI's reign, but he was made Lord High Chancellor under Mary and vigorously prosecuted Protestants such as John Rogers and John Bradford. He continued in office during the early part of Elizabeth's reign and died a wealthy man, though later his villainies were exposed by *Foxe's Book of Martyrs*. ▶ Reformation London

George III (reigned 1760-1820)   Although seen as a villain by the Americans because of injustices suffered by the colonists, he was a faithful husband and father, a popular monarch who loved his people and mingled with them freely, a patron of music and collector of books (Samuel Johnson was once invited to peruse his splendid library and was treated with a friendly conversation with the king), and above all a devout Christian. Unlike the first two Hanover kings or his profligate son George IV, his private life was sober and decent. According to David L. Edwards, he even refused to live at Kensington Palace and Hampton Court because he felt his predecessors had disgraced them. He had no use for some of the popular liberal clergy of his day, but he had a great admiration for George Whitefield, John Wesley and the Countess of Huntingdon.

Unfortunately, a long period of insanity toward the end of his life, during which the Prince Regent's immoral escapades became a major public scandal, eroded the respect for the monarchy which George III had built earlier. ▶ Classical London **M** Statue on horseback near Trafalgar Square, H-6 Portraits, National Portrait Gallery, H-9 Portrait (by Benjamin West), Queen's Ballroom, Windsor, N-6 Tomb in St George's Chapel, Windsor, M-6

Gibbons, Grinling (1648-1720) Gibbons was a Rotterdam-born wood carver who in 1671 was discovered by John Evelyn doing a wooden replica of Tintoretto's 'Crucifixion' at Deptford. Evelyn showed the work to Christopher Wren and Samuel Pepys and later to the royal family. Gibbons was employed by Wren to do the choir stalls at St Paul's Cathedral and work in other London churches. Examples may be seen in St Mary Abchurch and St Clement Danes. He was the most skillful wood carver of his age, producing pieces for Kings College Chapel at Cambridge and several royal palaces. He is buried in St Paul's, Covent Garden. ▶ Restoration London **M** Portrait, National Portrait Gallery, H-9 Many fine examples of work at Windsor Castle, N-6

Gibbs, James (1682-1754) He was the architect of four famous London churches: St Martin's-In-the-Fields, St Mary-le-Strand, St Peter's, Vere Street and St Marylebone Parish Church. He also designed the upper part of the tower of St Clement Danes. ▶ Classical London **M** Portrait, National Portrait Gallery, H-9 Portrait, north aisle of St Martin-in-the-Fields, H-13 Buried in Old St Marylebone Churchyard, E-8

Gladstone, William (1809-98) Gladstone was one of England's greatest political figures of the Victorian age, serving for sixty-two years as a member of Parliament and on the cabinet, three times chancellor of the exchequer and four times prime minister. Educated at Christ Church, Oxford, he had considered becoming a clergyman but was persuaded by his father, a member of Parliament, to go into politics. He was a devout Christian, a student of the Bible and a man of prayer, and consistently attempted to act as a Christian in public life. Known as the 'Great Commoner', he was a leader of the liberal party, a champion of the rights of the common people, an advocate of justice and a foe of slavery.

Not only was Gladstone an able politician, reformer and public leader, but he was also an accomplished classical scholar, a theologian and a skillful author. His works include *The State in Its Relation with the Church, Church Principles, The Impregnable Rock of Holy Scripture, Studies on Homer and the Homeric Age* and *Gleanings from Past Years*. Undergirding all of his work and thought was his firm faith in Christ. ▶ Victorian London **M** Statue & grave, North Transept of Westminster Abbey, C-10 Residence, 11 Carlton House Terrace, B-2 Portrait,

National Portrait Gallery, H-9   Monument, Strand west of St Clement Danes, J-5

'Glorious Revolution' The end of the era of misrule under the Stuart kings and of religious oppression by the government came with the 'Glorious Revolution' of 1688. William, Prince of Orange, the ruler of the Netherlands whose wife was Mary (the eldest daughter of Charles II), was invited to replace James II. When William landed on the south coast of England in November 1688, James started out with an army to meet him, but was deserted by almost all of his followers. William allowed James to make his escape to France and immediately took over the reigns of government. He was the first king to be placed in office by Parliament.

Soon after offering the crown to William and Mary as joint sovereigns, Parliament passed a law known to history as the 'English Bill of Rights'. This was followed by a Toleration Act, which allowed Protestant Dissenters to form congregations and worship publicly in their own way. Quakers were allowed to affirm instead of having to take an oath. The Roman Catholics still had to worship in private, but they were not persecuted and, in time, became unofficially recognized.

Queen Mary, who was very popular, died six years after receiving the crown. William carried on as king until his death resulting from a fall from a horse in 1702. He was succeeded by Mary's sister Anne. As William and Mary had no children and Anne's family had all died, Parliament feared that a Roman Catholic might again come to the throne. To keep this from happening an 'Act of Settlement' was passed determining that Sophia, a granddaughter of James I and a Protestant, should succeed Anne. Also included in this act was a provision that every future ruler of England must be a member of the Church of England and not marry a Catholic. As Sophia was married to George, elector of Hanover in Germany, the dynasty upon Anne's death in 1714 passed from the Stuarts to the house of Hanover.

▶ Restoration London   M Statue of Anne in front of St Paul's, L-15 Portraits of William and Mary, Anne, George I in the National Portrait Gallery, H-9   Statue of William III on horseback (as Roman general), St James Square, B-8

Gordon, Charles George (1833-85) Known popularly as 'Chinese Gordon' and 'Gordon Pasha', he was a professional soldier who served with distinction in the Crimean War and in various engagements in China. For a time he was Governor-General of Egypt, served in various other administrative posts, and was made major-general in 1884. He died heroically defending Khartoum against an uprising of fanatical Muslims. He was a constant student of the Bible, which he was seen carrying more often than a sword or gun, and a man greatly trusted and beloved. His monument in St Paul's reads:

He saved an empire by his warlike genius, he ruled vast provinces with justice, wisdom and power, and lastly obedient to his sovereign's command, he died in the heroic attempt to save men, women and children from imminent and deadly peril. 'Greater love hath no man than this, that a man lay down his life for his friends.'

▶ Victorian London M Statue, Victoria Embankment Gardens (showing him with Bible in hand), C-3   Reclining effigy, north aisle of St Paul's, L-15 Portrait, National Portrait Gallery, H-9

Gordon Riots In the year 1780 London experienced a notoriously ugly outbreak of mob violence prompted by religious bigotry which historians have dubbed the 'Gordon' or 'No-Popery' Riots. Fortunately, perhaps, the revolutions taking place at this time both in France and America have eclipsed this unsavoury event and it is rarely remembered. But anyone well read in the works of Charles Dickens will know that *Barnaby Rudge*, one of the author's two historical novels, is built around the Gordon Riots.

The threat of Roman Catholic interference in the affairs of England seemed to any logical person quite dead by the latter half of the eighteenth century. Thus in 1778 Parliament passed a Catholic Relief Act to do away with the old laws suppressing the Catholics. But, as the common people were generally unrepresented in Parliament at his time, a wave of popular resistance to this new act swept the country and Protestant Associations sprang up everywhere. The leader of this agitation was an enthusiastic but mentally unsound Scottish nobleman named Lord George Gordon. His rallying slogan was, 'No popery!'

Gordon prepared an appeal to do away with the Catholic Relief Act and called for 20,000 Protestants to join him on 2 June 1780, to present the appeal to Parliament. Sixty thousand showed up, and the affair quickly escalated from a demonstration to a riot. The Parliament House was stormed and the members mobbed, Roman Catholic chapels in London were sacked and burned, houses and businesses of Roman Catholics and anyone known to be sympathetic to them were destroyed.

For six days the mob raged out of control. Newgate Prison was attacked and burned, the mob was swollen by hardened criminals, and in the end some 300 people were killed. Finally King George III personally sent troops to restore order, which was done rigorously with much loss of life. Twenty-five of the leaders were hanged, though Gordon himself was acquitted. ▶ Classical London

Graham, Billy, and the First Greater London Crusade In 1954 the Billy Graham Evangelistic Team accepted an invitation to conduct a twelve-week campaign in London. The Harringay Stadium in the north of the city was engaged, and churches in London and the surrounding area spent months in preparation. Hundreds of special prayer meetings were organized, and an army of counsellors was trained to deal with the large number of inquirers expected. It was probably the greatest instance of church co-operation in London's history.

The Crusade lasted from 1 March to 22 May. Dr Graham was assisted by Grady Wilson who was in charge of counsellors, Cliff Barrows who organized and led the choirs, and baritone soloist George Beverly Shea. Attendance at Harringay was estimated at 1,756,000. In addition, there were overflow services, relay services, open-air meetings and the great final rallies at the White City and Wembley Stadiums, boosting total attendance to well over two million.

Over 38,447 individuals received counselling during the Crusade. The names of those who made decisions to receive Christ as Saviour or to rededicate their lives were parcelled out to co- operating churches for follow-up. At least seven books were written dealing with the amazing impact of the Crusade (the first of several) on the lives of all sorts of people, from elderly pensioners to young celebrities of the entertainment world, from respectable churchgoers to dissipated alcoholics. Not the least of the results of this memorable event was the encouragement and inspiration experienced by those Christians who participated, as counsellors, choir members, ushers or by bringing a guest. ▶ Twentieth-century London

Grant, Charles (1746-1823)   Grant went to India in 1767 in the service of the East India Company and, following the deaths of two young daughters, became a committed Christian. He rose to great wealth and prominence, ultimately became chairman of the board of directors of the East India Company, and at his residence in Clapham was an active member of the Clapham Sect. Among other achievements, he supported the building of churches in India and elsewhere, procured the assignment of a grant for education and introduced Sunday schools into Scotland. ▶ Classical London

Gray, Thomas (1716-71)   One of the best-known poems in the English language, *Elegy Written in a Country Churchyard* (1750), was penned by Thomas Gray in a lovely country setting now just on the outskirts of Greater London. Because the grounds so graphically described in the poem were part of the property of nearby Stoke Poges Manor House, they and the church have been preserved in their original park-like surroundings.

In 1799 an elaborate monument was erected by John Penn, grandson of William Penn, who currently owned the manor house. The remains of Thomas Gray rest beside those of his mother in a simple tomb of brick built just outside the east end of the church. The church itself is very ancient: a small part of it dates to Saxon times; and Norman, Gothic and Tudor styles are in evidence. In Gray's time there was a spire set on an 'ivy covered tow'r', but the tower now has a small peaked roof.

If one is inclined to reflect on the brevity of human existence, this is a good place to spend a few quiet minutes thinking about Gray's lines:

> The boast of heraldry, the pomp of pow'r,
> And all that beauty, all that wealth e'er gave,
> Await alike th' inevitable hour:
> The paths of glory lead but to the grave.
>
> Nor you, ye proud, impute to these the fault,
> If Memory o'er their tomb no trophies raise,
> Where, through the long-drawn aisle and fretted vault,
> The pealing anthem swells the note of praise.
>
> Can storied urn, or animated bust,
> Back to its mansion call the fleeting breath?
> Can honour's voice provoke the silent dust,
> Or flatt'ry soothe the dull cold ear of death?

▶ Classical London M Stoke Poges Church & Churchyard, N-1

Grey, Lady Jane (1537-54) A niece of Henry VIII, she was an innocent pawn in the attempt by the duke of Northumberland to retain control of the crown upon the death of Edward VI in 1553. She is one of English history's most tragic figures. ▶ Reformation London

Hampton Court Hampton Court Palace occupies a lovely park on a bend in the River Thames a few miles southeast of Central London. The property once belonged to the Knights Hospitaller, but in 1514 was leased by the powerful Cardinal Wolsey. Wolsey had grown immensely rich as Henry VIII's Lord Chancellor, and here he set about to build the most splendid palace in all of England. Constructed of brick in a style later called 'Tudor', it had 280 guest rooms and required 500 servants to maintain it. Tradition says that when asked by Henry VIII what he meant by building himself so magnificent a palace, Wolsey smoothly replied that he intended it as a gift worthy of His Majesty. Whatever the circumstances, it became the possession of the crown in 1529.

Hampton Court Palace was a royal residence for some 231 years, from Henry VIII to George II. Over much of this time it was the centre of the brilliant social life of the royal court. From the standpoint of London's Christian history, however, its most important period was during the reigns of Henry VIII, Edward VI and Mary I, and one incident during the days of James I.

It was here that Henry VIII spent honeymoons with two of his brides, Anne Bolelyn and Catherine Howard. Edward VI was born at Hampton Court to Henry's third wife, Jane Seymour, in October 1537, and poor Jane died there less than a month later. When Edward became king at age nine he spent much of his time at his childhood

Hampton Court Palace. Here Henry VIII passed honeymoons with both Anne Boleyn and Catherine Howard. And here both queens received the sentence of death.

home. Edward's half-sister, Mary, also loved Hampton Court, though it was here she waited in vain for the child that was not to be. A half century later (1604) King James I held a council of churchmen at Hampton Court, known to history as the Hampton Court Conference.

When visiting Hampton Court, keep in mind that quite a large section of the palace was rebuilt at the end of the seventeenth century. This 'New Palace', constituting the royal apartments on the south and west sides, was designed by Sir Christopher Wren and constructed in classical Renaissance style. But the palace as seen from the west, where visitors enter, is probably the finest example of Tudor architecture in existence. The approach is by a bridge over a dry moat between rows of royal 'beasts', across a court and under a gateway named after Anne Boleyn, as it was embellished by Henry during her brief occupancy. On the opposite side of the gateway is a famous astronomical clock, made for Henry VIII in 1540. The Chapel Royal is of especial interest, with its fine fan-vaulted roof added by Henry VIII, as is the Haunted Gallery outside where Catherine Howard was seized after trying to reach Henry at his prayers and plead for mercy. Her ghost is said to walk by night with its severed head underneath its arm. Also of primary importance is the extraordinarily fine Great Hall where Henry VIII dined at various times with four of his queens.

▶ Reformation London   **M** Map location N-2

Hampton Court Conference   King James I, the first of the Stuart
dynasty of English monarchs, had a hearty dislike of the Reformed or
Presbyterian Church, which had originally taken hold in Scotland in
the days of his mother and John Knox. He particularly distrusted their
system of church organization because it put more of the control of the
local churches into the hands of the pastors and had a form of
representative government rather than bishops. Thus when in 1603,
the first year of his English reign, the Puritans prepared a petition
asking for further reforms in the Church of England, James
sidestepped the request. Instead, he arranged a debate between
bishops Bancroft and Bilson, who were strong Episcopalians, and the
Puritans L.Chalderton and Dr John Reynolds (or Rainolds) of
Oxford.

Since the king was living at the time at Hampton Court Palace, the
four-day conference was held there in his audience chambers in the
presence of a larger body of leading clergymen. The king acted as
chairman and occasionally entered into the discussion. Reports of the
proceedings are confusing, but apparently the king allowed a few
concessions to the Puritans. However, the climax came when Dr
Reynolds proposed that certain disputed points be referred to the
bishop and his 'presbyters'. James, who apparently had the mistaken
belief that the Presbyterians advocated doing away with the
monarchy, accused him of trying to set up a 'Scotch presbytery' in
England, and with other angry words stamped out of the room. The
conference thus seemed at the time to be a victory for the Anglican
conservatives.   ▶ Stuart & Commonwealth London

Handel, George Frederick (1685-1759)   Handel was one of the greatest
masters of baroque music, a distinction he shared with Johann
Sebastian Bach (who was born in the same year). He is closely
associated with London, where he lived for forty-seven years, and
where he produced numerous works frequently played today, for
example the *Water Music* and *Royal Fireworks Music*. But his
masterpiece is also his greatest contribution to the history of Christian
London, the oratorio *The Messiah*. This was first presented in London
in 1714 before an audience in Covent Garden Theatre which
included King George II and the royal family. The king rose to his feet
upon the singing of the Hallelujah Chorus and the audience with
him, a tradition still observed.

Handel, whose distinguished career began in his native Germany,
became music director for Georg Ludwig, Elector of Hanover, who in
1714 became George I of England. The composer preceded his patron
to London, and during his first ten years in England wrote several
important ceremonial religious compositions such as the *Coronation
Anthems*, *Utrecht Te Deum* and *Jubilee*. But he is probably best known
for the series of oratorios on biblical themes initiated in 1732 which,
besides *The Messiah*, include *Esther*, *Saul*, *Israel in Egypt*, *Sampson*,

Judas Maccabaeus, Joshua, Solomon and Suzanna and *Jephtha*.

The great master, who never married, eventually became the most famous composer in the world and very wealthy. He was one of London's favourite characters, enormously stout and good humoured. He was a faithful member of St George's, Hanover Square, and lived in a house, which is still standing, nearby in Brook Street. He was a generous benefactor to the Foundling Hospital, now the Thomas Coram Foundation for Children, which possesses his portrait, the original score of *The Messiah* and other valuable mementoes. Here and there in England are a few churches with organs which he is known to have played. ▶ Classical London M House at 25 Brook Street, E-3 Statue in Westminster Abbey, C-10 Portrait, National Portrait Gallery, H-9

Hawksmoor, Nicholas (1661-1736) Hawksmoor was deputy-surveyor at Chelsea Hospital under Christopher Wren and was involved in the architecture of numerous palaces and great homes. He was Wren's assistant in the building of St Paul's, and was the architect of St George's, Bloomsbury and St Mary Woolnoth. He was also surveyor-general of Westminster Abbey. ▶ Restoration London M Bronze bust, National Portrait Gallery, H-9

Helwys, Thomas The pastor of the first Baptist congregation in London, imprisoned by orders of James I. ▶ Stuart & Commonwealth London

Henry II (reigned 1154-89) He was the first of the Plantagenet kings, and a great friend and later enemy of Thomas a Becket. He accepted responsibility for Becket's murder and did public penance. ▶ Medieval London M Portrait with group of early English sovereigns, National Portrait Gallery, H-9

Henry VII (reigned 1465-1509) A descendant of a daughter of John of Gaunt, the duke of Lancaster, he was thus a contender for the English throne on the Lancastrian side. In 1465 he slew Richard III, the reigning Yorkist monarch, at the Battle of Bosworth Field and succeeded to the throne. He was a shrewd and able administrator, much given to thrift and even miserliness. His eldest son, Arthur, was betrothed to Catherine of Aragon, the daughter of the Spanish Catholic monarchs Ferdinand and Isabella. Arthur died before his father, and Henry, unwilling to return the huge royal dowry, betrothed his second son, Henry, to Catherine. It was during his reign that the 'New Learning' of the Renaissance began to impact upon England. ▶ Renaissance London M Bust of Henry VII in Victoria & Albert Museum, A-9 Portrait in National Portrait Gallery, H-9 Buried in Chapel of Henry VII, Westminster Abbey, C-10

Henry VIII and the English Reformation We have surveyed in the 'overview' of Reformation London the sweeping changes in English church life and practices brought about by Henry VIII between the years 1527 and 1540. Five main factors, combined with Henry's forceful personality, seem to lie behind these unprecedented moves:

First, it is a generally overlooked fact that the young king, whom history knows for the enormous faults and excesses of his later life, was a child of the New Learning himself—well taught in the ancient languages; well read enough to write a book denouncing Luther; a champion in archery, tennis, riding and tilting in armour; and able both to compose music and to play well on all musical instruments. He gathered about him the learned men of the day, including the fearless John Colet, dean of St Paul's, and the brilliant lawyer and theologian Thomas More. The anti-clerical spirit prevalent among these intellectuals planted in his mind a dislike of monks and image-and-relic worship, and a respect for the study of the Bible, which he somehow balanced off against his doctrinal orthodoxy on the matter of transubstantiation.

Secondly, we need to understand the circumstance of Henry VIII's first marriage. Henry VII had arranged the marriages of his two daughters and his eldest son, Arthur, to his greatest political advantage. Arthur's wife, Catherine, was the daughter of none other than Ferdinand and Isabella of Aragon, Spain's great Catholic monarchs. However, Catherine was but sixteen at the time of the wedding, and Arthur fourteen. In a year and a half Arthur was dead, and Ferdinand demanded the dowry back. The problem remained unresolved until Henry VII died in 1509, at which time the new king, Henry VIII, married his brother's widow who was seven years his senior. As such a union was against canon law, it was necessary for the pope to make a special dispensation. After a number of pregnancies produced only one living child, a girl, Henry VIII had good cause to wonder if he had not indeed violated one of God's commandments.

Thirdly, in 1529 Henry was apparently deeply in love with Anne Boleyn, one of his wife's ladies of honour, and wished to divorce Catherine so that he might marry Anne and produce the desired heir through her.

Fourthly, Henry VIII needed money. He saw no reason why he should not lay hands on the rich Roman Catholic properties in his realm that in many cases had outgrown their usefulness and that were controlled by a foreign power which had opposed his wishes.

Fifthly and finally, as we have already pointed out, the spectre of a disputed succession haunted Henry VIII, leading him to take extreme measures in order to better his chances for a male heir.

While we are inclined to hiss at Henry VIII as one of the great villains of English history, he is at the same time fascinating and charming. Unlike Stephen, John or James II, who brought to their reigns nothing but grief and chaos and whom we can merely despise, Henry VIII seems, for all his cruelty, like a man of destiny. So far as the history of Christianity is concerned, he set in motion for the church in England a much-needed Reformation, one that in the long

run was considerably more moderate in terms of wars and violence than the Lutheran and Calvinistic Reformations on the Continent.
▶ Reformation London   **M** Portraits, National Portrait Gallery, H-9
Armour, Tower of London, M-19   Buried in St George's Chapel, Windsor, M-6

Hill, Rowland (1744-1833)   Next to George Whitefield, the most famous Calvinistic Methodist minister in London was Rowland Hill, a preacher of remarkable eloquence and wit who was a well-known figure in the City for some fifty years. Educated at St John's College, Cambridge, he was refused ordination because of his evangelical views but became a highly successful itinerant evangelist throughout England, Scotland and Wales. During the Gordon Riots in 1880 he preached to the huge crowds in St George's Fields, Southwark, and at this time money was subscribed to build him a chapel for a settled ministry. This was the famous Surrey Chapel, a landmark on Blackfriars Road, Southwark, for a great many years (now gone).

Many stories of Rowland Hill's wit were circulated during and after his day. Once, when preaching near the docks at Wapping, he began by saying, 'I am come to preach to great, to notorious, yes, to Wapping sinners!' On another occasion, when some passers-by had taken shelter in his chapel during a rain storm, he declared that he had heard of people making religion a cloak, but never an umbrella. One Sunday while reading prayer requests, he came across one that asked prayer for 'the Rev. Rowland Hill, that he will not go riding about in his carriage on Sundays'. He looked up and said gravely, without any loss of composure, 'If the writer of this piece of folly and impertinence is in the congregation, and will go into the vestry after the service, and let me put a saddle on his back, I will ride him home instead of going in my carriage!'

Surrey Chapel was famous for its congregational singing, accompanied by an organ. Hill himself composed hymns set to popular music, and is said to have remarked that he did not see why the devil should have all the good tunes. He took a great interest in the humanitarian possibilities of science through an acquaintance with Dr Jenner, and he published a pamphlet on the value of innoculation. A vaccine board was established at Surrey Chapel and some 10,000 or more children were vaccinated there. The first Sunday school in London also was organized at Surrey Chapel and involved many hundreds of children. Hill raised large amounts of money for patriotic and charitable purposes on a number of occasions. He played a leading part in the founding of the Religious Tract Society, the London Missionary Society, and the British and Foreign Bible Society.   ▶ Classical London   **M** Portrait, National Portrait Gallery, H-9

Hogarth, William (1697-1764)   Hogarth was a London artist whose fame rests on his 'extraordinary faculty for depicting the vices and follies of his time'. Though not known to be a religious man, he was a kind of prophet to eighteenth-century London in showing up the moral rot at the heart of the supposed 'Age of Reason'. His pictures, usually engraved by himself, were in many instances series of six or more scenes. Among his most famous are *A Rake's Progress*, *Marriage a la Mode* (his masterpiece, now in the National Gallery), and *The Election*. Well-known single plates are *The March to Finchley*, *Beer Street* and *Gin Lane*.

Hogarth had a considerable interest in the Foundling Hospital and in 1740 painted a portrait of Captain Coram for that institution. He later became governor of the Hospital and persuaded other artists to contribute paintings. Exhibitions of these works ultimately led to the founding of the Royal Academy. ▶ Classical London   M Engravings in the National Gallery, H-8   Bust and self-portrait in the National Portrait Gallery, H-9   House open to the public, Chiswick

Holy Trinity, Brompton

On the right side of the Brompton Oratory is an avenue of lime trees leading back to the parish church of the district, Holy Trinity, Brompton. The building is a mellow Gothic-revival structure with a clock tower at the west end. If one proceeds around the west end a lovely park comes into view, once the old burial ground (tombstones and bodies removed in 1954), and a pathway leads along under the trees to a typical country church gate. This gate was originally built on the Brompton Road side but was placed on the north boundary in 1908.

Holy Trinity, Brompton, was consecrated in 1829 to serve a parish which at that time ran as far west as Earl's Court. It could seat 1,505 people (899 of whom rented pews), and seems to have been considered more utilitarian than beautiful. Numerous changes and improvements have been made over the years, however, including the addition of a chancel in 1879. The interior now presents an attractive appearance with a five-bay clerestoried nave, a gallery above, and a broad chancel with marble steps, at the rear of which is a striking gold mosaic reredos (made in Italy and installed in 1885).

Today this former country church is full of life and vitality, serving a large congregation in the heart of crowded and fashionable southwest London. The old crypt has been made into modern meeting halls, offices and a bookshop, and it can be entered on ground level through glass doors on the northwest. Some 600 or more attend services on Sunday mornings and there is also a well-attended Sunday evening service and activities throughout the week (including an outreach to the poor and homeless in the area). Holy Trinity, Brompton, is united with the newly opened St Paul's, Onslow Square, and also with St Barnabas, Kensington and St Marks, Battersea Rise. ▶ Victorian London   M Map location A-5

Holy Trinity, Sloane Street

Built in 1888-90 on the site of an earlier nineteenth-century church, Holy Trinity is notable primarily for its decoration and furnishings. Contributions from numerous artists, including Sir Edward Burne-Jones, have made this into what is said to be the finest exhibition of Arts and Crafts work of any church in London.　**M** Map location A-6

Hospitals　The name of modern medical facilities comes from the medieval 'hospices', or places of shelter for aged and infirm persons operated by the church.　▶ Medieval London

Howe, John (1630-1705)　John Howe was born in Leicestershire in 1630, where his father was thrown out of the ministry by archbishop Laud for his espousal of Puritanism. Educated at Cambridge and Oxford, Howe was for a time chaplain to Oliver Cromwell. After 1660 he refused to conform, served a dissenting congregation in London for a while, and then was pastor to an English congregation in Utrecht. He returned to London in 1687. Howe, like Baxter, was anxious to promote Christian unity and wrote extensively on the subject. Among his chief works are *Blessedness of the Righteous*, *Delighting in God* and *Unity Among Protestants*.　▶ Restoration London

Hughes, Hugh Price (1847-1902)　Hugh Price Hughes was the leading Wesleyan in Victorian London, and the editor of the *Methodist Times*. A forceful preacher, he was the founder of numerous churches, central halls and city missions, and a highly successful campaigner for Methodist expansion both in the British Isles and overseas.　▶ Victorian London

Humanism　Humanism, or the Humanities, also known in England as the 'New Learning', was an intellectual movement growing out of the Renaissance. Humanist scholars in the north of Europe, Erasmus of Rotterdam in particular, went beyond the limits of the theological learning of medieval Scholastics to study the ancient biblical languages. This, in turn, aided the Reformation by enabling theologians and Bible translators to refer to the original text rather than having to rely on the Latin translation.　▶ Renaissance London

Hunt, William Holman (1827-1910)　Hunt is one of the most famous English painters of religious subjects of modern times. Born in London and a member of the Royal Academy, he joined with D.G. Rossetti, J.E. Millais and a few other young painters in 1844 to form the Pre-Raphaelite Brotherhood. The aim of this group, to resist contemporary art tastes, was warmly defended by the essayist John Ruskin. Hunt went to Egypt and Palestine on several occasions to paint accurate backgrounds for biblical scenes. His works include 'The Scapegoat', 'Triumph of the Innocents', 'The Awakened Conscience', 'Our Saviour Entering the Temple', 'The Shadow of Death', 'Nazareth', 'Christ Among the Doctors', 'Shadow of the Cross', and 'Plains of Esdraelon'. His best-known painting, 'The Light of the World', hangs in Keble College, Oxford, but in 1904 he reproduced a life-sized copy for St Paul's Cathedral (in the south aisle). Other works may be seen in the Tate Gallery. ▶ Victorian London **M** Map location of the Tate Gallery, C-8

Huntingdon, The Countess of (1707-91) Selina Hastings, the Countess of Huntingdon, was, together with George Whitefield, co-founder and leader of the Calvinistic branch of Methodists. As a consequence, this church movement was known as 'The Countess of Huntingdon's Connexion'. During her lifetime the Countess financed some sixty-four chapels and is said to have given over £100,000 to charity. Yet she herself lived on £1,200 a year and was known often to possess no more than the gown she was wearing. The Prince of Wales said to one of her critics at court, 'When I am dying I shall be happy to seize the skirt of Lady Huntingdon's mantle to lift me up to heaven'. Such was the esteem of her among the poor that during the Gordon Riots the mob refrained from burning Spa Fields Chapel when they learned she was associated with it.

The Countess, a relative of the royal family on both sides, became a Methodist through the influence of her sister-in-law, the Lady Margaret Hastings, after the death of Selina's husband and two sons. She early joined Wesley's Fetter Lane Chapel, and in 1747 she made George Whitefield one of her chaplains. Later she sided with Whitefield in the controversy with Wesley over Calvinism. The Countess opened her home in Park Street for preaching services, and her chaplains ministered to the wealthy socialites of the Countess's acquaintance. A charity school was later built nearby on the site of the Countess's garden. ▶ Classical London

James I (reigned 1603-25) James I, who as the son of Mary, Queen of Scots, was the great-great grandson of Henry VII, was also the grandson of James V, king of Scotland. As James VI of Scotland, he had been a king from very early childhood, and he considered himself chosen by God to decide the course that religion should take both in Scotland and England. Consequently it was not long before the tension between the established Church of England and the Puritans of Presbyterian persuasion became as great as between the Catholics and Protestants of an earlier time. James also reversed the foreign policy of Henry VIII and Elizabeth I in an unsuccessful attempt to make a marriage alliance between his son Charles and a Roman Catholic Spanish princess.

Personally, James was a staunch high-churchman, and he encouraged talented preachers such as Lancelot Andrewes. He was also interested in theology and wrote a book on witchcraft. But he was incapable of understanding any expression of Christianity outside of his own narrow experience. Against popular opinion, he refused to send aid to the Protestants in Germany during the Thirty Years War even though his daughter was married to one of their leaders.

Throughout his reign he engaged in a bitter feud with the Puritan-dominated Parliaments, refusing to acknowledge their right to make legislation of which he himself did not approve. In short, the reign of James I created of England a divided religious camp, with the growing Puritan population and their leaders becoming ever more discontented. Upon his death in 1625 he was succeeded by his son Charles. ▶ Stuart & Commonwealth London   **M** Portrait, National Portrait Gallery, H-9   Buried in Westminster Abbey, C-10

James II (reigned 1685-88)   Charles II died in 1685. By this time the fear of civil war should the royal line not continue had overcome the strong objection to a Catholic king, and James II peacefully succeeded to the throne. Trouble soon began, however, when the duke of Monmouth, an illegitimate son of Charles II and a Protestant, attempted to invade England. Monmouth was quickly defeated and put to death, and the king appointed a wicked judge named Jeffreys to administer justice to those suspected of being sympathetic to the rebellion. More than 300 were sentenced to be hanged, and nearly 900 were sold into virtual slavery in the West Indies.

James moved now to swing the laws in favour of the Roman Catholics, completely disregarding the wishes of the people. His strategy was to override Parliament and make a Declaration of Indulgence, doing away with the laws against Dissenters. The Protestant Dissenters generally recognized what the king was up to and refused to support him. In 1688 a second Declaration was made, and James ordered that it be read in the churches. In Westminster Abbey, when one of the bishops tried to do this, the congregation walked out. In one of the London churches a minister preached on this text from Daniel: 'Be it known unto thee, O king, that we will not serve thy gods, nor worship thy golden image which thou hast set up'.

So low was the popular opinion of James that all of London erupted in a tumult of joy when the archbishop of Canterbury and six other bishops were found 'not guilty' of an accusation of sedition. To complicate matters, the queen early in 1688 bore a son, frustrating the hopes of many that the Protestant Queen Mary with her husband William of Orange would come to the throne of England when James died. When finally James saw his position and began to reverse himself, it was far too late. ▶ Restoration London   **M** Portrait, National Portrait Gallery, H-9   Statue outside National Gallery, H-8

Jerusalem Chamber   The fourteenth-century abbot's retiring room in Westminster Abbey where Henry IV died in 1413 and where committees have met to work on Bible revision.   **M** Map location of Westminster Abbey, C-10

Jesuits   Members of the Society of Jesus founded in 1540 by Ignatius Loyola. They were the foremost Catholic intellectuals during the Counter-Reformation, effective in winning back many lapsed Catholics in England after 1578. A number of Jesuits were apprehended and suffered the supreme penalty for treason.

Jewish Museum This is a collection of antiquities illustrating Judaism and Jewish history. Located in Woburn House on Tavistock Square.

Jews in Medieval London A street called Old Jewry, which runs between Poultry and Gresham Street not far from Guildhall, was the heart of London's Jewish ghetto in medieval times. There is evidence that Jews resided in London from the early Saxon period. Edward the Confessor's laws mentioned them as being under the king's protection. And William the Conqueror invited to England many Jews from Rouen, some of whom settled in London. Apparently they had peace up to the reign of Stephen (1135-54) when the king, unfortunately urged on by certain of the clergy, exacted various fines. During this time vicious rumours began to be circulated regarding their supposed blasphemous rites.

Henry II (1154-89) granted the Jews cemeteries outside the towns, though he too levied fines and banishments. Richard I (1189-99) was responsible for at least two massacres of the Jews, though later he established a tribunal for them. John (1199-1216), with characteristic wickedness, tortured, blinded and imprisoned thousands of Jews who did not pay the huge sums he demanded.

All through the long reign of Henry III (1216-72) and on into the beginning of the reign of Edward I (1272-1307) the Jews suffered periodic persecution, indignity, torture and the most cruel of deaths, especially when the crown was in need of money. Finally, in the year 1290, some 15,000 or more Jews left England by ship, abandoning houses and other possessions which were seized by the king. Even this did not bring peace at last to some of the sons of Abraham. They were betrayed by sailors and left ashore, where they were put to death miserably. The Jews did not come back to England for some 400 years, when some began to return during the Commonwealth under Oliver Cromwell. ▶ Medieval London **M** Map location of Old Jewry, K-5

John of Gaunt (1340-99) He was duke of Lancaster and the fourth son of Edward III, and had almost the power of a king during the minority of Richard II. Thus Savoy Palace, his London town house, was a target of Wat Tyler's mob. He opposed the church's right to exercise authority in temporal matters, and he protected John Wyclif for political reasons. He accompanied Wyclif to what was to be an examination before the bishop of London in 1377 and disrupted the proceedings, causing the meeting to break up in confusion.
▶ Medieval London

Johnson, Samuel (1709-84) Dr Samuel Johnson was one of the greatest men of letters in the history of England. He dominated the literary scene in London from 1764 until his death twenty years later, for some years presiding as chairman of a literary fellowship called The Club. Members included the most brilliant figures of the day, such as the painter Sir Joshua Reynolds, the actor David Garrick, writers Oliver

Dr Samuel Johnson, the giant of eighteenth-century letters, was a clear and convinced Christian.

Goldsmith, Edmund Burke and Edward Gibbon, and others.

Johnson himself produced a wide variety of writing: classical-style poetry such as his famous *Vanity of Human Wishes*, prose romance, a literary journal called *The Rambler*, a series of biographies called the *Lives of the Poets* and a host of other works. In 1755 he published, in two huge volumes, the first standard dictionary of the English language, which was unrivalled for a hundred years and gained him the name 'The Great Lexicographer'. Some 116,000 quotations are included, testifying to Johnson's almost unbelievable knowledge. He is best known to posterity, however, through the records of his brilliant conversation in *The Life of Samuel Johnson* and *Journal of a Tour to the Hebrides* by his younger companion and biographer, James Boswell.

Samuel Johnson gave the superficial impression of an egotist who had to have the last word in every conversation. He was undoubtedly one of the most peculiar of all great English writers—and one of the most beloved by succeeding generations. As one critic puts it, 'His massive common sense, his real tenderness of heart, his generosity, his sincere piety, his transparent honesty, endear his memory'. Lord

Macaulay wrote in 1856: 'Our intimate acquaintance with what he would himself have called the anfractuosities of his intellect and his temper, serves only to strengthen our conviction that he was both a great and a good man'. Elton Trueblood, in the preface to an edition of Johnson's prayers, says, 'Dr Johnson was a deeply religious man and a conscious upholder of Christian doctrine all his days'.

Johnson was for many years a member of St Clement Danes (J-13), and a plaque in the gallery marks where his pew was (before the war). Today his statue stands outside the east end, facing Fleet Street. His house, on Gough Square just north of Fleet Street, miraculously escaped the bombing and is a shrine for Johnson lovers from around the world. The Good Doctor was an enthusiastic citizen of London, saying to Boswell on one occasion (20 September 1777), 'Sir, when a man is tired of London he is tired of life, for there is in London all that life can afford'. ▶ Classical London **M** Portrait, National Portrait Gallery, H-9   Statue, east side of St Clement, Danes, J-7   House on Gough Square open to the public, J-6

Jones, Inigo (1573-1652) He was the first to apply Renaissance principles to designs for public buildings in London, including St Paul's, Covent Garden (H-15), the Queen's Chapel, St James (B-3) and Old St Paul's. ▶ Stuart & Commonwealth London **M** Portrait, National Portrait Gallery, H-9   Buried in St Benet's, Paul's Wharf, L-3

Jordans Meeting House and Burial Ground A short way south of Milton's Cottage is the Jordans Meeting House, built in 1688. The property is owned and preserved by the Society of Friends as their earliest meeting place still in existence and as the burial place of William Penn and his family.

In the days of persecution for Nonconformists following the Restoration in 1660 there were several meetings of Friends in this district, including one at Old Jordans Farmhouse owned by William Russell. This meeting was frequently disturbed by constables and informers in the summer of 1670. In 1671 Russell sold a quarter of an acre to Thomas Ellwood and others to be used as a graveyard. Russell's infant daughter was the first to be buried here. Two years later it is recorded that George Fox was present at least once at the meeting at Old Jordans.

The Declaration of Indulgence by James II in 1688 led to the construction of a number of new Friends meeting houses in the area. A building for this purpose was put up on property adjoining the burial ground and became known as Jordans Meeting House, It was, and still is, a plain brick building consisting of a meeting room attached to a cottage and stables. This was in regular use by Friends until the early nineteenth century, when it lapsed into occasional use. Since 1919, meetings for worship on Sunday mornings have taken place at Jordans Meeting House. The Old Jordans Farmhouse and the Mayflower Barn have been purchased and are used as a hostel.

William Penn, in 1672, married Gulielma Maria Springett, stepdaughter of one of the leaders of the Old Jordans meetings. The Penns settled nearby at Basing House, Rickmansworth, and while there four of their infant children were buried at Jordans. In the following years Penn poured his energy into founding the new colony of Pennsylvania. In 1689 a fifth infant was buried at Jordans graveyard, and in 1694 Penn laid to rest here his wife of twenty-two years. Two years later his son Springett Penn, who was most sympathetic with his father's faith and aims, was buried near his mother. Not long after this Penn married Hannah Callowhill of Bristol, who accompanied him to America. They returned to England in 1701, and apparently Penn visited Jordans frequently. At his death in 1718 he was buried next to his first wife. ▶ Restoration London **M** Map location N-5

King James Version of the Bible Ironically, the great 'King James Version' of the Bible was a direct result of the suggestion of the Puritan Dr Reynolds at the Hampton Court Conference. King James readily agreed to this proposal for two reasons. First, he recognized that the official Bible for public reading, the Bishop's Version, was cumbersome in size and awkward in style. And second, he well knew that the popular Geneva Version contained notes heavily biased toward Reformed doctrines. (But he never 'authorized' the version named after him, even though it is now officially known as the AV or Authorized Version. It was only 'appointed' to be read in churches.)

The work was entrusted to forty-seven translators working in three panels on the Old Testament, the New Testament and the 'Apocrypha'. The translators worked as much as possible with the original languages, their prime tool being the Greek New Testament produced by Erasmus of Rotterdam, called the 'Textus Receptus' or 'Received Text'. They also drew upon modern-language versions and other English versions (in fact, approximately 80% of the phraseology originated with Tyndale). Interpretative notes were eliminated.

While the translators themselves (with the possible exception of the great preacher and poet Launcelot Andrewes) are rarely remembered, this version achieved literary distinction rivalled only by Shakespeare. Many passages (e.g. Psalm 23, Isaiah 53, Matthew 5, 1 Corinthians 13, Hebrews 11) are classics of the English language. First published in 1611 by Robert Barker, stationer to the king, it remained the most popular English Bible until the second half of the twentieth century. ▶ Stuart & Commonwealth London **M** A first edition of the King James Bible may be seen in the British Library, H-1

King's Weigh House Chapel One of the earliest and most famous Presbyterian chapels in London, it was located on Eastcheap in a building formerly used as a royal weigh-house for merchandise. A Presbyterian congregation under this name (though not on the original location) lasted into the nineteenth century.

Kingsley, Charles (1819-75)   The famous author of *Westward Ho*,
Hereward the Wake and *The Water Babies* was educated at King's
College, London, and was a curate at St Luke's, Chelsea, for a time.
He was a Christian Socialist and a critic of John Henry Newman and
the Tractarians, leading Newman to write his *Apologia*.   ▶ Victorian
London   **M** Portrait, National Portrait Gallery, H-9

Knights   London was the base of two priories of military monks during the
Crusades and later, the Knights Templar and the Knights Hospitaller
of St John of Jerusalem.   ▶ Medieval London

Lambeth Palace   Lambeth Palace, which is just across the river and
slightly upstream from the Houses of Parliament, has been for some
seven centuries the official residence and headquarters of the
Archbishop of Canterbury. It has been the scene of numerous events
of great importance in the Christian history of England and of London
in particular. Today it houses a library containing the most complete
collection of books and manuscripts in the world relating to the
Church of England. The library is open for research to qualified
scholars, and the Palace itself is open to visitors upon appointment.

The story of Lambeth Palace takes us back to the latter part of the
twelfth century, when an archbishop named Baldwin decided to
move his residence away from Canterbury. He did this for two
reasons: to be nearer to the palace at Westminster, and because of
conflicts with the monks of the Priory of Christchurch, Canterbury.
The conflict continued for a time despite the move, however, as the
monks appealed to the Pope, who in 1199 gave orders to have the
buildings at Lambeth destroyed. But early in the thirteenth century
the great Archbishop Stephen Langton, who supported the barons
against King John, restored the archiepiscopal residence at Lambeth
and actually became the first archbishop to live there. All of his
successors have resided at Lambeth to this day.

In early times the archbishops lived somewhat like feudal lords,
behind defensive walls and gates, guarded by armed retainers. Thus
the entrance to Lambeth Palace is beneath medieval towers through
heavy wooden gates known as Morton's Gateway. This was built in
the fifteenth century to replace an earlier gateway which had been
broken down during the Peasant's Insurrection. Another tower,
dating from 1434-35, can be seen on the left of the central hall as
viewed from the river. This is called the Lollard's Tower (though the
actual prison for Lollards was in the precincts of Old St Paul's), and it
obviously served as a prison of some sort in medieval days. One can see
the grim cell at the top with rings in the wall, a massive door and a
peephole. Interesting graffiti still remain on the walls.

The main building of Lambeth as seen from the riverside, or on the
left of the courtyard from Morton's Gateway, is a beautiful hall in the
Gothic perpendicular style, crowned by a lantern and weather vane.
This is the Great Hall, also known as Juxton's Hall because it is a

reconstruction done in 1663 under Archbishop William Juxton. Inside is a magnificent hammer-beam roof of oak. The Hall was used for banquets and early convocations and church councils. During the reign of Henry VIII a special commission was held here under Archbishop Thomas Cranmer that framed the oath acknowledging the king's supremacy over the church. The present Great Hall houses the marvellous Lambeth Library mentioned previously, with its priceless illuminated Lambeth Bible (1150), MacDurnan Gospels (ninth century), and some 3000 manuscripts and 150,000 printed books. It is also the meeting place of the Lambeth Conference, which assembles every ten years to discuss affairs of the worldwide Anglican communion.

Historically, the most important part of Lambeth is the chapel, the original of which was the first building to be completed under Stephen Langton. Here John Wyclif was summoned in 1378, here Archbishop Thomas Cranmer did much of the work on the first Book of Common Prayer, and here in 1558 Matthew Parker was consecrated, later to become the architect of the 'Elizabethan Settlement'. During the Commonwealth period in the seventeenth century the stained glass windows were smashed and the Chapel used for secular purposes. But at the return of Charles II it was restored by Archbishop Juxton along with the Great Hall. The original Chapel suffered badly from the bombing and was gutted to the walls, with only the thirteenth-century doorway remaining intact. However, a careful restoration by Lord Mottistone and Mr Paul Paget succeeded in recreating an interior much like the medieval one, including the vaulted roof, carved pews and screen, and fine stained-glass windows.

Other parts of Lambeth Palace of historic interest include the Guard Room and the Picture Gallery, both of which are hung with paintings of former archbishops. The Guard Room, where armed guards once waited, contains a fine arch-braced roof which is much more ancient than the room itself. It was in the Guard Room where Thomas More was probably questioned for his refusal to take the Oath of Supremacy. Here also the Lambeth Conference first met in 1867. Among the paintings is one of Archbishop William Laud done by Van Dyck. In the Portrait Gallery (which once was an open gallery above the Cloister, now gone) Queen Elizabeth I attended a Lenten service in the days of Matthew Parker. Parker's picture hangs here, as do one of Archbishop Thomas Cranmer done by Holbein and one of the famous Archbishop William Temple, who occupied Lambeth during World War II.   **M** Map location C-4

Langton, Stephen (died 1228)   Archbishop of Canterbury from 1207, he played a leading part in the struggle of the barons against King John, leading to the framing of the Magna Carta. He was also the first to reside at Lambeth Palace.   ▶ Medieval London

Latimer, Hugh (c. 1485-1555)   Latimer was a bold Reformer, a theologian and one of England's most famous martyrs. But he is also known as one of London's great popular preachers. While a student at Cambridge he was opposed to the Reformation but became convinced through Thomas Bilney. He quickly rose to prominence and, because of pressure from the Catholics, was examined by Cardinal Wolsey but acquitted. In 1530 he was appointed royal chaplain, then received a pastorate in West Kington, Wiltshire.

Accused of too vigorously promoting the Reformation, Latimer was recalled to London and threatened with excommunication. However, he was saved by his favour with the king. He was again appointed royal chaplain and then bishop of Worcester. He fell from the king's good graces in 1539 through his opposition to Henry VIII's return to Roman Catholic doctrines, and was ultimately imprisoned in the Tower.

Latimer's best preaching years were during the reign of Edward VI. His famous *Sermon on the Plough* was given at Paul's Cross in January 1548. Between 1548-50 he gave a series of Lenten sermons at the royal court. He was also a contributor to the *First Book of Homilies* (written sermons that could be used by clergymen unaccustomed to preaching) and probably the author of the twelfth in that collection, 'A Faithful Exhortation to the Reading of Holy Scripture'. Latimer was burned along with Nicholas Ridley at Oxford in 1555 during Mary's reign. ▶ Reformation London M Portrait, National Portrait Gallery, H-9

Laud, William (1573-1645) In 1629 King Charles I dissolved Parliament and began what is called his 'personal government', which lasted eleven years. During this period his principal advisor on all matters of religion was William Laud, bishop of London and, later, archbishop of Canterbury. Laud loved form and ceremony and was eager to revive pre-Reformation liturgical practices. He was also extreme in his belief in the importance of submission to authority, especially the authority of the king and his ministers. He encouraged the reintroduction into churches of stained-glass windows, crosses and crucifixes, and practices such as bowing whenever the name of Jesus was mentioned and making the sign of the cross in baptism. To many people, he seemed to be preparing the way for a reintroduction of Roman Catholicism.

Laud strongly resisted the more extreme Puritans and in some cases imposed severe penalties. He caused a number to have their ears cut off, their noses slit, to stand in the pillory and to suffer large fines and long imprisonments. Between 1634 and 1637 he conducted 'metropolitan visitations' in which he or another official inspected the practices of a great many parish churches. If the clergyman did not follow the exact form of the prayer book and also bow whenever the name of Jesus was mentioned, Laud would refer him for discipline. In this way numerous nonconforming ministers were removed from office.

Despite the fact that Laud was a tireless worker and responsible for many positive reforms in the Church of England, he was understandably one of the most hated men in the land. When the king was finally forced to call Parliament in 1640, Laud was ordered to be arrested and placed in the Tower. He was executed for treason in 1645. ▶ Stuart & Commonwealth London **M** Portrait by Van Dyck, Lambeth Palace, C-4 Portrait, National Portrait Gallery, H-9 Portrait (copy), Laud Chapel, St Katharine Cree, M-12

Liddon, H.P. (1829-90) Liddon was a high-church Anglican divine, a professor and administrator at Oxford and a member of the Tractarian group. In 1866 he gave an outstanding lecture, *The Divinity of Our Lord and Saviour Jesus Christ*, which was published and became his best-known work. But his chief fame rests on his preaching as a canon of St Paul's Cathedral from 1870 to 1890, in which he marshalled his great knowledge of Scripture and theology, his strong sense of logic and order, and his superb command of the English language.
▶ Victorian London **M** Portrait, National Portrait Gallery, H-9

'Light of the World', The A famous painting by Pre-Raphaelite artist Holman Hunt depicting Christ with lantern in hand knocking at a door. A copy is in the south aisle of St Paul's Cathedral. Underneath is a verse from Revelation 3:20, 'Behold I stand at the door, and knock; if any man hear my voice, and open the door, I will come into him, and will sup with him, and he with me'. The essayist John Ruskin wrote in 1854 the following explanation of the picture:

> On the left-hand side of the picture is seen this door of the human soul. It is fast barred; its bars and nails are rusty; it is knitted and bound to its stanchions by creeping tendrils of ivy, showing that it has never been opened. Christ approaches it in the night-time, in his everlasting offices of Prophet, Priest, and King. He wears the white robe, representing the power of the Spirit upon him; the jewelled robe and breastplace, representing the sacerdotal investiture; the rayed crown of gold, interwoven with the crown of thorns, but bearing soft leaves for the healing of the nations. He bears with him a twofold light: first, the light of conscience, which displays past sin, and afterwards the light of peace, the hope of salvation.

▶ Victorian London **M** Map location of St Paul's Cathedral, L-15

Lindisfarne Gospels An illuminated Gospel book and one of the British Library's most prized possessions, it was produced in the ninth century by monks on the Island of Lindisfarne off the coast of Northumberland. On permanent display in the British Library.
▶ British London **M** Map location of the British Library, H-1

Livingstone, David (1813-73) Britain's best-known medical missionary and the most famous African explorer of the nineteenth century. The discoverer of Lake Ngami and Victoria Falls, he made a 30,000-mile journey across the continent said to be 'the greatest journey of exploration ever made by one man'. He was an effective foe of the slave trade, as attested by a stirring memorial in the centre aisle of the nave, Westminster Abbey. ▶ Victorian London **M** Map location of Westminster Abbey, C-10 Portraits, National Portrait Gallery, H-9 Statue outside Royal Geographical Society, facing Kensington Road at junction of Exhibition Road. Mementoes on view inside; apply at the door. Plaque on house which he occupied in 1857 at Hadley Green.

Lollards, Lollard Movement John Wyclif is recognized as the 'Morning Star of the Reformation' because his work inspired the first translation of the whole Bible into English and sparked a movement to read and obey the Bible involving tens of thousands of English people over a period of 150 years. His writings also touched off a spiritual revival in Bohemia led by Jan Hus and others. In 1401 the bishops persuaded Parliament to pass an act increasing the power of the church over heresy and forbidding any preaching or religious teaching without the authority of a bishop. This was the first such civil law in English history. Many of the Lollards including Wyclif's close associates now came under heavy pressure. Some recanted, while others fled or continued their work secretly.

While the activities of the Lollards were in the main carried on in small groups with no attempt to organize or to go counter to the established church, there were also many instances of martyrdom that have become part of historical record. In the first year of the act against heresy a priest named William Sawtrey was burnt at Smithfield in London, and others followed him to the stake in the next several years.

In 1413 a powerful lord and heroic veteran of foreign wars, Sir John Oldcastle, was imprisoned in the Tower of London for espousing Wyclif's doctrines and sheltering Lollard preachers. Sentenced to death by burning, Oldcastle said, 'Ye judge the body, which is but a wretched thing, yet am I certain and sure that ye can do no harm to my soul. As to these articles, I will stand to them even to the very death, by the grace of my eternal God!' A bit later Oldcastle was rescued, and an ill-advised plan was laid to muster an army of 100,000 Lollards under his leadership. In the end sixty Lollards of all ranks were hanged. Oldcastle himself was burnt in chains over a slow fire at Smithfield. Significantly, the Lollard movement was so closely associated with Wyclif and the English translation of the Scriptures that it became the practice to burn Lollards with a portion of a Wyclifite Bible hanging around their necks. ▶ Medieval London

London Bridge London Bridge today is a plain structure of steel and concrete, over which vehicle traffic flows from the City's financial district to Borough High Street and on to the southern suburbs. Built in 1973 to replace the 1831 bridge, it is the newest of London's eleven

St Magnus Church stood for centuries at the end of London Bridge, until the bridge was moved.

motor-traffic crossings over the Thames. It is, however, a successor to the most famous bridge in all the world, Old London Bridge, and to a medieval monument with strong Christian connections. Here is its story:

London Bridge goes far back into antiquity, so far that no one knows exactly when it was first built. We are told that in Saxon times it was destroyed and rebuilt on several occasions, and that at the Conquest in 1066 it was a bridge of timber with a fortified gate like the other gates of London. Even after the Normans came, with their superior engineering skills, it was constantly being rendered useless— once, in 1091, by a terrific whirlwind that swept up the Thames.

Toward the end of the twelfth century, however, the church came into the picture. The chaplain of St Mary Colechurch in the Poultry, Peter by name, was unusually skilled in bridge building and proposed that a stone bridge be constructed. A fund-raising campaign was started and money was contributed by the king and citizens alike. So popular was this campaign that it was the talk of the land, and the children made up songs about it, as follows:

London Bridge is broken down,
Dance over my Lady Lee;

> London Bridge is broken down,
> With a gay ladee.

The new bridge, started in 1176, took thirty-three years to build. It was 926 feet long, 20 feet wide, and stood 30 feet above the water. It had a drawbridge and nineteen pointed arches. Later, houses and shops were built on it. Over the tenth and longest pier a chapel was erected and dedicated to St Thomas a Becket. Peter de Colechurch died during the construction and was buried in this chapel in 1205. The chapel had two levels, and the lower one was accessible by stairs from the river. No bridge in medieval Europe could compare with it for size and strength. Until the Reformation the maintenance of this most important edifice was in the hands of the Brethren of St Thomas of the Bridge.

The London Bridge of Peter de Colechurch lasted for over 600 years. It was, however, often in need of repair due to fires, storms, ice floes, and so on. But as London's main gateway to the southern ports it was indispensable and usually so crowded with traffic that it was difficult and even dangerous to cross on foot. From the fourteenth century onward it was the practice to place the heads of traitors over the bridge gates. In early Reformation times the head of Sir Thomas More was so displayed. The piers of the bridge were protected by huge boat-shaped buttresses of logs, called starlings; the narrow openings under the bridge consequently created the effect of a dam, with the water upstream spilling over into the lower river like a series of rapids. As hundreds of boats plied the Thames ferrying passengers up and down stream, 'shooting the bridge' was a necessary hazard. Also the slower movement of the upper river made it more susceptible to freezing. On 9 January 1684, John Evelyn records in his *Diary*:

> I went across the Thames on the ice, now become so thick as to bear not only streets of booths, in which they roasted meat, and had divers shops of wares... but coaches, carts, and horses passed over.

By the late eighteenth century London Bridge had been deserted by the merchants who formerly had shops there, and had fallen into hopeless disrepair. A new bridge was proposed in 1789, but it took another thirty-three years before Parliament finally accepted a plan for a replacement, designed by Sir John Rennie. In 1824 work began 100 feet westward, and in 1831 the new bridge was opened with great ceremony by King William IV. After this, the old bridge was finally demolished. When nothing was left above water but the starlings, workmen excavated the old Chapel of St Thomas and the grave of Peter de Colechurch on the centre pier. London Bridge's Christian origins then disappeared forever. ▶ Medieval London M Map location, D-1

Macaulay, Zachary (1768-1838) As a young man he worked on an estate in Jamaica that used slave labour, and was an opponent of the practice all his life. He rose to be governor of Sierra Leone. He later joined other evangelicals of the Clapham Sect in working toward the abolition of slavery. He also took an active part in the British and Foreign Bible Society and the Church Missionary Society. His son was the celebrated historian and essayist Thomas Babington Macaulay. ▶ Classical London

Magna Carta   The concept of rulers being under the authority of a law greater than themselves finds its source in the Old Testament and in the writings of the apostles. Thus the creation of the Magna Carta (Great Charter) and King John I's submission to it at Runnymede Meadow, 15 June 1215, takes a place of importance in the Christian history of London. Moreover, in the development of English constitutional rights the Christian church has obtained a more just and balanced place in society than under other systems of government.

The Magna Carta was drawn up by a group of barons who determined to curb the misuse of power by the corrupt King John, specifically to keep him from over-taxing their lands to finance military campaigns in France. They were supported by the great archbishop Stephen Langton, who acted as one of the arbitrators. John had been forced by a papal interdict and excommunication to accept Langton as archbishop. As early as September 1213, Langton had secured the support of the prelates for a proposal forcing John to abide by the liberties promised by Henry I. By early 1215 the barons had renounced their loyalty to John and on 17 May had captured London. By June the king had no other choice but to meet with the barons and concede the liberties which they had drawn up in the Great Charter.

Significantly, the first clause is a guarantee of freedom to the church:

> First, that we have granted to God, and by this present charter have confirmed for us and our heirs in perpetuity, that the English Church shall be free, and shall have its rights undiminished, and its liberties unimpaired...

Clauses 39 and 40 are the most famous:

> No free man shall be seized or imprisoned, or stripped of his rights or possessions, or outlawed or exiled, or deprived of his standing in any other way, nor will we proceed with force against him, or send others to do so, except by the lawful judgement of his equals or by the law of the land...
> To no one will we sell, to no one deny or delay right of justice.

The liberties obtained at the time were limited to 'all freemen of our realm', but it was a first and most important step toward the constitutional government which today characterizes free nations the world over. A copy of the Magna Carta itself may be seen in the British Library. The site of the signing (or sealing) is marked by an impressive monument at Runnymede Meadow (now a picnic site on the banks of the Thames between Staines and Windsor.

▶ Medieval London   **M** Runnymede Meadow, N-3   British Library, H-1

Man Born To Be King, The   A famous series of radio plays based on the life of Christ, written by Dorothy Sayers in 1941 for the BBC and later published in one volume.   ▶ Twentieth-century London

Martyrs: Protestant   From the enactment of the first law against 'heretics' in 1401 to the Act of Toleration in 1680, innumerable English men and women have suffered the supreme penalty for putting the authority of the Bible over that of pope, bishop or king. Many of these were put to death out in the counties, but Smithfield (J-8) was the primary place of execution in London for Lollards and Protestants. The extensive research and dynamic literary style of John Foxe resulted in popularizing the stories of the martyrs and had much to do with establishing England as a Protestant nation.

Martyrs: Roman Catholic   Between 1534 and 1680 numerous laws were made in England against Roman Catholics, at first forbidding them to deny the validity of Henry VIII's marriage to Anne Boleyn but eventually outlawing priests and 'Popery' completely. Hundreds of individuals were put to death under these laws: many priests, some monks and a considerable number of lay people. The most famous of these are Sir Thomas More and Bishop John Fisher, but many of the others were highly educated and distinguished churchmen. Some, like More and Fisher, were beheaded at the Tower, and others died in regional towns. But the majority suffered at Tyburn, often by being hanged, drawn and quartered as traitors.

Roman Catholics in England have always considered as martyrs those who were executed during this 'Penal Period' in church history. However, it has only been since 1850, when the Roman Catholic hierarchy was reestablished in England, that official investigation has taken place. The result of this extremely careful and complicated process has been the public recognition of a number of persons whose lives and deaths have shown them to be genuine martyrs of the church. Of these, forty-two have been canonized (that is, recognized universally as saints), including More and Fisher, and 136 have been beatified (recognized by papal decree as worthy of regional veneration and referred to as 'blessed'—such as the Blessed John Haile). Still another eighty-five are under active investigation, and there is a final group, the 'Dilati', for whom there is insufficient evidence.

Martyr's Memorial   A bronze plaque on the side of St Bartholomew's Hospital facing Smithfield, near the execution site, memorializing

John Bradford, John Rogers, John Philpot and the many others who died for their faith in the Bible under Mary Tudor during the years 1555-57. ▶ Reformation London M Map location, J-8

Mayflower Barn On the property of Jordans Meeting House is a barn said to have been constructed in 1625-26 with timbers from an old ship. The Mayflower, famous ship of the Pilgrim Fathers' voyage in 1620, was broken up in 1624, and there is some evidence that its beams might have been the ones used in this barn. Visitors to Jordans are usually invited to visit the barn, which is in full view from the public road. ▶ Stuart & Commonwealth London M Map location N-5

Maypoles, Maypole Dancing The celebration of the arrival of spring on 1 May with Maypole dancing goes back to the Celts, who paid homage to trees and leaf-covered branches as part of fertility rites. All over Britain on 1 May in early times bonfires were lit, people from every walk of life went gathering flowers, or 'Maying', and there was dancing, often very wild, around a flower-decked village Maypole. In London there was a Maypole in the Old City near St Andrew's church on Leadenhall Street. This was removed in Reformation times because of a riot. Maypoles were generally opposed by the Puritans because of their pagan implications. But at the Restoration in 1660 a huge Maypole was erected in the Strand, near the church of St Mary-le-Strand, which finally blew down in 1672.

Medieval Church Buildings in London In the days of William Fitz-Stephens there were in London thirteen 'conventual' churches (attached to monastic houses or convents) and 126 parish churches. Today there are in Old London eight churches and chapels whose main fabric dates back to medieval times—that is, before the reign of Henry VIII and the English Reformation. They are:

All Hallows, Barking, M-1   Ely Chapel, J-4   St Bartholomew-the-Great, Smithfield, K-9   St Ethelburga-the-Virgin, M-9   St Helen's, Bishopsgate, M-10   St John, Clerkenwell, J-16   St John the Evangelist, Tower, M-11   Temple Church, J-20

Medieval churches outside the Old City of London proper include:

Southwark Cathedral, D-6   Westminster Abbey, C-10   St George's Chapel & Albert Memorial Chapel, Windsor, N-6

The eight City churches all survived the Great Fire. And of the eleven, All Hallows, St Saviour's and Temple Church suffered rather badly from the bombing in World War II. All have been affected by neglect and misuse, if not outright vandalism. But by the grace of God and the loving efforts of various men and women within and without the clergy, they have all been skillfully restored. Great is their historical and architectural value, but greater still is their silent testimony that Christian worship has gone on in this city uninterrupted for at least 1,300 years. ▶ Medieval London

Mellitus (died 624) A Benedictine monk sent by Pope Gregory I to assist Augustine at Canterbury in Britain. In 604 he was consecrated as bishop of the East Saxons and a cathedral was built for him by King Ethelbert on Ludgate Hill in London. In 610 he was banished to France upon the death of the East Saxon king Sigebert but returned to become the third archbishop of Canterbury. ▶ Saxon London

Messiah, The Handel's celebrated oratorio, traditionally sung at Christmas throughout the western world, was written in London in 1741 and first presented in 1742. It is said to be the most performed major choral work in history. ▶ Classical London

The Methodists The amazing Evangelical Revival that swept over Britain and the American Colonies in the eighteenth century stemmed largely from the preaching of John Wesley and George Whitefield. The preaching and especially the hymns of Charles Wesley also played a significant part. This movement, which affected primarily the working classes and was strongly opposed by many of the educated and influential churchmen, was born, ironically, in the university.

In the year 1726 the young Charles Wesley became a student at Christ Church College, Oxford. The product of a godly home and a most illustrious mother, Charles began to invite friends to meet together for the purpose of spiritual betterment. Later his brother, John, became a fellow at Lincoln College and the group, including also George Whitefield and up to twenty others, began to meet in John's rooms. They attempted to practise discipline and regularity in their Christian exercises, thus acquiring the epithet 'Methodists' from the other students.

The 'Holy Club', as the group came to be called, followed the example of the Moravian Brethren and earlier religious societies of the Anglican Church in applying their Christianity in practical service. They visited prisoners, helped the poor and maintained a school for neglected children. Years later, after all three of the young men had experienced God's power in preaching, the Holy Club became the model for the various societies formed following the Great Awakening. It was the inspiration for the movement's social concerns that so greatly affected England. ▶ Classical London

Metropolitan Tabernacle Charles Spurgeon was first called to preach at the New Park Street Chapel, Southwark, in 1853 at the age of nineteen. This was one of the oldest Baptist chapels in London. The young preacher's remarkable gift soon drew overflowing crowds, and it was decided to enlarge the chapel to accommodate them. While preparations were under way, Spurgeon commenced his services in a large rented hall and then moved to the Royal Surrey Gardens, a music hall. Here the crowds grew to 10,000. He also preached at the Crystal Palace, where he was heard at one time by 23,654 people.

By this time the church decided to abandon plans to enlarge the New Park Street Chapel and build anew on a property at the Elephant & Castle. Spurgeon hastened the decision by a threat; as he says in his autobiography, '…either the Tabernacle must be erected, or I would become an evangelist, and turn rural dean of all the commons in England, and vicar of all the hedge-rows'. The building, with its broad portico of Corinthian columns, cost £31,000 and could seat 5,000. It was called the Metropolitan Tabernacle, the 'tabernacle' following a tradition established by Spurgeon's hero, George Whitefield. Spurgeon himself said, 'We believe this building to be temporary, meant for the time in the wilderness without the visible king'.

In 1898 the first Metropolitan Tabernacle burned to the ground. A fund-raising campaign was mounted, with money coming from all over the world to raise the £45,000 needed to rebuild. The pastor at that time was Thomas Spurgeon, one of Charles Spurgeon's twin sons. The new Tabernacle opened debt free, with a seating capacity of 3,000. Disaster struck again with the bombing in World War II. The third Metropolitan Tabernacle, which exists today, was opened in 1959, again debt free. It has a rebuilt sanctuary seating 2,000 with space for another 500 in the basement. A restoration of the original facade faces the Elephant & Castle. A centenary celebration was held in March 1961, featuring Dr Martin Lloyd-Jones of Westminster Chapel as speaker. ▶ Victorian London   **M** Map location, D-2

Meyer, F.B. (1847-1929)   Meyer, a graduate of London University and Regents Park Baptist College, while a pastor in York helped to launch the American evangelist D. L. Moody on his British campaigns. Meyer became pastor of Regents Park Church in 1888 and, later, of Christ Church, Westminster Bridge Road. He was a popular preacher in his own pulpits and a frequent speaker at Keswick, Northfield and Portstewart conventions. His devotional studies on biblical characters are still widely read. ▶ Victorian London

Milton, John (1608-74)   Milton's life spans the three turbulent periods of the first Stuart kings, the Commonwealth and the Restoration, and he was writing some of the finest works in the history of English literature during this time. But the poet's triumph, *Paradise Lost*, was completed during the reign of Charles II. This accomplishment becomes even more remarkable when one realizes that the poet had become blind by 1652 and most of the work was done by dictation. The last part of this great epic was completed in 1665, the Plague Year, and the poet was living with his third wife in a still-surviving cottage at Chalfont St Giles, a village just north of the City. It was published in 1667, and Milton received the princely sum of £20 for it.

Paradise Lost is an heroic poem in the tradition of the Greek classics of Homer. But the material comes not from the Greeks but from the Hebrews, and the subject is the biblical drama of Heaven and Hell and all that lies between—the revolt of Satan and his rebel angels, the expulsion of the rebels from Heaven, Satan's plot against the Almighty to corrupt the newly created earth, the temptation and fall of Adam and Eve, and the prophecy of Christ's ultimate triumph over Satan. The theme, as Milton says in the prologue, is to:

> …assert (or vindicate) Eternal Providence,
> And justify the ways of God to men.

John Milton was born in a house on Bread Street off Cheapside in 1608. His parents were Puritans. He was brought up in an atmosphere of culture and refinement, attended St Paul's School and spent seven years at Christ's College, Cambridge. Archbishop Laud's policies repelled him from the Anglican ministry, and he became a Presbyterian and later an Independent. He was secretary to the Council of State during Cromwell's time, which put him in some danger after the Restoration. Milton lived in various houses in London, none of which have survived. He died in 1674 and was buried near his father in the chancel of St Giles, Cripplegate. ▶ Stuart & Commonwealth London **M** Memorial plaque on wall of St Giles, Cripplegate, K-11 Memorial window, St Margaret's, Westminster, C-7 Monument in Poet's Corner, Westminster Abbey, C-10 Portrait, busts, National Portrait Gallery, H-9

Milton's Cottage Just at the western edge of today's Greater London on a country road running south from Amersham (between Watford and High Wycombe) is the picturesque village of Chalfont St Giles. Here on the main road is the cottage where Milton spent a year, 1665-66, to escape the plague raging in London. And here was completed the great epic, *Paradise Lost*. The cottage has some relics of the poet and is open to the public daily except Tuesday, February-October.
▶ Restoration London **M** Map location, N-4

Miracle Plays or Mystery Plays These were medieval dramas put on by the city corporation and guilds, representing sacred history or lives of the saints. They were played principally on festivals, Corpus Christi Day, Christmas, Whitsuntide and Easter. Acted usually on wheeled stages and pulled about to various points in the city, they tended to mix their serious subjects with slapstick humour and farce. For example, the star of the Nativity play is Mack, the sheep stealer, who hides a lamb in a baby's crib and who for punishment is tossed in a blanket. While many Miracle Plays were staged in London, we know more about those put on in Coventry, York, Chester and Wakefield because of the material that has survived. ▶ Medieval London

Missionary Societies in London The first English foreign missionary society was the Corporation for the Propagation of the Gospel in New England, created by act of Parliament in 1649 to give support to the work of John Eliot among the Indians. The first in the modern sense was the Baptist Missionary Society (1792), associated with the famous William Carey. The first in London was the London Missionary Society (1795), which sent Robert Morrison to China, John Williams to the South Pacific, Robert and Mary Moffat and their celebrated son-in-law David Livingstone to Africa, and James Chalmers to New Guinea. Today there are over one hundred Protestant missionary societies headquartered in London. ▶ Classical London

Mithraic Temple   The ruins of a place of worship of the Roman mystery religion devoted to Mithras was found during excavations for new buildings on Queen Victoria Street in the 1950s and reconstructed in the forecourt of one of the office blocks. ▶ Roman London   **M** Map location, L-1

Monastic Communities in Medieval London   We are indebted to William Fitz-Stephens, writing in the days of Henry II in the twelfth century, for the information that in his days there existed in London 126 parish churches and 13 churches attached to monasteries. By the time of the Reformation the number of religious institutions and properties had grown to the following:

Eight abbies (monastic communities under the rule of an abbot):

The Black Friars (Dominicans), founded in 1221. Their property was located between Ludgate and the river; today Blackfriars Bridge passes the site.

The Grey Friars (Franciscans), who occupied a site on Newgate Street off Warwick Lane, later the famous 'Blue Coat' school of Christ's Hospital. The war ruins of Christ Church, Newgate Street, occupy the site today.

The Augustinian or 'Austin' Friars, founded in 1253, who had their house on Old Broad Street leading off Threadneedle Street. Their church was assigned by Edward VI in 1550 to Protestant refugees from Europe, later becoming the Dutch Church. The original building was destroyed in the bombing and a new Dutch Church was erected in 1950-54. But the area is still known as 'Austin Friars'.

The White Friars (Carmelites), founded in 1241, who had a house east of the Temple which was destroyed in 1537.

The Crutched Friars (that is, they wore a cross sewn on the backs of their cloaks) who had their abbey near St Olaves, Hart Street.

The Carthusian Order, who occupied what is now the Charterhouse.

The Cistercians, whose Abbey of St Mary Graces was at East Smithfield, an open area east of the Tower. It was destroyed in the Dissolution.

The Brethren de Sacca or 'Bonhommes', a small community under Augustinian rule located in Old Jewry. It, too, disappeared in the Dissolution.

The very early Benedictine Abbey of St Peter is not mentioned by

Fitz-Stephens as it was at Westminster, not part of London in medieval times.

Then there were five priories; that is, communities under the rule of a prior rather than an abbot, but subject to the abbot of another community:

The Knights Templar and the Knights Hospitaller of the Order of St John of Jerusalem, whose story is told elsewhere.

The Priory of Holy Trinity, Aldgate, which was located just north of St Katharine Creechurch on Leadenhall Street.

The Priory of St Bartholomew's, Smithfield, part of whose church remains today as the parish church of St Bartholomew the Great, Smithfield.

The Priory of St Mary Overy, Southwark, on the south bank of the Thames where Southwark Cathedral now stands.

Next, there were four nunneries:

The Priory of the Nuns of St Helen, off Bishopsgate Street where the Church of St Helen's stands today.

The Benedictine Priory of St John the Baptist, Holywell, which was north of the City in Shoreditch.

The Abbey of the Nuns of St Clare (or 'Poor Clares'), also called the Abbey of the Minoresses, which was located between Aldgate Street and Tower Hill.

The Benedictine Nunnery of St Mary, Clerkenwell, which lay north of the Priory of St John of Jerusalem.

Of colleges, or *collegium*, communities of religious men not under the rule of an abbot or prior, there were five:

St Martin le Grand, near Aldersgate.

St Thomas of Acon (or Acre), which was near Guildhall.

The College of 'St Esprit and Mary' in the Vintry Ward. College Street off Upper Thames Street derives its name thus. This was founded by the famous Richard Wittington.

The College of St Michael, Crooked Lane, just north of London Bridge.

Corpus Christi, which was located by the old church of St Lawrence Pountney, between Cannon Street and the river.

There were also eight hospitals, most of which were outside the city walls because of well-justified fear of contagion:

St Giles In the Fields, a leprasarium near Tottenham Court Road where the present church of St Giles In the Fields stands.

St James Hospital for female lepers, where St James Palace is today.

St Mary of Rounceval, by the present day Charing Cross.

The Papey was a hospice for infirm priests, located in Bevis Marks.

St Bartholomew the Less, at Smithfield where St Bartholomew's

Hospital stands today.

The Lock Spital, later the Hospital of St Mary Spital for lepers, north of Bishopsgate.

The Hospital of St Katharine's By the Tower, now St Katharine's Docks.

Elsing Spital, a hospital for a hundred blind men, located near Cripplegate.

Later the famous Hospital of St Mary of Bethelehem (nicknamed Bedlam) for the insane was founded just outside the walls near Bishopsgate.

Finally there were the town estates of the various bishops, who as members of the House of Lords needed to spend part of the year in London. A remnant of one of these, the chapel of the former estate of the Bishops of Ely located just north of Holborn Circus, is now the Catholic Chapel of St Etheldreda.

Monmouth, Humphrey He was the London merchant in whose home William Tyndale worked on the translation of the New Testament until forced to move to the Continent. He is buried in All Hallows, Barking, M-1, but his monument was destroyed in the bombing.
▶ Reformation London

Monument, The This famous London landmark, located on Fish Street close to Thames Street and London Bridge, is a fluted Doric column 202 feet high. It was designed by the scientist Robert Hooke to commemorate the Great Fire of 1666 and was built by Wren between 1671 and 1677. It is supposed to be located exactly 202 feet from where the fire broke out in Pudding Lane. A winding staircase leads to a caged gallery from which a splendid view may be obtained of St Paul's, the Tower and Old London generally. A 42-foot-high flaming-gilt urn at the top symbolizes the fire, whose history is given on the base. Originally the religious prejudice of the late seventeenth century was expressed in this account, which blamed the disaster on the 'popish faction'. Thus these lines from Pope's *Essay on Man*:

> Where London's column, pointing at the skies,
> Like a tall bully, lifts the head and lies.

This reference was removed in 1831, after the repeal of the Test and Corporation Acts. ▶ Restoration London **M** Map location, D-3

Moody, Dwight L. (1837-99) Moody, an American evangelist, together with his musical associate Ira Sankey, held meetings in London in 1873 with record-breaking attendance. This was the beginning of a religious revival, known as the 'Second Great Evangelical Awakening', that swept over most of Britain. ▶ Victorian London

Moravians or Moravian Brethren Names for the Church of the United Brethren, which began with refugees from Moravia who re-settled on the estates of Count Nicholas von Zinzendorf in Saxony (now East Germany). This was essentially a missionary movement, as numerous of the Brethren took the Gospel to far corners of the earth. John Wesley first encountered them on his voyage to Georgia, and it was at a Bible reading at one of their houses in London that he was spiritually awakened. The Moravians had a chapel on Fetter Lane where Zinzendorf himself preached for a time. ▶ Classical London

More, Thomas (1478-1535) Thomas More was a brilliant scholar, influenced by the 'New Learning' growing out of the Renaissance, and a good friend of dean John Colet and Erasmus of Rotterdam. The latter, in fact, was More's house guest on several occasions and a frequent correspondent. Trained at Oxford, More was a devout Catholic and had considered entering holy orders. He decided instead on law. He was very successful, entered Parliament in 1504 and became known for his fairness and clemency, as well as for his interest

Sir Thomas More, martyred for resisting Henry VIII's claims to be head of the church.

in social reform. During this period he published his most famous work, *Utopia*, which describes an ideal state where people had all things in common but were allowed freedom of religion.

More and his wife were generous and hospitable and had many friends among learned and influential people in politics and the royal court. They often invited guests to their homes, both in the City and later on the riverside at Chelsea, where there was much lively and witty conversation around the dinner table. More also lived a deeply religious life. He not only had a private chapel in his home but in 1528 rebuilt a chapel for his private worship in the parish church next to his property. This, as well as the epitaph which he wrote for himself, may still be seen in Chelsea Old Church (A-1).

The king, who had great confidence in Thomas More and knighted him in 1521, appointed him lord chancellor in 1529 when that office was vacated by Thomas Wolsey. But More's rise to the top administrative post in the land was short lived. In 1531 Henry VIII had induced a convocation of the clergy to acknowledge him as supreme head of the church, and More as a convinced Catholic could not support him in this. Neither could he give his approval to Henry's plan to obtain a divorce. He used the excuse of ill health to resign from the chancellorship in 1532 and tried to remain silent. But the king felt threatened even by the silence of so influential a man, and More was committed to the Tower and brought to trial for treason in 1534. He stuck steadfastly to his refusal to approve of the divorce even though his daughter pleaded with him in prison. He went calmly to the block that same year. ▶ Reformation London ■ Commemorative window, St Lawrence, Jewry, K-12 Modern statue outside Chelsea Old Church, A-3 Portrait, National Portrait Gallery, H-9 Portrait on triptych, Altar of the English Martyrs, Brompton Oratory, A-1

'Morning Star of the Reformation' A term used by John Foxe to describe John Wyclif in the *Actes and Monuments*. It is on Wyclif's monument in the crypt of St Paul's Cathedral. ▶ Medieval London ■ Map location of St Paul's, L-15

Museum of London This is the museum of London's history. It is located in modern quarters in the Barbican off Aldgate Street, a development built up after the bombing near a corner of the old London Wall. The collection is arranged chronologically, beginning with pre-historic London and ending with World War II and the early post-war period. It includes artifacts, diagrams, clothing, dioramas, vehicles, books, photographs, films and much more, and makes numerous references to London churches and the religious life of the City. There is an excellent bookshop. Admission is free.

An item of particular interest to Christians of all backgrounds is located outside on the side of the building to the right of the main entrance. It is a large bronze replica of the page from John Wesley's Journal dated 24 May 1738, giving an account of a meeting that he attended 'very unwillingly' in Aldersgate Street (the Barbican structure covers the actual site). It reads in part:

> I felt my heart strangely warmed. I felt I did trust in Christ, Christ alone, for salvation; and an assurance was given me, that he had taken away *my* sins, even *mine*, and saved me from the law of sin and death.

M Map location, K-4

Museums London is especially rich in museums and galleries with exhibits of particular interest to Christians. These include: British Library, H-1 British Museum, H-2 The Courtauld Institute Galleries, G-1 Museum of London, K-4 National Gallery, H-8 National Portrait Gallery, H-9 Tate Gallery, C-8 Victoria & Albert Museum, A-9

Nash, John (1752-1835) Nash was the architect who designed Regent's Street including All Souls, Langham Place and also Regent's Park, under the Prince Regent, later George IV. ▶ Classical London
M Portrait & bust, National Portrait Gallery, H-9 Bust, Porch of All Souls, Langham Place, F-2

National Gallery The National Gallery faces Trafalgar Square on the north side. It is one of the world's great art galleries, and it exhibits numerous paintings with biblical subjects, especially from the Renaissance period and earlier. There are special collections of works by Leonardo da Vinci, Rembrandt, Rubens, Van Dyck, among a great many others. **M** Map location, H-8

National Portrait Gallery This unique gallery, located at the side of the National Gallery facing St Martin's Lane, is a treasure-house of portraits of England's famous men and women, including many of the sovereigns. Numerous well-known Christian figures associated with London are included. The museum shop has postcards of many of the portraits, and photo prints may be specially ordered. **M** Map location, H-9

New English Bible The 'King James' or 'Authorised' version of the Bible, first published in London in 1611, was for 270 years the only English Bible generally accepted by Protestants as authoritative. However, by the second half of the nineteenth century Bible scholars began to recognize that a revision was greatly needed. There are four reasons why this was so:

> Many English words had changed in meaning since Elizabethan times;
> A number of ancient biblical manuscripts had been discovered since 1911;
> The scientific method had been applied to the examination of

biblical materials, making it possible to be more accurate in their use;

Scholars knew a great deal more about the Hebrew and Greek languages.

In 1870 the Church of England initiated a move to produce a revision of the *Authorized Version*, and interdenominational teams of translators were appointed in both England and the United States. The English New Testament Company began work in the historic Jerusalem Chamber of Westminster Abbey (C-10) on 22 June 1870. The New Testament of this, the *Revised Version*, was published in London on 17 May 1881. The Old Testament was published in 1885. The American translators, however, had certain preferences which were not included in the English publication and thus continued their work for several more years. The result was the *American Standard Revised Version*, published by Thomas Nelson & Sons in New York in 1901.

Shortly after World War II, in 1946, the various church bodies and Bible Societies in Great Britain recognized that not just a revision of the King James but an entirely new translation of the Bible in modern English was necessary. The actual work of translation was entrusted to four panels dealing with the New and Old Testaments, the 'Apocrypha' and the literary revision as a whole. The joint committee began meeting in 1948, again in the Jerusalem Chamber. The result of their work was the *New English Bible*, the New Testament first appearing in 1961 and the entire Bible with Apocrypha in 1970. Donald Coggan, the archbishop of Canterbury at the time, was particularly interested in the project and his portrait in Lambeth Palace shows him holding a copy. ▶ Twentieth-century London

Newman, John Henry (1801-90) Newman is perhaps the best-known today of the 'Tractarians' associated with the Oxford Movement. He was an evangelical in early life but at Oxford gradually moved to a High Church position. While vicar of St Mary's, the university church, he became deeply involved in attempting through writing and preaching to demonstrate that the Church of England occupied a middle position between Protestantism and Romanism and is a descendant of the Apostolic Church. In 1843 he resigned St Mary's and was received into the Catholic Church. His autobiographical defence against his critics, *Apologia Pro Vita Sua*, brought him into great prominence. He was made a cardinal in 1879. ▶ Victorian London **M** Portrait, bust, National Portrait Gallery, H-9 Statue outside Brompton Oratory, A-1

Newton, John (1725-1807) John Newton, who became one of the leading evangelicals within the Church of England in the late eighteenth century, is best known for his hymns, 'Amazing Grace', 'Glorious Things of Thee Are Spoken', 'How Sweet the Name of Jesus

St Mary Woolnoth, whose vicar for twenty-eight years was John Newton, slavetrader turned hymnwriter.

Sounds', among many others, written in collaboration with the poet William Cowper. Newton was the son of a merchant sea captain, and his early life included sailing with his father, service with the royal navy, desertion and involvement in the West African slave trade. At one point in his life he was actually the servant of a white slaveholder's black wife, who humiliated and degraded him.

During a violent storm on the North Atlantic during a voyage back to England in 1747, Newton turned to God. However, he continued in the slave trade until 1755. Back in his home city of London he was influenced by George Whitefield and John Wesley, decided to take holy orders in the Anglican Church, and was ordained in 1764.

Newton was curate of the parish church in Olney, Buckinghamshire, for fifteen years. His friendship with Cowper helped the poet through a period of mental illness and resulted in the famous *Olney Hymns*. In 1779 Newton became vicar of St Mary Woolnoth near the Royal Exchange, London, where he remained for the rest of his life. He preached to large con- gregations, at one time giving a series of sermons based on the texts used in Handel's *Messiah*. He was a counsellor to Charles Simeon, Hannah More, Thomas Scott and William Wilberforce, and he played a significant part in the

latter's campaign to abolish the slave trade. ▶ Classical London
M Memorial plaque in St Mary Woolnoth, L-11

Nonconformists, Nonconformity 'Nonconformity' in the his- tory of
English Christianity means, strictly speaking, the position of the
various Protestant bodies such as Presbyterians, Baptists and
Separatists when, after 1660, a series of laws was passed making it
impossible for them to remain within the Church of England. From
that time onward church bodies were either Church of England or
Nonconformist. Until the Act of Toleration under William and Mary
there was outright persecution of Nonconformists, and there were
certain restrictions of rights until the early nineteenth century.

However, in a broader sense Christian Nonconformity in England
goes back at least to Wyclif, who in the fourteenth century refused to
conform to certain non-biblical doctrines of the Roman Catholic
Church. Until the Reformation began in Germany in 1517,
Nonconformity was generally a matter of individuals committing
themselves (usually, but not always, in a quiet way) to the authority
of the Bible over that of the Pope (or later, the king). They were
Nonconformists because they were officially heretics if they believed
this way, declared so by an act of Parliament in 1401.

After 1517 we read of groups of scholars at the universities,
especially Cambridge, gathering together to read and discuss Luther's
writings and later preaching these doctrines which did not conform to
the official doctrines of the emerging Church of England. However, it
was during Elizabeth's reign that underground congregations began to
form in London. These had different systems of church government
than the state church, primarily Reformed or Presbyterian and
Separatist. In 1593 an 'Act Against Puritans' was passed, stipulating
that anyone who failed to attend an approved church and instead
worshipped with a 'conventicle' (underground church) 'shall be
committed to prison, there to remain without bail... until they shall
conform'. From this time until 1640, when the Puritans gained the
upper hand in Parliament, these bodies were suppressed. Between
1640 and 1660 it was the Episcopalian system that was suppressed.

Nonconformists after the Restoration Besides the ravages of the
Plague and the Great Fire, London in the 1660s continued to be
battered by religious controversy during the Restoration period.
Charles II, son of the executed monarch, had declared himself willing
to approve any bill that Parliament might pass in favour of liberty of
conscience. But the members of Parliament, even though many were
Presbyterians, were reacting to the lack of any restraint on religious
nonconformity that existed during the Commonwealth. They
hastened to re-establish the Anglican Church in its old form,
including all the former bishoprics. In 1662 an Act of Uniformity was
passed, requiring all clergy to give full approval to the prayer-book.
This was clearly a signal of intent to make any religious activity

outside the established church difficult if not impossible. Some 2,000 courageous ministers whose consciences would not permit them to accept this provision resigned from their livings.

Thus began a long 'outlaw' period for the Separatists, Presbyterians, Baptists, Quakers and other nonconforming Protestants. The Corporation Act, the Five Mile Act and the Test Act were other measures directed at harrassing 'conventicles', making it difficult and risky for Nonconformist congregations to gather, Nonconformist ministers to preach or for Nonconformists to hold any public office. In contrast to earlier times, however, these laws did not pass downward from the king but arose from the conservative representatives of the people who feared the extremes of Protestant sectarianism on the one hand and 'popery' or Roman Catholic power on the other. ▶ Restoration London

Nonconformist Chapels in London   Before the seventeenth century there were no Nonconformist chapels at all— only secret gatherings which the authorities called 'conventicles'. Then, as Nonconformist bodies grew (there were around three dozen groups in London in 1646), some congregations took over unused church buildings or other existing properties. One of the earliest of these in Old London was the King's Weigh House at the west end of Eastcheap. It had been first a church then was turned into the King's Weigh House, where merchants weighed their goods on official scales. Two ministers who had been forced out by the Act of Uniformity founded there a Presbyterian chapel which lasted well into the nineteenth century.

Another famous Nonconformist chapel, also extinct, was located at 32 Fetter Lane. This was started by a minister named Turner who had served faithfully in the City during the Great Plague. Richard Baxter says in his journal, 'I began a Tuesday lecture in Mr Turner's church ... with great convenience and God's encouraging blessing; but I never took a penny for it from anyone'. Records indicate that this same chapel was attacked in 1709 by a mob, who carried the contents away and burnt them in Lincoln's Inn Fields. Later it became a chapel of the Moravians, and the great Count Nicholas Zinzendorf preached here sometime after 1738. Here, too, John Wesley ministered in the early part of his career.

Not far away, at 96 Fetter Lane, was a Baptist congregation founded by Dr Thomas Goodwin, who ministered during the trou- bled times between 1660 and 1681. Goodwin was an outspoken and controversial figure who held both Calvinistic and Arminian doctrines. This building was rebuilt in 1732 and lasted into the nineteenth century. One of its better-known pastors was the Rev. John Spurgeon, father of the famous Charles Haddon Spurgeon of Metropolitan Tabernacle.

Southwark, which had less-stringent laws than London, was home to several early Nonconformist chapels. There was, for example, a

Presbyterian chapel in Park Street where Richard Baxter also preached for a time. On Zoar Street, a short distance westward, a Congregational chapel was established in the 1680s under John Chester. Here John Bunyan preached to great crowds on one or two occasions. The Baptists built a chapel in a secluded court called Goat's Yard in 1672. The first minister was Benjamin Keach, a popular preacher, and it is said that his chapel would hold a thousand people. He was the author of a *Baptist Catechism* which is still in print. The Baptists also had a building on the riverside, the 'Baptisterion', where they could hold public baptisms by immersion. The passageway leading to it was called, appropriately enough, 'Dripping Alley'.

By the early eighteenth century the Nonconformist meeting places in London alone had increased to nearly forty—there were still more in Southwark and Westminster. Many of these consisted of buildings converted from other uses or rented halls. But as the eighteenth century progressed it became possible for these congregations to construct buildings specifically for their own use. The four most famous were Spa Fields Chapel, Surrey Chapel, Whitefield's Tabernacle and Wesley's Chapel.

> The Spa Fields Chapel was built in Clerkenwell on a site originally occupied by an amusement palace. In 1777 the property was purchased by the Countess of Huntingdon and rebuilt for use by the Calvinistic Methodists.
>
> Surrey Chapel was constructed in 1783 for use of the Rev. Roland Hill and his large congregation. It was in Southwark on the road leading south from Blackfriars Bridge. Like Spa Fields Chapel, it was round, with a cupola on top to let in light.
>
> George Whitefield's first chapel (which he called a 'tabernacle', alluding to its temporary nature) was constructed in 1741 in the Moorfields not far from Wesley's Foundry. In 1756 he put up a plain brick building on Tottenham Court Road, which was known as 'Whitefield's Tabernacle' for nearly two centuries. It and all the others are now only memories.
>
> Wesley's Chapel on City Road is the last and only Nonconformist chapel still standing in London.
>
> **M** Wesley's Chapel, K-17

Norfolk, Duke of   He was the Catholic peer who, during the reign of Elizabeth I, was involved in a conspiracy to wed Mary, Queen of Scots, in an attempt to depose Elizabeth and place Mary on the throne of England. He was beheaded in the Tower.   ▶ Elizabethan London

Nunneries in London   There were four nunneries in medieval London. The remains of the church of one, St Helen's, is incorporated into the parish church of St Helen's, Bishopsgate.   ▶ Medieval London   **M** St Helen's, Bishopsgate, M-10

Oates, Titus (1648-1705)   Oates was an ordained Anglican turned Catholic, who in turn was expelled from Catholic schools in Spain. He returned to London in 1673 with alleged information about a plot to assassinate Charles II and make the duke of York, a Catholic, king of England. For a time there was a great reaction against the Catholics and active persecution, while Oates became a hero. When the plot was found to be false he was convicted of perjury and exposed in the stocks to public degradation.   ▶ Restoration London

Old St Paul's   One of London's great sights is the magnificent cross-topped dome of St Paul's Cathedral rising supreme amidst the steeples, towers and highrise office buildings of the modern city. But the dome goes back less than 300 years, and before its time a much larger medieval cathedral stood here whose spire once soared nearly 100 feet higher. Old St Paul's was so important a part of medieval London that its story needs to be told separately.

This was the most ancient church foundation in London, the most splendid ecclesiastical structure in the City and the centre of its religious and, to some extent, its civic life. It lasted from 1240 to 1666, roughly on the site where St Paul's Cathedral stands today. It was the fourth known church to be built here. At 596 feet, it was the largest church in England and the third largest in all Europe. The steeple was 489 feet high and could be seen from as far away as Greenwich.

The first St Paul's Cathedral, a wooden building consecrated in 604, was replaced by a stone structure built by Bishop Erkenwald. After destruction by the Vikings, it was rebuilt by the Saxons in 962, and this building burned down in 1087. Construction of the medieval St Paul's went on for some 250 years. Even after its consecration the further addition of a choir took place, which greatly increased its length. The steeple was put up in 1315 (and burned during a lightning storm in 1561).

Old St Paul's was affected in one way or another by all the great events in London's history throughout the Middle Ages. Pilgrims (like modern tourists) came by the thousands from all parts of the kingdom to visit the shrine of St Erkenwald, covered with pure gold, and to gape at other marvellous relics such as some hair of Mary Magdalene, the blood of St Paul, milk from the Virgin's breast, the hand of St John and some pieces of the skull of Thomas a Becket. (Becket had sent an envoy to St Paul's who publicly proclaimed the excommunication of the bishop of London.) In the early thirteenth century archbishop Stephen Langton secured a pledge from a large gathering of prelates and barons at St Paul's to support the Magna Carta and all the liberties of England. Wyclif came to St Paul's in 1377 accompanied by John of Gaunt and Lord Percy, Earl Marshall of England. Later one of the Lollard priests nailed twelve articles to the door of St Paul's denouncing false doctrine and clerical vice. And

Henry VII came here twice after his victory at Bosworth Field to offer thanksgiving.

In Reformation times Old St Paul's was the scene of several occasions of great ecclesiastical pomp involving the ambitious Cardinal Wolsey. In 1522 Wolsey said mass before King Henry VIII and the Emperor Charles V, surrounded by more than twenty prelates waving incense. But in the reign of Edward VI the cathedral was stripped of its images and crucifixes, vestments and altar cloths were sold, and a plain table was used for communion; the ceremonials returned during Mary's short reign. Several heresy trials were conducted here under the vicious Bishop Bonner. In Elizabeth's day the victory over the Spanish Armada was celebrated amid great rejoicing by a sermon at Paul's Cross, and later the queen herself came to offer her thanks to God.

Despite its honoured position as London's earliest Christian foundation and the episcopal see of the capital city, Old St Paul's was used very irreverently by the general citizenry. As early as King Edward III (1327-77) a proclamation was issued prohibiting buying and selling in the cathedral, throwing stones and shooting arrows at jackdaws nesting in the church walls and playing at ball within the building. But numerous warnings and punishments notwithstanding, Old St Paul's seems always to have been more a Vanity Fair than a place of worship. 'Cheats, gulls, assassins, and thieves thronged the middle aisle of St Paul's; advertisements of all kinds covered the walls; the worst class of servants came there to be hired; worthless rascals and disreputable flaunting women met there by appointment.'

By the seventeenth century Old St Paul's was badly in need of repair. James I tried and failed to raise money for the work, but William Laud, the new bishop of London appointed by Charles I, succeeded in getting a new west end built, to a classical design by Inigo Jones. However, the work was cut short by the strife between the king and Parliament. The remaining building funds were seized, and after the king's execution the building was badly defaced and the choir used for a cavalry barracks. Much of the gold, silver and valuables was sold off, partly to raise money for Cromwell's artillery. After the Restoration, Wren was called in to try and make a plan to revive the old cathedral once again. However, the Great Fire enabled the architect to apply his genius to an entirely new structure.
▶ Medieval London

Oldcastle, Sir John (c.1378-1417) A prominent soldier and member of Parliament, he was arrested for his Lollard views. Although he escaped, he was eventually put to death at Smithfield. Oldcastle's reputation was maligned by his enemies and in some quarters he was made the object of derision. Shakespeare's comic figure Sir John Falstaff was drawn from this source. ▶ Medieval London

Oratorio A musical work with a dramatic theme, usually from the Bible.

George Frederick Handel is the most famous composer of oratorios, several of which are still performed. ▶ Classical London

Oratory A special place for divine services, in particular the celebration of the Roman Catholic mass. It also refers to the community made up of 'oratorios' who serve the oratory. The oratory was introduced into London by Frederick William Faber and John Henry Newman in the nineteenth century. ▶ Victorian London

Owen, John (1616-83) John Owen, born in Oxfordshire, received divine orders at Oxford but left the university rather than submit to Laud's High Church policies. He espoused the Parliamentarian cause, and when the Civil War broke out he moved to Charterhouse Yard, London. He preached before Parliament in 1649, the day after the execution of Charles I. He was one of Cromwell's chaplains and later dean of Christ Church College, Oxford, where William Penn came under his influence. Owen was tolerated and allowed to preach after the Restoration. In 1673 he became minister of a large congregation in Leadenhall Street, London. His written works include *Exercitations on the Epistle to the Hebrews*, *On the Holy Spirit*, *The Divine Origin of the Scriptures* and *Union Among Protestants*. ▶ Stuart & Commonwealth London, Restoration London **M** Portrait, National Portrait Gallery, H-9

The Oxford Movement In 1828 the Test and Corporation Acts were repealed, and Roman Catholics and Nonconformists gained permission to sit in Parliament. This triggered a strong reaction from several conservative leaders of the Anglican church at Oxford, notably John Henry Newman, vicar of St Mary's, the University Church; John Keble, editor of the *Christian Year*; and Edward B. Pusey, regius professor of Hebrew at Oriel College. This group believed that the Church of England was the true descendant of the ancient Catholic Church and that Anglican bishops were in the line of authority given by Christ to the apostles. These views were propagated very successfully by means of a series of theses which they called *Tracts for the Times* (hence the name 'Tractarians'). The general emphasis of this movement was upon the glory of the past and the place of tradition in the church.

The Oxford, or Tractarian, Movement created a storm of controversy in that, while on the one hand they resisted liberal trends in the Church of England and reawakened public interest in the Christian heritage of the English nation, on the other they seemed to overlook the accomplishments of the Reformation and to be reintroducing the doctrines and practices of the medieval church. Newman eventually left the Church of England and became a Roman Catholic cardinal.

As noted in the introduction to Victorian London, the Oxford Movement inspired the reconstruction of many church interiors. In this they reflected, to the Victorian mind, a more adequate picture of earlier Christian traditions. They played a major part in saving St Paul's Cathedral from neglect and disrepair, restoring its former glory, and brought to London the Oratory of St Philip Neri and its impressive church, known as Brompton Oratory. ▶ Victorian London

Pageantry in Medieval London In the cities during the Middle Ages the church played an important role as a source of popular diversion. Medieval London was a city vibrant with life—noisy, odoriferous and colourful. While the lot of the masses was hard, with work from dawn to dark the year round and the threat of starvation or the plague never far away, there were also a great many special events in the City which were occasions for excitement and merriment.

Some of this free entertainment consisted of affairs put on by London itself, such as the annual Lord Mayor's show or splendid 'ridings' by the sheriffs, aldermen or other officials. Others were magnificent events having to do with royalty or the nobles— coronations, victory celebrations and the like. And of course there were morris-dancing, mummers, May-pole dancing and other folk diversions in the spring, and minstrels, jugglers and street shows in the market and at various fairs.

But a good number of the special events were church holy days. For example, each guild had a celebration in honour of its patron saint, which called for a solemn mass before the feasting. There were many other saints days too, such as the vigils of St John the Baptist, St Paul and St Peter, the Feast of St Bartholomew… And of course there was feasting and merriment on Christmas, Easter and Twelfth Night, the Beating of the Bounds on Ascension Day, Mystery Plays in the churches, and colourful ceremonials on the occasion of important weddings and funerals all the year round. Thus it is not difficult to see how much the people of London counted on the church to make their lives, if not holier, at least a bit more interesting. ▶ Medieval London

Paradise Lost This is an epic poem written by John Milton in the tradition of the Greek and Roman classics, except that the theme is taken from the Bible. It is considered one of the greatest literary works in the English language. ▶ Restoration London

Parker, Joseph (1830-1902) In marked contrast to his contemporary H.P. Liddon, Joseph Parker ceased his formal education at age sixteen, but his outstanding gifts resulted in his ordination by the Congregational church at the age of twenty-three. Parker was called in 1869 to the Poultry Street Chapel in London, which in 1874 was replaced by the famous City Temple (H-9). He was a man of impressive appearance, commanding voice and impeccable diction. For over twenty-five years he preached three times a week, one of London's great pulpit masters alongside Liddon and Spurgeon. The *People's Bible* in twenty-five volumes was based on his seven- year preaching cycle through the entire Bible. ▶ Victorian London
M Plaster case of bust, National Portrait Gallery, H-9

Parker, Matthew (1504-75)   He was archbishop of Canterbury under
Elizabeth I from 1559 and played an important part in the Elizabethan
Settlement, helping to reinstate the prayer-book and the *Thirty-nine
Articles of Religion*. In earlier life he was identified with the Reformers
at Cambridge, and from 1535 he was chaplain to Anne Boleyn.
Parker was an able administrator and a scholar, whose valuable library
was bequeathed to Corpus Christi College, Cambridge.   ▶ Elizabethan
London   **M** Portrait, Lambeth Palace, C-4

Parnell, John Vesey (1805-83)   Parnell was fifth baronet and second
Baron Congleton. Educated in France and at Edinburgh University,
he was associated with the Plymouth Brethren from 1829, first in
Dublin and later in London. He spent much of his life preaching and
ministering among them.   ▶ Victorian London

Paul's Cross   At the northeast corner of Old St Paul's stood a covered
outdoor pulpit called Paul's Cross. This was used for proclamations
and topical sermons on events of the day. It seems to have been open
to use by any of the clergy who wanted to hold forth on some issue of
general interest, much like Speaker's Corner in Hyde Park today. It
was here that Hugh Latimer preached his famous 'Sermon on the
Plough'. But unpopular speakers took considerable risk of life and
limb, as a crowd could be ugly and there was no such thing as police
protection. Wyclifite Bibles were burned publicly here and Tyndale's
New Testaments as well. While Old St Paul's has completely
disappeared, the outline of Paul's Cross may still be seen outside the
northeast end of the present building.   ▶ Medieval and Reformation
London   **M** St Paul's Cathedral, L-15

The Peasant's Revolt   From the eleventh century onward, and especially
in the fourteenth century, the bubonic plague, which at that time was
called the 'Black Death', appeared periodically. During the years
1348-50 and thereafter, this terrible, swift and usually fatal sickness
decimated the ranks of every class of people in England, particularly
the labouring class. As the shortage of laboring hands began to
impact upon the landowners, higher wages were demanded and paid.
But the government, which was entirely in the hands of the upper
classes, soon reacted by passing laws forbidding labourers to ask more
than they had received before the plague.

Enforcing these laws, however, was exceedingly difficult, and the
result was increased tension and bitterness between the peasants and
the government. Moreover, the war with France which dragged on all
through the fourteenth century required heavier taxes, and this
burden also fell most heavily on the peasants and 'villeins' or small
farmers. Certain popular preachers went about the country discussing
social conditions in their sermons, which intensified the discontent.

In 1381 the war tax, called a 'poll tax' because it was collected from
every household, did not yield enough revenue and the tax collectors

were sent back to the villages to find those who had avoided payment. The people began attacking the tax collectors and rioting broke out all over southeast England. A great body of the peasants, under a leader named Wat Tyler, invaded London and for two or three days had the city in its power. They burned the city palace of the duke of Lancaster along with properties of unpopular nobles and of the Knights Hospitaller. In addition, they executed Archbishop Sudbury, the lord chancellor, and other officials and citizens.

The rioters wanted to lay their petitions before the king, Richard II, a boy of fifteen. Richard met with them and craftily promised everything they demanded. The next interview was at Smithfield, and the king was accompanied by the lord mayor of London and some attendants. When Tyler rode forward to lay new demands before the king a dispute arose, and one of the lord mayor's men sprang up and stabbed Tyler, who fell from his horse and was then dispatched by the others. Before the peasants could react the young king cried out, 'Are you seeking a leader? I will be your leader'. As they followed him out of the city gates they were ambushed by the king's troops and dispersed.

Because the evils which had brought about the ill-fated rebellion were in some points the very same evils that Wyclif and his followers were preaching against, Wyclif was very cleverly made the whipping boy for the rebellion. But no attempt was made by the government to acknowledge or redress the wrongs against the peasants. ▶ Medieval London

Penn, Admiral Sir William (1621-70) A distinguished naval commander, he was knighted and made commissioner of the navy after the Restoration. As Samuel Pepys' superior, he is frequently mentioned in the *Diary*. He was the father of the Quaker William Penn. ▶ Restoration London

Penn, William (1644-1718) The most famous Quaker of all is William Penn, founder of Pennsylvania. Penn, whose naval-officer father was often away at sea, was raised by his mother in Chigwell, Essex, and received a good education. As a young man he was greatly influenced by John Owen and by the Quaker Thomas Lee. Expelled from Oxford for his Nonconformist views, he eventually joined the Society of Friends. He was imprisoned on several occasions and used both his pen and the pulpit to defend Quakerism and to advocate political and religious freedom. Between 1677 and 1678 he helped send more than 800 Quakers to New Jersey.

In 1681, in consideration of a debt to his father, he received from Charles II a grant of land now consisting of Pennsylvania and Delaware. He founded the colony of Pennsylvania as a 'holy experiment' for establishing liberty and equality in the exercise of religion. Penn was briefly imprisoned under William and Mary on a charge of being a Papist but later came into royal favour. His book, *No Cross, No Crown*, was written during his time in the Tower. He died in 1718 and was buried along with other members of his family in the grounds of Old Jordans. ▶ Restoration London **M** Quaker Meeting House, Jordans, N-5

Pepys, Samuel (1633-1703) Pepys was a very influential citizen of London and was personally involved in the return of Charles II to England. He rose to a high position in the naval office and was largely responsible for the rehabilitation of the British navy in Restoration days. He was a personal friend of many prominent Londoners and government officials, including Admiral Sir William Penn, the father of William Penn, and John Evelyn, one of the founders of the Royal Society.

Though a devout Christian personally and a longtime member of St Olave's Church, Hart Street, Pepys was not a member of the clergy nor officially involved in the church. But he is included in this history of Christian London because his famous *Diary*, kept between the fateful years of 1659 and 1669, contains a gold mine of eyewitness observations of London churches, their clergy and the religious affairs of the time. Here is a sample:

> *Aug. 10th, 1662 (Lord's Day)* Being to dine at my brother's, I walked to St Dunstan's, the church now being finished; and here I heard Dr Bates, who made a most eloquent sermon; and I am sorry I have hitherto had so low an opinion of the man, for I have not heard a neater sermon a great while, and more to my content.

Pepys thus gives us the reaction of the man in the pew to the result of the Act of Uniformity which forced so many of England's Nonconformist ministers to leave their callings. The minister mentioned here , William Bates, gave his last sermon on 17 August, using a text from Hebrews 13:20, 'Now may the God of peace...' We know this because Pepys also recorded his farewell words.
▶ Restoration London **M** Portraits, National Portrait Gallery, H-9
Bronze bust (modern) outside Admiralty building, Seething Lane, M-4

Philpott, John (1516-55) Educated at Winchester and Oxford, he was archdeacon of Winchester under Edward VI but was arrested during Mary's reign for opposing the doctrine of transubstantiation. He is one of three martyrs burned at Smithfield whose names appear on Martyr's Memorial. ▶ Reformation London **M** Martyr's Memorial, Smithfield, J-8

Pilgrim Fathers Strictly speaking, the Pilgrim Fathers (leaders of the group that sailed on the Mayflower and founded Plymouth Colony in 1620) were not associated with London but rather were a group of Separatists from the village of Scrooby in Nottinghamshire. However, there is a Pilgrim Fathers memorial in St Bride's Church

Samuel Pepys' celebrated diaries paint a vivid portrait of London church life in his day.

relating to Edward Winslow, an early governor of the Plymouth Colony and organizer of the Society for the Propagation of the Gospel among the Indians in New England, whose parents were married in that church. ▶ Stuart & Commonwealth London **M** St Bride's, Fleet Street, J-12

Pilgrim's Progress An allegory of the Christian life written by John Bunyan during his second imprisonment in 1676-77, it vies with *Foxe's Book of Martyrs* as the most-read Christian book next to the Bible. It traces the adventures of a man who, clothed in rags with a great burden on his back and a book in his hand, is directed by Evangelist to a distant shining light and a wicketgate. After a great many experiences during which his burden falls off at the foot of the cross, the man (Christian) fords the river and enters the Celestial City. Many of the characters and places in the story, such as the Giant Despair, Worldly Wiseman and Vanity Fair have become familiar figures in the English language. Scenes from *Pilgrim's Progress* are on John Bunyan's monument in Bunhill Fields Burying Ground. ▶ Restoration London **M** Map location of Bunhill Fields, K-1

Plague Year, The In the summer of 1665, five years after Charles II had ascended the vacant throne, an epidemic of the bubonic plague swept through London. This disease, carried by fleas from infected rats, caused a swift and horrible death. It was, of course, a re-occurrence of similar epidemics which took place in medieval times for the same reasons—sanitary conditions in the City had not changed a great deal. The churchyards were soon full, and pits were dug outside the walls to receive the corpses. At night wagons went about the streets, the drivers ringing bells and crying, 'Bring out your dead!' Before it was over some 100,000 Londoners had perished. A graphic description of the disaster was later given by Daniel Defoe in his book *Journal of the Plague Year*, published in 1722. A number of London's clergymen and doctors risked their lives to serve the suf- fering populace during this dreadful affliction. ▶ Restoration London

Prayer-book Informal name of the *Book of Common Prayer*.

Pre-Raphaelites A group of mid-nineteenth-century London artists led by Dante Gabriel Rossetti who sought to emulate painters earlier than Raphael (1483-1520), one of the great artists of the Italian Renaissance. Rossetti at first used only the initials PRB, and when it became known that these stood for 'Pre-Raphaelite Brotherhood' the group was attacked as being part of the Oxford Movement and secret Romanists. However, they were supported by the essayist John Ruskin and gained wide popularity. While the Brotherhood soon separated, one of them, Holman Hunt, continued in style and theme to maintain the original ideas. ▶ Victorian London

Puritans During the reign of Queen Elizabeth (1558-1603), as a result of the availability of the Bible in English, a great many English people including those of the upper classes became Christians in a personal way. They began to exert pressure on the Church of England to put more emphasis on the Bible and on Christlike living and less on form and ceremony. A number of these Christians were greatly influenced by the Reformed doctrines of John Calvin in Switzerland and the Scottish Reformer John Knox. Some of their leaders had been in Geneva during the reign of Mary, and they were eager to teach the Reformed doctrines. Also the annotated version of the Bible produced in Geneva was printed in London and became very popular.

These people were referred to as 'Puritans' because they put a great deal of emphasis upon the authority of the Bible, upon living moral lives and upon 'purifying' the church of what they considered pagan elements—clerical robes, use of incense, the ringing of bells, bowing toward the altar, and so on. They rejected the role of bishops and a church hierarchy, and they favoured a state church governed by representative bodies made up of clergy and leading laymen. Local churches in this system were bound to abide by the decisions of these governing bodies, called 'presbyteries' or 'consistories' (the word 'presbyter' comes from the Greek word *presbyteros*, meaning 'elder'). The national church of Scotland was eventually set up along these lines.

During much of the seventeenth century the Puritans struggled to replace the Episcopalian system with the Reformed or Presbyterian. They received very bad set-backs under Elizabeth and James I, but later nearly succeeded. In the end, however, the excesses of the Civil War and the Commonwealth led the English people to restore the King and episcopacy. After the Savoy Conference in 1661, Puritanism disappeared forever. ▶ Elizabethan, Stuart & Commonwealth London

Pusey, Edward (1800–82) Pusey was a fellow at Oriel College, Oxford, a scholar of Oriental languages, and eventually regius professor of Hebrew. He is best known as an associate of Keble and Newman in the Oxford Movement, and was the author of tracts on baptism and the eucharist. While enthusiastically supporting reconciliation with the Roman Catholic Church, he remained an Anglican when Newman became a Catholic, and thus was widely influential in the restoration of ritualism in the Church of England. ▶ Victorian London **M** Family group portrait, Royal Portrait Gallery, H-9

Quakers The name 'Quaker', like the name 'Puritan' (and, indeed, the name 'Christian'), was originally a term of derision—in this case applied to the Society of Friends founded by George Fox. It is said to have been used first by a judge at Derby where Fox was imprisoned as a blasphemer, after Fox had exhorted the magistrate to 'tremble at the word of the Lord.'

The Quakers from early times have put much emphasis upon the Spirit of God speaking in and through them. Generally, they have rejected ceremonies, the sacraments and clergy, considering the 'inner light' as important as Scripture. They have consistently practised and promoted pacifism and social services. A great number of Quakers were imprisoned at Newgate after the passing of the Act of Uniformity in 1660. But by the late 1660s there were many Friends meeting houses in the London area, more in the country districts than the City itself. One of these, Jordans Meeting House in Buckinghamshire, still exists. ▶ Restoration London **M** Quaker Meeting House, Jordans, N-5

Queen's Chapel, Palace of St James The Queen's Chapel is located across a small roadway from St James Palace near the Pall Mall, and behind it is concealed Marlborough House. It is so called from the fact that, in about 1623, Inigo Jones was ordered to 'prepare with great costliness' a chapel for the services of the Infanta of Spain, the intended bride of Charles I. The new queen, as a Roman Catholic, would wish to hear mass, which would not be possible in the Chapel Royal. This marriage did not take place, but later the chapel was opened with great ceremony for Charles's queen, Henrietta Maria. It was also used by Charles II's queen, Katharine of Braganza. During the time of William IV permission was given by the bishop of London for German Lutheran services to be held there.

The exterior of the chapel is in Palladian style and quite plain. Inside, the classical double-cube hall has a superb elliptical coffered ceiling constructed of timber. The interior retains its seventeenth-century fittings, with an altarpiece of the Holy Family by Annibale Carracci. The building was restored after World War II and is open to the public for services. ▶ Stuart & Commonwealth London

Rahere A courtier in the time of Henry I, he established the priory and hospital of St Bartholomew at Smithfield in the early twelfth century. His effigy is in the chancel of St Bartholomew the Great. ▶ Medieval London **M** St Bartholomew the Great, Smithfield, K-9

Raikes, Robert (1735-1811) He was publisher of the *Gloucester Journal* and a very influential promoter of the Sunday-school movement (but not the founder). His statue is in the Victoria Embankment Gardens below the Strand. ▶ Classical London **M** Portrait and medallion, National Portrait Gallery, H-9 Statue on Victoria Embankment, H-10

Raleigh, Sir Walter (1552-1618) Sir Walter Raleigh—courtier, fighting seaman, explorer, scholar and gifted writer—epitomizes the greatness of the Elizabethan Age. He was badly treated by King James, imprisoned in the Tower for thirteen years and ultimately beheaded. His *History of the World* was written in the Tower. It accepts the Old Testament chronology and was much appreciated by the Puritans. Shortly before his execution he wrote the following lines:

> Even such is time, which takes in trust
> Our youth, our joys, and all we have,
> And pays us but with age and dust;
> Who in the dark and silent grave,
> When we have wandered all our ways,
> Shuts up the story of our days:
> And from which earth, and grave, and dust,
> The Lord shall raise me up, I trust.

▶ Elizabethan London   **M** Statue, Ministry of Defence, Whitehall, C-5 Memorial plaque near the east entrance of St Margaret's, Westminster, C-7   Portraits and miniature, National Portrait Gallery, H-9

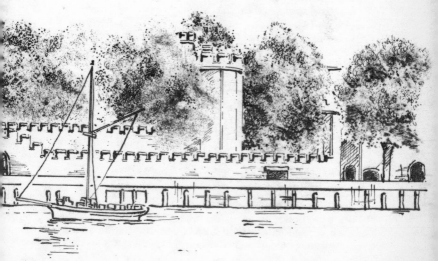

The cells of the Tower of London housed some of the greatest characters of English history, including Sir Walter Raleigh, whose final letter to his wife contains moving prayers.

'Reformation Parliament'   In 1529 parliament, in co-operation with the wishes of Henry VIII, passed the first of a number of statutes designed to transfer control of the church from Rome and the pope into the hands of the English sovereign. At first it passed laws correcting the excessive fees of church courts. In 1532 and 1534 two Acts of Annates were passed cutting off all money payments from the English clergy to the pope. The Acts of Appeals in 1533 forbade any appeals from church courts in England to Rome, thus paving the way for Henry VIII's divorce from Catherine. In 1534 the Act of Supremacy gave Henry the title of 'Supreme Head on earth of the Church of England' with the same power over the church that he had over the state. The 'Reformation Parliament' sat in successive sessions over seven years, and played a major role in the hands of Henry in bringing about the English Reformation.

Relics   Material remains of saints, such as bones, hair, teeth, and so on, which are venerated by the faithful as being a means through which God works miracles. During medieval times both St Paul's and Westminster Abbey possessed numerous relics.   ▶ Medieval London

Restitutus   A bishop of London in Roman times.   ▶ Roman London

Richard I, the Lion-heart (reigned 1189-99)   Richard's short and much-romanticized reign was spent mostly away from England, first as leader of the Third Crusade and then on other campaigns on the Continent. When he came to the throne, at the age of thirty-two, the Roman Catholic Church was again calling for a crusade to free the Holy Land from the Infidel. After a period of years as a Latin kingdom, Jerusalem had been captured by Saladin, a Kurdish general who had also made himself sultan of Egypt.

Richard started out on the campaign with Frederick Barbarossa of Germany (who was drowned en route) and Philip Augustus of France, and he succeeded in capturing Acre in 1191. But months of fierce fighting, with legendary heroics on both sides but especially on Richard's part, failed to wrest the Holy Sepulchre from Saladin's grasp. Eventually Richard made a truce with his enemy and in 1192 set out for home, only to be captured and held for ransom by Leopold, Duke of Austria. He finally reached English soil in 1194 but soon was engaged in war with his former comrade, Philip Augustus. He died in Normandy from an arrow which pierced his helmet, shot at a hazard by a sentry who failed to recognize him. Richard is often portrayed as England's ideal Christian knight and crusader.   ▶ Medieval London
M Statue on horseback, Old Palace Yard, Westminster, C-6

Ridley, Nicholas (c.1500-55)   Ridley, educated at Pembroke College, Cambridge, became chaplain to Archbishop Cranmer in 1537 and bishop of London in 1550. During his episcopate he became convinced of Reformed views on transubstantiation and, in turn, convinced Hugh Latimer. He took part in the compilation of the *Book* *of Common Prayer* in 1549 and 1552. At the death of Edward VI in 1553 he supported the attempt to have Lady Jane Grey succeed to the throne. He was subsequently imprisoned and burnt at the stake with Latimer in 1555. ▶ Reformation London **M** Portrait, National Portrait Gallery, H-9

Romaine, William (1714-95) Evangelical Anglican and outstanding gospel preacher, also a capable Hebrew scholar. From 1748 he was associated with the London churches of St George's, Billingsgate, St Dunstan's-in-the-West and St Anne's, Blackfriars (now united with St Andrew-by-the-Wardrobe). A friend of George Whitefield and the Countess of Huntingdon, he drew large crowds in London and elsewhere on preaching tours, sharing with Whitefield and the Wesleys a desire to see the gospel spread throughout the nation. ▶ Classical London **M** Portrait, National Portrait Gallery, H-9

Roman Catholics under Elizabeth The Protestant Reformation, which spread so rapidly through much of Europe including England, brought on a powerful reaction, sometimes called the 'Counter-Reformation', by the Roman Catholic Church. This consisted of moral reform, clearer statements of Catholic doctrines, better training of the clergy and a vigorous attempt to stem the tide of Protestantism. England felt the effect of this in several ways. The new, highly disciplined order of Jesuits infiltrated the British Isles and won back many lapsed Catholics. Elizabeth was excommunicated by the pope in 1570, and many plots were hatched to replace her with her cousin Mary, Queen of Scots. Elizabeth reacted by a series of severe laws against Roman Catholics labelling them traitors. A secret plan was discovered, called the 'Ridolfi Plot', in which Philip of Spain was to invade England, Elizabeth was to be deposed and replaced by Mary, Queen of Scots, and the latter was to marry the Catholic Duke of Norfolk. For this the duke, highest peer in the land, was beheaded in the Tower in 1572.

Yet another major Catholic intrigue, called 'Babington's Plot', was uncovered in 1586, also involving Mary, Queen of Scots. Mary, the daughter of Henry VIII's sister, had previously been married to the king of France before her marriage to the king of Scotland, and she was an ardent Catholic. She returned to Scotland at a time when the Protestant movement was gaining rapidly under the leadership of the reformer John Knox. In time Mary was driven from the throne because of a series of disgraceful romantic adventures, and her infant son James was named king. Spirited about from place to place in England, she was always a threat to Elizabeth, yet Elizabeth was extremely reluctant to act against her. The Babington Plot finally forced her hand, and Mary was beheaded in 1587. Even then Elizabeth blamed the decision on her council.

The execution of Mary was the signal to Philip of Spain that an invasion of England for the Roman Catholic cause was long overdue.

In July of 1588 the great 'Invincible Armada' of 150 galleons set sail and was met in the Channel by the lighter and more manoeuvrable English men-of-war under brave sea captains like Drake and Hawkins. The combination of English fighting skill and bad weather took its toll of two-thirds of the Spanish fleet. So devastating was this defeat and subsequent English naval attacks over the next ten years that all hope vanished of restoring England to the pope's domains during Elizabeth's reign. ▶ Elizabethan London

Roman Catholics under Charles II Within England, the Roman Catholics were actually a small minority when Charles II came to the throne in 1660. However, Parliament looked upon them as a threat for two reasons. One, the king favoured the Catholics (and actually declared himself a Catholic in 1669), and the duke of York was one openly. Second, the great Roman Catholic powers of France and Spain were always ready to send over their armies should there be a Catholic uprising in England.

To make matters worse, in 1678 a Londoner named Titus Oates invented a preposterous story of a Roman Catholic plot to murder Charles and put his brother James on the throne. This triggered a violent wave of reaction, and many Catholics were accused of conspiracy and imprisoned. A number suffered the extreme penalty, including some whose lives were known to be above reproach. By 1681 feeling against James becoming king ran so high that Charles, fearing the London mob would break into the Parliament House at Westminster, convened that body at Oxford. ▶ Restoration London

Rossetti, Christina (1830-94) Christina Rossetti, one of the important minor poets of the Victorian Age, was, like her more-famous brother Dante Gabriel, born in London. She lived there most of her life. She was closely associated with the Pre-Raphaelite movement through her brother, though she was not a part of it. At one time she was engaged to the painter James Collinson, a member of the Brotherhood, but broke the engagement when he left Anglicanism and returned to the Roman Catholic Church.

Miss Rossetti was very deeply influenced by the Oxford Movement, and her life was closely bound up with high-church activities. In poor health most of her days, her appearance reproduced in some of Dante's paintings tended to become the model of the Pre-Raphaelite ascetic type.

She showed literary promise early in life, and her first book of poetry was printed by her maternal grandmother when she was seventeen. Then followed several poems printed in *Macmillan's Magazine* in 1861. *Goblin Market and Other Poems*, published in 1862, is her most famous work. In addition to several other volumes of poetry, she produced nursery rhymes, short stories, children's stories and a number of religious tracts. Many of her poems are truly 'Victorian', that is, much concerned with death and a very serious kind of spirituality. But some have a timeless quality and are still familiar, as this last stanza from 'A Christmas Carol', sometimes known by its first line, 'In the deep midwinter':

> What can I give him,
> Poor as I am?
> If I were a shepherd
> I would bring a lamb,
> If I were a Wise Man
> I would do my part.
> Yet what I can I give him,
> Give my heart.

▶ Victorian London   **M** Portrait, National Portrait Gallery, H-9
Commemorated in reredos with paintings by Burne-Jones in Christ Church on Woburn Square (near Courtauld Art Institute)

Royal Chapels (or Chapels Royal), Royalty   The present queen of England, Elizabeth II, stands in a royal line going back to Cerdic, first king of the West Saxons, who died in the year 534. Most of the early West Saxon kings, including Alfred the Great, lived and died in Winchester, and their burial chests may be seen to this day in Winchester Cathedral. From Edward the Confessor (who reigned from 1042 to 1066) onward, however, the kings and queens of England have lived in or near London. Their places of worship, special religious ceremonies and the tombs where their remains are laid are of great significance to the nation and of major interest to visitors.

The practice and defence of the Christian faith has from earliest times been considered the duty of English sovereigns, and coronations are in most of their aspects Christian ceremonials. At a coronation, which always takes place in Westminster Abbey, the new king or queen is first presented to the people by the archbishop of Canterbury and other high officers in what is called the 'recognition'. The coronation oath is then administered by the archbishop, and the sovereign is presented with a Bible by the moderator of the General Assembly of the Church of Scotland. Next is the anointing of the sovereign with oil, a symbolic act from the Old Testament indicating that the Spirit of God is poured out on the new monarch. After being invested with spurs, bracelets and a sword, these articles are then placed on the altar.

Next the sovereign is clothed in royal robes and, sitting in the coronation chair, receives the orb, the ring and the sceptres from the archbishop, who also places a crown on the king or queen's head. A benediction is pronounced, the sovereign is enthroned and receives the homage of spiritual and temporal peers. The last part of the ceremony is a communion service, indicating that the monarch is following the command of Christ, 'This do in remembrance of me'.

The anthems of the coronation consist primarily of hymns and anthems, the oldest of which, 'Zadok the Priest', is taken from 1 Kings 39 and 40 in the Old Testament. The music for this was composed by Handel for the coronation of George II.

There are in or near London several chapels where the English sovereign worships on occasion and where special ceremonies are held. These are:

Westminster Abbey: Always used for coronations, sometimes for royal weddings. Map location C-10

Royal chapel in Buckingham Palace: Used by the sovereign for private services while in residence.

Chapel Royal, St James Palace: The sovereign attends special services here during the year. It also has been used for royal weddings. Map location B-1

St George's Chapel, Windsor Castle: The monarch attends services here while in residence. Royal funerals and burials also take place here. Map location N-6

St Paul's Cathedral: The queen attends special services here. Most recently it was used for the royal wedding of Prince Charles and Princess Diana. Map location L-15

In addition to royal chapels where the monarch currently attends services, there are also in or near London chapels associated with the crown that have great historical significance. They are:

The Queen's Chapel, St James Palace: One of the first Renaissance buildings built by Inigo Jones, it is open to the public both for visiting and for services on Sundays. Map location B-3

The Queen's Chapel of the Savoy: This is associated with the queen through her right to the Duchy of Lancaster and is also the Chapel of the Royal Victorian Order. Open to the public for visiting and for services on Sunday. Map location H-16

The Chapel Royal at Hampton Court: A beautiful sixteenth-century chapel associated with Henry VIII and other sovereigns who resided at Hampton Court Palace. Open to visitors daily. Map location N-2

Finally there are the royal chapels where England's past monarchs are interred. They are:

Royal Chapels, Westminster Abbey: Burial place of Edward the Confessor, Henry VII, Queen Elizabeth I and many of Britain's royalty from the eleventh to the seventeenth century. Map location C-10

St George's Chapel, Windsor Castle: Here are entombed the monarchs not buried in Westminster Abbey, beginning with Edward IV interred here in 1483 and including Henry VIII and all the monarchs from George III to the present day (excepting Victoria, who is buried at Frogmore House nearby). Map location N-6

The Chapel Royal of St Peter-ad-Vincula, Tower: In this chapel lie the remains of Queen Anne Boleyn and Queen Catherine Howard, beheaded in the Tower under Henry VIII. Map location M-16

Rural Churches in London Before the massive urban sprawl of the nineteenth century there were numerous villages and hamlets close to the City, and some of the churches and chapels from these remain today though the country has long disappeared. The following few still have surroundings that give the illusion that they are far away from the metropolis, even though the reverse is true:
St Giles-in-the-Fields, H-12   Holy Trinity, Brompton, A-5   St James, Clerkenwell, J-15   St Luke, Chelsea, A-8   St Pancras Old Church, G-5

Sacheverell Riots In 1709 a sermon preached in St Paul's by Dr Henry Sacheverell against Nonconformist (or Whig) ministers led to his impeachment by Parliament. Rioting broke out by those in sympathy with his views and several Nonconformist meeting houses were sacked and the contents burned. Sacheverell went unpunished and actually made political gain from the incident. He is buried in St Andrew's, Holborn. ▶ Restoration London

St Alban, Wood Street See *Towers*.

St Alphage, London Wall See *Towers*.

St Andrew-by-the-Wardrobe First mentioned in a manuscript of 1244, this church on Queen Victoria Street near where the old Blackfriars monastery once stood was rebuilt by Wren during the years 1685-93. In 1774 a west gallery was added, followed by a number of alterations by the Victorians. It was burnt out by fire bombs in December 1940, and it was restored by Marshall Sisson in 1959-61.

'By the Wardrobe' alludes to a large house built by Sir John Beauchamp and bought by Edward III in 1359. It was subsequently converted into the office of the Master of the Wardrobe and used as a repository for the ceremonial robes and other regalia of England's monarchs until the Great Fire. The early name for this church was 'St Andrew juxta Baynard's Castle', after a fortress which once stood by the riverside. The church may have been built when the noble family of Fitzwalter took up residence in the castle.

The tower and walls of St Andrew's survived the bombing, and today it has the plain look of the original Wren building. Its churchyard in front is landscaped and, as it is on a slope, the church itself is clearly visible. Inside there are some fine early furnishings from other churches but little that is original with this one.

In the late eighteenth century the celebrated evangelical preacher William Romaine regularly packed the church from 1766 to 1795. Later the newly formed Church Missionary Society held its first meetings here. Until 1985 the British and Foreign Bible Society occupied the building next door and made use of the north aisle of St Andrew's. It is still a parish church, combining with several other parishes in the area. In recent years it has offered lectures by prominent churchmen on Sunday afternoons during the winter. Call the church office for information. ▶ Restoration London **M** Map location, J-9

St Andrew's, Holborn

This church is located at Holborn Circus on a triangle formed by Holborn, St Andrew's Street and Shoe Lane. Thus it is on the very western edge of Old London and not within the area once encompassed by walls. It has one of the most commanding positions of any church in London, being on a rise above Holborn and having no buildings to obstruct its view.

St Andrew's appears in a charter of King Edgar, in the year 951, which mentions that it is on the boundaries of Westminster. The early wooden building was succeeded by a Norman one of stone, and this in turn was rebuilt in the fifteenth century. The old church escaped the Great Fire but was so decayed that it was rebuilt by Wren in 1684-87. In 1941 it was bombed into a shell. It enjoyed a successful reconstruction in 1961.

There is a little garden on the west side facing the street, from which one can see figures of a boy and girl above the Gothic doorway. These are charity children, and the figures used to be on the wall of the old parochial school in Hatton Garden. The inside of the church, completely burned out, now is furnished with many fine objects from other churches. The organ, from the chapel of the Foundling Hospital, was made by Renatus Harris, and George Handel helped in its design and later gave recitals on it. The stained glass is a reproduction of some surviving from Wren's time and some done by Joshua Price in 1718.

Among the associations of St Andrew's is Thomas Coram, founder of the Foundling Hospital in Bloomsbury, whose tomb is at the west end. Samuel Wesley, father of John and Charles, was ordained priest here in 1689. Henry Sacheverell, famous controversial divine of the seventeenth century who preached in St Paul's against the 'Glorious Revolution' of 1688, is buried under the high altar. ▶ Restoration London **M** Map location, J-10

St Andrew Undershaft

This venerable church near Leadenhall Market in the heart of Old London was first mentioned in the twelfth century. However, it was rebuilt on more than one occasion, the latest being between 1520 and 1532 during the reign of Henry VIII. Its exterior combines perpendicular gothic features, such as the fine south door, with Tudor stone. Like St Helen's, it is especially associated with lord mayors and other City dignitaries. There are a half-dozen interesting monuments of important personages and a number of fine brasses. The painter Hans Holbein is believed to have resided in the parish, and a brass tablet on the south wall honours him.

The famous May-pole to which the name refers was a fir shaft higher than the church steeple—hence 'under shaft'. Each May 1 it was hung with flowers and was the centre of day-long revels, essentially pagan in nature. On this holiday in 1517, later called 'Evil May Day', a riot broke out in which city apprentices attacked foreign merchants, particularly the Lombards, and a number of people were killed. The king then banned the May Day holiday, and the shaft was hung on hooks in an alley. In 1550, according to John Stow, an eccentric curate of St Katharine Cree named Stephen preached a sermon at Paul's Cross against the May-pole, condemning it as an idol because it was attached to the name of a church. The people who lived in the alley where the shaft was kept then sawed it into lengths and burned the pieces. Stow goes on to describe the eccentric antics of Stephen: 'I have oft times seen this man, forsaking the pulpit of his said parish church, preach out of a high elm tree in the midst of the churchyard'.

The good old London historian John Stow himself was a member of St Andrew Undershaft, and a monument with his likeness may be seen on the north wall. Each year a ceremony is held near the anniversary of his death on April 5, when the lord mayor, attended by sheriffs, renews his quill pen and presents a copy of the *Survey* to the writer of the best essay on London received that year.

Although it has been restored several times, St Andrew Undershaft was undamaged by either the Great Fire or the bombing. It presents a delightful contrast to the ultramodern office building across the street. But it is not just an historical monument; it serves as a chapel of ease to the very active St Helen's nearby, with a special ministry to under-thirties working in the City. ▶ Reformation London **M** Map location, M-5

St Anne & St Agnes The earliest mention of this church is about 1200. Although the double dedication to the oldest and youngest female saints is quite early, it was commonly called 'St Anne In the Willows'. Stow says that in his time there was 'no such void place for willows to grow, more than the churchyard, wherein do grow some high ash trees'. The old building was destroyed in the Great Fire and rebuilt by Wren between 1676 and 1687. It was bombed in December 1940 and left in a state of ruin until restored by Braddock & Martin-Smith in 1963-68.

St Anne & St Agnes is nicely situated back from the street in a tree-shaded churchyard. The grounds include those of St John Zachary, which was once next door but was not rebuilt after the Great Fire. Restoration has exposed the original brick, an improvement over the stucco added in the nineteenth century. The little building has a quaint bell turret with a weather vane topped by the letter 'A'. The interior, modelled after the Nieuwe Kerk at Haarlem in the Netherlands, is a cross within a square.

The building is leased to St John's Evangelical Churches of London, a Lutheran body, and services are held in Estonian, Latvian and English. The Lutheran Church was first established in London to serve German workers who came to help rebuild the city after the Great Fire. Furnishings of the church are sparse, in keeping with the Lutheran tradition, and none of it is from the original St Anne & St Agnes. Except during services the church is open only by special arrangement. ▶ Restoration London   **M** Map location, K-8

St Augustine with St Faith's See *Towers*.

St Bartholomew the Great, Smithfield

This is the oldest church *building* still standing in London. Its story takes us back to the reign of Henry I (1100-35), son of William the Conqueror. In the court there was a wit and minstrel named Rayer or Rahere, who early in Henry's reign made a pilgrimage to Rome. On this trip he became gravely ill with malaria and, while delirious with fever, saw a vision of St Bartholomew. The saint commanded him to found a church in his name at a certain place outside the walls of London. Rahere miraculously recovered, and upon his return he petitioned the king to give him the piece of land, Smithfield, to establish a hospital and priory. In his petition Rahere also asked permission to hold an annual fair in honour of St Bartholomew. Henry granted both requests.

Rahere built the hospital on the east side nearest the city walls and the priory on the north, work probably commencing on both projects in 1103. Using his talents as jester, he pretended to be half-witted and persuaded children and idlers to fill in with stones the swamp that covered most of the area. He claimed to have witnessed several miracles attributed to his patron saint, which brought widespread fame to the priory. The annual St Bartholomew's Fair was immensely popular and brought much revenue to the two institutions. By the time of his death both the hospital and priory were flourishing. In the fifteenth century he was honoured with a handsome tomb and effigy on the north side of the chancel, which has been beautifully restored and remains to this day.

In 1244 the priory was visited by Boniface, archbishop of Canterbury. This man, uncle of the queen, was a political appointee who had been imported from France by King Henry III and was not even ordained. He made slighting remarks to the canons of St Bartholomew's and was told by the sub-prior that they, having a learned bishop, did not need his visit. The archbishop, with an oath, tore off the sub-prior's rich cope and shoved him violently against a pillar. The canons then forcefully threw off the archbishop and in turn were beaten by his armed retainers. This nearly touched off a riot. In the words of John Stow, 'the whole city was in an uproar, and ready to have rung the common bell, and to have hewn the archbishop into small pieces', had he not hid himself at Lambeth.

In the later Middle Ages St Bartholomew the Great was one of London's richest and most influential priories. A significant part of its wealth was due, as earlier suggested, to the yearly St Bartholomew's

Fair, where clothiers and drapers had 'booths and standings within the churchyard of the priory, closed in with walls, and gates locked every night'. In the year 1410, during the reign of Henry IV, the priory was rebuilt. The garden became famous for its mulberry trees, and it was the custom for schoolmasters to bring their scholars here to hold logical controversies in public under these trees. Records indicate that early miracle plays were often performed at Smithfield near St Bartholomew's. In 1409 the parish clerks played *Matter from the Creation of the World* for eight consecutive weeks.

In the first part of the sixteenth century a famous prior named Bolton made extensive repairs and built an oriel window on the south side of the chancel, so he could watch mass being celebrated without leaving his lodgings. When the dissolution of monasteries was ordered by Henry VIII the last prior, named Fuller, turned St Bartholomew's over to the crown on 25 October 1539. The chancel was retained as a parish church (by petition of the residents, after falling into the hands of the infamous Richard Rich), but the nave was destroyed. In time much of the property became ruinous and, despite a couple of attempts at restorations in the eighteenth century, the various parts of the building not used for church purposes were turned to commercial uses. For a time there was a print shop in the Lady Chapel, and Benjamin Franklin is known to have worked here. The beginning of the fine restoration to be seen now occurred in the late nineteenth century under Sir Aston Webb.

When visiting St Bart's see the delightful half-timbered gatehouse over the west gate, the churchyard where the old nave once stood, the original choir and chancel bounded by great Norman pillars and arches, the rebuilt Lady Chapel, the remains of the old transepts and cloister. Take note of the effigy of the founder over his tomb and Prior Bolton's oriel window on the south side of the chancel. A guidebook to the church is available in the little bookshop. ▶ Medieval London ◼ Map location, K-9

St Bartholomew-the-Less St Bartholomew-the-Less came into existence as a hospital chapel at the same time as the nearby priory, both being founded by Rahere in 1123. It has been on the present site since 1184, but the earliest parts of the remaining building are the fifteenth century tower and west end. In 1789 George Dance the Younger replaced the decayed nave with a wooden octagon, and this in turn was rebuilt in stone and iron in 1823 by Thomas Harwick. This architect's grandson did further work on it in 1865, and bomb damage required an extensive restoration after World War II. A new doorway that accommodates wheelchairs has been opened at the south end of the east wall. Note the nineteenth-century octagonal lantern perched on the old tower, topped by an attractive weather vane.

Although still the chapel for St Bart's Hospital, this has been a

parish church since the Dissolution (the hospital is its parish).
Entering by the door under the tower, note the two fifteenth-century
brasses of William Markby and his wife in the vestry on your left.
There is a sixteenth-century canopied tomb on the west wall of the
tower to John Freke, surgeon, and on the north wall of the nave is a
monument to Lady Elizabeth Bodley, wife of Sir Thomas Bodley who
founded the Bodleian Library at Oxford. The stained glass windows of
the apse were done after the war by Hugh Easton and depict the Virgin
and Child in the centre, with St Luke (the physician) on the left and
St Bartholomew and Rahere on the right.　**M** Map location, J-11

St Benet's Welsh Church　This church is a landmark on Upper Thames
Street just south (that is, on the river side) of St Paul's Cathedral. In
early days when the Thames was like the main street of London, Paul's
Wharf nearby served as a boat landing for St Paul's Cathedral and the
surrounding area.

A church on this site was noted in the year 1111. The present
building was built by Wren in 1677-85. It has suffered very few
changes, the worst being a fire in 1971 that damaged the organ and
galleries, and it is said to be one of the best preserved of Wren's
original creations. Since 1879 St Benet's has been the Metropolitan
Welsh Church, and services are conducted in the Welsh language.
Inigo Jones, the architect who introduced the Renaissance style to
London (and a Welshman), is buried here. Normally not open except
for services, the building is a pleasant sight, its tower with white
shutters and contrasting dark brick and white stone surmounted by a
weather vane rising cheerfully above the heavy traffic of Thames
Street.　▶ Restoration London　**M** Map location, L-3

St Botolph, Aldersgate　This church is next to Postman's Park on St
Martin le Grand before it becomes Aldersgate Street at the Barbican.
The present building dates from 1789-91, though it was probably
founded in Norman times. It serves as the Centre for After Care of
Prisoners, and public services are also held during the week. At the
gate to the park near the church is a plaque commemorating the
conversion of the Wesley brothers, which occurred nearby. In
Postman's Park itself is a wall with touching memorials to persons who
have given their lives to save others.　▶ Classical London　**M** Map
location, K-10

St Botolph, Aldgate　St Botolph, a seventh-century Saxon abbot,
somehow became the protector of travellers during the Middle Ages,
something like St Christopher. Thus there were chapels dedicated to
him at four of London's gates, three of which have survived. Aldgate
was the easternmost gate of the City, and this church is now on the
street called Aldgate at the corner of Houndsditch. It was first built in
the twelfth century or maybe earlier, but the present building was put
up in 1741-44 by George Dance the Elder, architect of the Mansion

House. It was damaged in the war and again by a fire in 1966, but has been well restored. It serves as the headquarters of the Diocesan Council for Jewish/Christian Understanding. The crypt is used partly as a mission for homeless men, partly for a boys' club. ▶ Classical London　**M** Map location, M-6

St Botolph, Bishopsgate　Churches have stood on this site since at least 1212, quite possibly earlier; some evidence of a Saxon building has been found. The present building was erected in 1724-28 by James Gold. It is still a parish church. Its pleasant tower and clock provide a picturesque sight looking north on Bishopsgate with open ground in the foreground. The galleried interior in classical style is nicely lit by a dome and lantern installed in the nineteenth century. It possesses the original pulpit and lectern and an organ originally installed in 1764. ▶ Classical London　**M** Map location, M-7

The classical-style St Botolph, Bishopsgate.

St Bride, Fleet Street　Post-World War II excavations have established what was long suspected about this famous church just off Fleet Street: it occupies the site of Roman buildings and of a very early Christian church, perhaps the first in London. Seven church-building foundations of different sizes and ages have been identified, as well as numerous other objects dating from Roman times to the nineteenth century.

The latest building prior to the Great Fire was built in the fifteenth century, but aside from the undercroft nothing remains of this structure. It was rebuilt by Wren in 1670-75 except for the tower and spire, which were added in 1701-3. It was gutted by incendiaries in December 1940 and restored in 1957.

St Bride's is one of London's most celebrated churches, both because of its appearance and in its association with famous people and events. The most prominent physical feature is the 226-foot-high steeple of Portland stone, made up of four stages of diminishing octagons with open arches and pilasters. This steeple was struck by lightning three times in the early eighteenth century, and in 1764 George III consulted with Dr Benjamin Franklin regarding the best type of lightning rod. Later in this century a pastry cook nearby named William Rich invented the wedding cake modelled after St Bride's steeple. The twelve bells of St Bride's were known for their pealing.

The burnt-out inside has been restored to resemble the original, and it contains much that is representative of the best craftsmanship of the second Elizabethan Age. One of the most notable features is the oak reredos, which is a memorial to the Pilgrim Fathers. Near the font is a memorial to Virginia Dare, the first English child to be born in America, whose parents were of this parish. In addition, an altar commemorates Edward Winslow (1595-1655), who was a member of this parish. Winslow became governor of Plymouth Colony and made several trips back to England in the interest of the colonies. On one of these he was imprisoned for four months by Archbishop Laud on the charge of having taught in the church as a layman. He was the author of The Glorious Progress of the Gospel among the Indians in New England and was instrumental in organizing the Society for the Propagation of the Gospel in New England.

Other famous figures of Christian history associated with St Bride's include Wynken de Worde, who brought Caxton's press from Westminster to St Bride's in 1500, John Taylor who became vicar in 1543 and was later burnt at Smithfield under Bloody Mary, Samuel Pepys who was christened here, and John Milton, Izaac Walton and Samuel Johnson, all of whom lived nearby.

In the crypt there is a museum exhibiting many of the finds made during the excavation. These include a tesselated pavement and walls from Roman times, part of a Saxon font, medieval carvings, and various samples of medieval glass left from the Great Fire. St Bride's is sometimes called the 'Cathedral of Fleet Street' and has close ties with the world of journalism. ▶ Restoration London M Map location, J-12

St Clement Danes This famous church is prominently situated on an island in the centre of the Strand, between the east end of Aldwych and the Royal Courts of Justice. Its date of origin is before the Conquest, and records indicate it was rebuilt of stone in the early part of the eleventh century. It survived the Great Fire, but Wren had it pulled down and replaced in 1680-82. The upper tower was designed by James Gibbs and added in 1719. It was burnt out in 1941, restored in 1955. With St James, Piccadilly, it shares the distinction of being one of two Wren churches outside of London proper.

The 'Danes' in the name probably resulted from an order by King Alfred to the Danes in London who had married English women, to dwell 'between the Isle of Thorney (Westminster) and Cael Lud (Ludgate, the western gate of the walled city)'. Probably the first church building here was built by these ninth-century Danes. Stow, however, cites two other possible sources for the name. One is that Harold Harefoot, illegitimate son of King Canute the Dane, might be buried here. Harold became king of the Saxons from 1037 to 1040 and was buried at Westminster. But when Hardicanute, the lawful heir, came to the throne, he had the body dug up and thrown into the Thames. A fisherman was said to have buried it at St Clement's. The second source dates to the days of Ethelred the Unready, one of the last Saxon kings (deposed 1013). A band of Danes went on a rampage and were said to have been cut down in the neighbourhood of St Clement's.

The most important association of St Clement Danes is with Dr Samuel Johnson, the literary lion of the late eighteenth century. A brass plate in the north gallery which once was affixed to the original pew reads:

> In this pew and beside this pillar, for many years attended divine service the celebrated Dr Samuel Johnson, the
> philosopher, the poet, the great lexicographer, the profound moralist and chief writer of his time. Born in 1709, died 1784. In the remembrance and honour of noble faculties, nobly employed, some inhabitants of the parish of St Clement, Danes have placed this slight memorial, AD 1851.

Dr Johnson is also commemorated by a statue outside the east end of the church.

Two notable persons of Christian history buried at St Clement Danes are Ann, wife of John Donne, the great poet and dean of St Paul's, and Bishop George Berkeley, the eighteenth-century writer and philosopher who sought to oppose materialism and rationalism on their own ground.

Many English children are familiar with the lines,

> Oranges and lemons
> Say the bells of St Clemen's

The famous (re-cast) bells ring out the tune of this nursery rhyme at 9.00 a.m., 12.00 noon, 3.00 p.m. and 6.00 p.m. On or about 31 March a service is held at which oranges and lemons are distributed to children.

The interior of St Clement Danes, completely gutted by fire from incendiary bombs in 1941, is now most impressive for its lightness and

143

openness. This is due to white columns, light-colored pews contrasting with the dark oak of the Grinling Gibbons pulpit (1685) and exceptionally wide aisles. This is the official church of the Royal Air Force, and over 700 badges of R.A.F. squadrons are fixed in the floor of the entryway. In lighted cabinets around the nave are books of remembrance containing the names of 120,000 airmen who died in the defence of Britain. An American shrine beneath the north gallery contains the names of 19,000 members of the US Air Force who also died during World War II. ▶ Restoration London M Map location, J-13

St Clement, Eastcheap This is the smallest parish church in London, secluded on a narrow lane near the junction of King William and Canon Streets. It dates to the twelfth century or earlier. Because it is located quite near to Pudding Lane where the Great Fire started (now marked by the Monument), it was one of the first to be destroyed. It was rebuilt by Wren in 1683-87. The church once stood on Eastcheap, the main shopping street, when that thoroughfare ran further west. The interior, whose walls are irregular, is distinguished by a pleasing ornamental ceiling. ▶ Restoration London M Map location, L-4

St Cyprian, Clarence Gate The area of this church north of Marylebone Road was divided off as a parish in 1866 through the efforts of Charles Gutch. It being a poor part of London at the time, Gutch felt called to minister there even though no church building existed. His place of worship for many years was a structure created out of two houses with a coalshed in between. A building site was obtained shortly after Gutch's death in 1896. The resulting building, designed primarily by Sir Ninian Comper, is plain on the outside but richly decorated and furnished, within its 'twentieth-century-medieval' style. This is in keeping with Gutch's deep interest in the Oxford Movement and his desire to return Protestant worship to medieval ornateness. Comper himself described it as 'the last development of a purely English parish church with lofty aisles and clerestory'. M Map location E-4

St Dunstan's-in-the-East See *Towers*.

St Dunstan's-in-the-West The lantern bell tower and bracketed clock of this octagonal church are familiar landmarks on Fleet Street just across from the Temple. We have placed it in Victorian London, even though it was built slightly before Victoria's reign (1829-33), because it is not classical in design. However, it is not exactly neo-gothic either. It is like no other church in London: a credit to the architect, John Shaw, who is commemorated above the south door.

Outside the church may be seen the statue of Queen Elizabeth I, the oldest stone representation of the great queen in existence. It was taken from the old Lud Gate when the walls were removed, as were the figures of King Lud and his two sons. The clock was made in 1671 for the old church and was removed by the marquis of Hertford and installed on his property. It was returned in 1936. Two of the most famous preachers at St Dunstan's-in-the-West were William Tyndale, the Bible translator, and John Donne, dean of St Paul's. Their likenesses may be seen on the west and east sides of the entry arch. Finally, note the two giants who strike the bells. Their counterparts may be seen in Venice near the Cathedral of St Mark.

The octagonal interior has seven vaulted recesses, with the chancel and altar in the north bay. The northwest chapel is shut off from the rest of the church by a beautiful eighteenth-century painted screen, and is used by the Romanian Orthodox congregation. Through the screen can be seen a window dedicated to the beloved angler Isaak Walton (see Stuart and Commonwealth London), who held several offices in the church. He is depicted with some of the subjects of his *Lives*. On the west side is a window commemorating Bishop John Fisher, who was beheaded under Henry VIII. The new north window depicts four famous Saxon and Norman archbishops: St Dunstan, Lanfranc, Anselm and Stephen Langton. The altar and reredos are fine carved work of the seventeenth century, and there are numerous early monuments.

Before its reconstruction, St Dunstan's-in-the-West was thirty feet closer to the then narrow street, with shops against the east and west walls. The vicinity of the churchyard was a favourite locality of booksellers and publishers, including Thomas Marsh of the 'Prince's Arms' who published Stow's *Chronicles*; Richard Marriot, who published John Donne's *Sermons* and Isaac Walton's *The Compleat Angler*; and Matthias Walker, one of three publishers who gave John Milton five pounds down and a total of twenty pounds for *Paradise Lost*. ▶ Classical London **M** Map location, J-14

St Ethelburga-the-Virgin This small parish church is one of London's oldest, as its Saxon dedication indicates. The present building dates to the first part of the fifteenth century, but a fourteenth- century (west) window survives. It is not very distinguished in appearance, either inside or out, the interior resembling a small country church. Until the early 1930s the entrance was between two shops that fronted on the street.

There are, however, four striking stained-glass windows by Leonard Walker, three of which commemorate the voyages of Henry Hudson. Hudson and eleven of his crew took the sacrament here in 1607 before their first attempt to discover a northwest passage. An east window, done by Kempe in 1871, depicts Ethelberga (not Ethelburga—note spelling), the daughter of King Ethelbert of Kent who welcomed Augustine. She married King Edwin of Northumbria, and her chaplain, Paulinus, was instrumental in the conversion to Christianity of what is now Northumbria and York. ▶ Medieval London **M** Map location, M-9

St Ethelburga-the-Virgin is one of London's oldest church buildings.

St Etheldreda This is the former chapel of Ely House, now a Catholic chapel. Details of its long history are given under Ely Chapel.
M Map location, J-4

St George's, Bloomsbury St George's is a parish church, fronting on busy Bloomsbury Street, which serves especially the University of London and the British Museum, located just a block away. It was built by the famous architect Nicholas Hawksmoor, an assistant to Christopher Wren, and completed in 1730. Anthony Trollope, author of the Barchester novels of the nineteenth century, was baptized here. It also figures in a minor way in one of Charles Dickens' little stories in *Sketches by Boz* called 'The Bloomsbury Christening'.

The facade of St George's, Bloomsbury, with its massive Corinthian columns, was modelled after the description given by Pliny of the tomb of Mausolus in Carla. In our times its grand classical design appears dignified and in keeping with its neighbour, the British Museum. But to many of the Victorians it was, as described in a guidebook of the day, 'at once the most pretentious and the ugliest ecclesiastical edifice in the metropolis'. The detached tower and steeple, topped by a statue of King George I in a Roman toga (a gift of a local brewer), especially came under ridicule. Horace Walpole spoke of it as 'a master stroke of absurdity' and penned the following epigram:

When Harry the Eighth left the Pope in the lurch,

The people of England made him 'Head of the Church';
But George's good subjects, the Bloomsbury people,
Instead of the Church made him 'Head of the Steeple'.

▶ Classical London   **M** Map location, H-11

St George's Chapel, Windsor   This magnificent building at Windsor
Castle, dedicated to the patron saint of the Knights of the Garter,
ranks with Henry VII's Chapel in Westminster Abbey and Kings
College Chapel at Cambridge as the finest example of perpendicular
Gothic in all of England. It was built between 1478 and 1528 and is
made up of two sections, the nave and the choir, separated by a
Gothic screen. Buried here are Henry VIII, Queen Jane Seymour and
King Charles I (centre aisle of the choir), and most of the sovereigns
from George II onward.

The choir, with its exquisite fan vaulting and intricately carved
stalls, is where the present queen attends divine services while in
residence at Windsor. Above the stalls hang the banners, swords and
helmets of the present Knights of the Garter. At the back of each stall
are ancient enamelled plates telling in Norman French the arms and
titles of the first knights of the order who occupied the seat. The
chapel is open to the public most days except during services.

▶ Medieval London   **M** Map location, N-6

St George's, Hanover Square   One of Wren's assistants, John James,
who was an under-surveyor of St Paul's Cathedral, was the architect
of this church. It was built in 1721-25, and a chancel was added
toward the end of the Victorian era. The colonnaded portico was the
first of several in this particular area, a design that was to be
particularly associated in later years with the Georgian period. It was
originally intended to serve a new parish growing up in what was
countryside north of Piccadilly and south of Oxford Street. Today its
fashionable surroundings make it a popular choice for society
weddings.

The most famous parishioner of St George, Hanover Square, was
(appropriately) George Frederick Handel. For thirty-four years, from
1724 until his death in 1759, the great composer resided nearby in
Brook Street and worshipped regularly at this church.   ▶ Classical
London   **M** Map location, F-4

St Giles, Cripplegate   St Giles Church originally stood just outside a gate
in the city wall near the northwest corner. The round base of one of
the battlements and some remains of the wall itself are incorporated
into the post-war Barbican development that surrounds it. The
original church was founded in 1090 in early Norman times. The
earliest part of the present structure dates to a rebuilding in 1545
during Reformation times. The tower was raised fifteen feet in 1682,
and various alterations were made in the nineteenth century. It was

burned out in 1940 and for nearly twenty years stood in ruins until restored in 1960 by Godfrey Allen.

The founder of St Giles, Cripplegate, was Alfune, an associate of the famous prior Rahere who founded St Bartholomew's, Smithfield. The site of the church, on swampy ground near the Walbrook where it flowed under the walls of London, caused construction problems in early days, and even today the water forms a pond below a retaining wall which runs around the perimeter of the building. Being at the north of the City and outside the wall, the church survived the Great Fire (but was not so fortunate during the wartime blitz).

Several of London's great Christian figures are associated with St Giles, including John Foxe the martyrologist; Launcelot Andrewes, court preacher and a translator of the King James Version of the Bible; and the renowned poet John Milton. Foxe, who returned from exile when Elizabeth became queen, was ordained a priest and, joining forces with John Day the printer, brought out the first English edition of his famous *Actes and Monuments* in 1563. He served in several minor ecclesiastical posts and was, for a short time at the end of his life, rector of St Giles. Upon his death in 1587 he was buried in this church. The site is not marked. Andrewes was vicar of St Giles from 1588 to 1605 but is buried at St Saviour's.

John Milton was a Londoner by birth, and his father, a scrivener or writer of legal papers, was interred in the chancel of St Giles. After living in numerous places in London Milton, toward the end of his life, resided in a house near Bunhill Fields. When he died in 1674 he was buried next to the grave of his father. The grave site was lost during the late eighteenth century due to some changes in the placement of the pews; in 1790 a search was made and the right spot found. A gravedigger and certain other hangers-on raised the coffin at night and desecrated the remains of the poet, taking away among other items a lock of hair (which eventually made its way into the museum at Milton's Cottage, Chalfont St Giles). Today a stone in the floor of the chancel marks the site. There is also a bronze statue of Milton in the south aisle and a modern bust by John Bacon.

During the Great Plague of 1665 the parish of St Giles suffered heavily because of the swampy location. Some 8000 people died; one day, August 18, there were 151 funerals. The churchyard became a campground for refugees from the Great Fire the following year. Today, however, the location of this church—apart from the street traffic and surrounded by water and gardens—gives it a pleasant distinctiveness. ▶ Reformation London **M** Map location, K-11

St Giles-in-the-Fields This church is on the south side of St Giles High Street, which continues the curve of High Holborn back to New Oxford Street at Tottenham Court Road. The origin of a church on or near this site was a chapel attached to a hospital for lepers established in 1101 by Matilda, Queen of Henry I. The chapel served both the inmates and the residents of the little village of St Giles. (St Giles was the patron saint of lepers, and churches dedicated to him were generally outside the city walls where lepers and invalids gathered.)

In medieval times and up to the nineteenth century, when New Oxford Street was built, the road to Tyburn ran from Cheapside, the city market, out of Newgate and eventually where St Giles High Street runs today. Consequently, carts bearing condemned criminals to execution at Tyburn passed this way, and it became a custom to toll the church bell when the cart went by. Another custom was for the local tavern to offer the condemned man a last bowl of ale. The bodies of some of these poor wretches were brought back to be buried in the churchyard. A number of Catholic martyrs, including the famous Oliver Plunkett, archbishop of Armagh, are buried in the churchyard as well.

The area grew considerably by the seventeenth century, and it was one of the hardest hit by the Great Plague of 1665. Later it became one of London's most notorious slums and a refuge for criminals. Church Lane, which once ran between St Giles High Street and New Oxford Street, is cited by a Victorian survey of London as a place to avoid even in daylight.

The present church, constructed in 1730-34 by Henry Flintcroft, has spacious grounds behind it, which still give a feeling of being 'in the fields'. The tall clock tower and spire rising amid the trees are a pleasant sight from the High Street. Inside is the original model of the present building. The nave has a beautiful barrel-vaulted plaster ceiling, but the stained glass was unfortunately destroyed in the blitz. There are several interesting memorials and, in addition to the fine mahogany pulpit of 1676, there is a plain pulpit in the north aisle brought from West Street Chapel where it was frequently used by the Wesley brothers. Services here are conducted using the traditional prayer-book of 1662. ▶ Classical London **M** Map location, H-12

St Helen's, Bishopsgate

St Helen's, one of London's finest medieval churches, has from early times been associated with City officialdom. Many of the lord mayors, aldermen, sheriffs and successful merchants and businessmen lived in the parish, and a number were buried in this church and commemorated by imposing monuments. In fact, St Helen's exceeds all other City churches in the number and splendour of its monuments. Among the prominent persons interred here are Sir John Crosby, grocer, woolman and the builder of famous Crosby Hall; Sir Thomas Gresham, the founder of the Royal Exchange and one of London's most illustrious citizens; Martin Bond, commander of the City Trained Bands before whom Queen Elizabeth made her stirring speech at the approach of the Armada; and Sir William Pickering, Queen Elizabeth's ambassador to Spain.

The second unique feature about St Helen's is that it possesses two naves side by side. This unusual arrangement came about in the year 1210, during the reign of Henry III, when a priory of Benedictine nuns was founded on the property next to the original church. This new priory included a hall, hospital, dormitory, cloisters and offices. The priory church was placed next to the parish church and the nave of the latter, which was somewhat shorter, was extended to form a united west wall. The two congregations were separated by arches and a screen, but apparently the close proximity between the nuns and the 'seculars' created some problems. The dean and chapter of St Paul's felt it necessary to reprove the nuns for wearing 'ostentatious veils' and the prioress for keeping a number of small dogs. Another warning concerned dancing and 'revelling', which was restricted to holidays and forbidden to 'seculars'.

The nunnery was suppressed in 1538. All the buildings except the church were taken over by the Leathersellers Company. At this time the screen was removed so that the two naves together became part of the parish church. There was originally a crypt under the nun's hall next to the church which had a canopied grating on the wall facing the nave so that the nuns unable to come into the church could watch mass. All the old priory buildings except the church were removed in 1799, but the 'nun's squint' on the north wall remains, a curious reminder of a bygone day.

Like St Bartholomew the Great and its neighbour St Ethelburga's, St Helen's has the distinction of having escaped the Great Fire and gone through the blitz without major damage. Today it has a very active evangelical congregation (possibly a tradition going back to the eighteenth century when George Whitefield preached here frequently). There is a particularly popular lunchtime Bible study for business people during the week. ▶ Medieval London **M** Map location, M-10

St James's, Clerkenwell Clerkenwell is a district in Central London just north of Holborn Circus. It is bounded by Clerkenwell Road to the south, Farringdon Road to the west and St John Street to the east. The name is derived from the Anglo-Saxon and means 'Clerk's Well'. It is thought that the clerks of the parish performed mystery plays in medieval times near some springs located in the area. The parish church is St James, Clerkenwell, and was founded in the fifteenth century. The present building was constructed by James Carr and reconsecrated in 1792.

The church is on a rise above Clerkenwell Green and on a little lane called Clerkenwell facing a quaint pub, amid a setting that could be a village rather than a city. It has an evangelical tradition going back to the Restoration of 1660, at which time the parishioners gained control of the minister's living so they could chose whom they desired. An object in the church of considerable interest to historians is the carved wooden tablet (on the south wall) commemorating the

Smithfield Martyrs. The dates range from 1400 to 1558, covering much more than the Reformation period. The church is not normally open to visitors outside service times, but the area is worth a look, being one of those picturesque corners of London that time seems to have forgotten. ▶ Classical London **M** Map location, J-15

St James's, Garlickhythe The first recorded mention of this church on the banks of the River Thames is in the year 1170. The old church was rebuilt in 1326 by Richard Rothing, sheriff. After the Great Fire it was rebuilt by Wren between 1676 and 1683 at a cost of 5,357 pounds, 12 shillings and 11 pence. It was restored and repaired on several occasions in the nineteenth century and was struck by a bomb from a German aeroplane in 1917. In 1940 it was hit by a bomb again, but this one did not explode. However, much damage was caused by fire from incendiaries and the building was thoroughly restored in 1954-63.

The term 'Garlickhythe' refers to the association of the area with the importation of garlic in medieval times. It means 'garlic-bank' or 'garlic-landing'. The church is noted for its novel Wren spire (in common with St Michael, Paternoster Royal; St Stephen's, Walbrook and St Bride's). It is 125-feet high, consisting of a plain square tower surmounted by a Renaissance three-stage steeple topped by a weather vane. A projecting clock with a quaint figure of St James was destroyed in the war.

The interior of St James, Garlickhythe, is Wren's highest, now restored to something more like the original than what the Victorians left. The organ is a genuine Father Smith and the pride of the church. The beautifully carved pulpit came from St Michael's, Queenhythe, when it was demolished in 1875. There are other fine furnishings, most of which came from other churches or are modern. An original bit is the row of eighteenth-century wig pegs at the west end.
▶ Restoration London **M** Map location, L-6

St James's, Piccadilly This Wren church is among the two built in Westminster rather than London proper, and it is unique in that it is not built on the site of an earlier church. It was badly damaged in an air raid in October 1940 and was restored by Sir Albert Richardson in 1954.

In the late seventeenth century fashionable new estates were being developed in the open area which is now the West End. St James' was built to serve one of these. (The name 'Piccadilly' is of somewhat older origin, being derived from the pickadils or ruffs worn by dandies in the early Stuart period.) Henry Jermyn, the builder, retained Christopher Wren as architect. Wren developed in St James something of the ideal church, large enough to hold 2,000 people but small enough so that all could see and hear the preacher. It is elegantly proportioned and graceful inside and out. The best view is from the slightly lower elevation of Jermyn Street opposite Piccadilly, as the estate was on that side.

Originally this church possessed several furnishings carved by the famous Grinling Gibbons and three of these, the organ case, the reredos (or altar backing) and white marble font, were stored elsewhere during the blitz. They are now back in their places, and well worth stepping inside to see. Notice also the modern stained glass (1954) in the east window. The scenes are of our Lord's life and passion. Visitors entering from the Piccadilly side will find a pleasant Garden of Rememberance. This was created from the bombed churchyard at the expense of newspaper proprietor Lord Southwood to commemorate the courage of the people of London. ▶ Restoration London ▪ Map location, B-4

St John's, Clerkenwell The present building on this site, located on St John Street just north of busy Clerkenwell Road, is not ancient, but the site itself was once part of the Priory of the Knights Hospitaller of St John of Jerusalem, whose property extended south to where St John's Gate still stands. It is one of several London churches impossible to date, being a mixture of several periods and not rebuilt entirely at any one time.

It was originally consecrated in 1185 by Heraclius, the patriarch of Jerusalem, who also consecrated the Temple Church. The building then consisted of a round chancel and a rectangular nave. This was burned to the ground in the Peasants' Revolt of 1381. It was reconstructed in the early sixteenth century, partly destroyed during the Reformation, reopened as a private chapel in 1623, turned into a Presbyterian chapel in 1706, gutted by a mob in 1721 and made a parish church in 1723. In the twentieth century it was returned to its first use as Priory Church of the Order of St John. In 1941 it was burnt out by enemy bombs but was restored and rededicated in 1958.

The exterior of St John's, Clerkenwell, with its pleasant memorial garden in the rear, is modern and gives no hint of its long and eventful history. The interior, however, is another story. In the main church one may see the colourful banners of the present-day Order of St John, and behind the altar is the famous fifteenth-century 'Weston Triptych' (two side wings only) painted by the school of Rodger van der Weyden. The crypt is an even greater surprise, being the original twelfth-century structure virtually unscathed. It shares the distinction, with the Chapel of St John the Evangelist in the Tower and St Bartholomew the Great, of being one of the three Norman church structures left in London. ▪ Map location, J-16

St John's Gate The extensive priory of the Hospitallers of St John of Jerusalem located northwest of Smithfield had, by the fourteenth century, become notorious for its luxury. Hence it was attacked and burned by Wat Tyler's mob during the Peasants' Revolt (1381). The priory buildings were restored after this, and in 1504 the main gate on the south was rebuilt. Later in the sixteenth century, when the priory was suppressed (1540), most of buildings were destroyed and taken away, but the gateway somehow survived. It remains today, under the custody of the new Order of St John. Along with the Norman crypt of St John's, Clerkenwell, it is a priceless remnant of the proud Crusader order. ▶Medieval London **M** Map location, J-17

St John the Evangelist, Tower

This is the oldest place of Christian worship in London, being part of the White Tower whose construction began in 1078. It is pure Norman (Romanesque), with a rare barrel vault and massive columns. The sanctuary is open to the nave, not the usual arrangement. A gallery runs around the nave above, and here William the Conqueror himself and his successors worshipped while in residence at the Tower.

Over the centuries numerous historic events have taken place within the walls of this chapel, primarily relating to England's sovereigns. Knights of the Bath chosen by medieval kings kept vigil here all night. In the year 1399 some fourteen noblemen were so honoured by King Henry IV. A bit earlier, in 1381, the year of the Peasants' Revolt, the mob dragged Archbishop Sudbury from here and beheaded him on Tower Hill. Ninety years later the body of Henry VI was placed in the Chapel of St John the Evangelist after he was murdered while at prayers in the Wakefield Tower.

In the turbulent times of the Tudor monarchs the body of Elizabeth of York, queen to Henry VII, lay in state in this chapel. And here in 1553 the innocent Lady Jane Grey prayed during the nine days before her execution. The following year Mary Tudor was betrothed by proxy here to Philip of Spain.

The Chapel of St John the Evangelist, located in the innermost part of a fortress and reserved for royalty and a privileged few, has been preserved for over 900 years in nearly perfect condition. Long used simply as a storeroom, it is once more a place of Christian worship. It is open to visitors daily. ▶Medieval London **M** Map location, M-11

St Katharine Cree (or Creechurch)

During the reign of King Henry I (1100-35) the queen, Matilda, founded the Augustinian priory of Holy Trinity, Christ's Church, on a plot of land just inside the walls of Old London near Aldgate. Matilda also united the older parishes of St Mary Magdalen, St Michael, St Katharine and Holy Trinity into the one parish of the Holy Trinity. The priory church thus became the parish church for all the people in the district. This edifice was built in the year 1108, and Stow tells us that the priory 'in process of time became a very fair and large church, rich in lands and ornaments, and passed all the priories in the city of London or shire of Middlesex'. Its prior also held the office of alderman and rode in the public processions in similar livery, 'saving that his habit was in shape of a spiritual person' (Stow).

In the year 1280 the attendance of the townspeople apparently became a problem to the canons of the priory, and thus the prior caused a chapel to be built for the laity in the churchyard between Christ's Church and the roadway coming from the Aldgate (now called Leadenhall Street). As the area was originally the parish of St Katharine, this new church was called St Katharine de Christ Church at Aldgate. The building lasted about 200 years and then was reconstructed.

At the Dissolution King Henry VIII gave the priory to Sir Thomas Audley, later lord chancellor. Sir Thomas wanted to build a house next to the roadway and offered to trade Christ's Church for St Katharine's, a smaller building. The parishioners refused the deal. He then tried to get someone to dismantle the great church in exchange for the materials, but there were no takers. In desperation Sir Thomas hired workmen to demolish it, hoping to gain back their wages by selling the materials. But, beginning with the steeple, the men carelessly threw down the stones, which broke in pieces. In the end, 'any man in the city might have a cart-load of hard stone for paving brought to his door for six pence or seven pence'. Sir Thomas eventually built his house on the site of the priory church, but it cost him a great deal more than he had reckoned on.

The old church of St Katharine continued through Stow's day, and he tells us that because the roadway was so often raised by new pavements it was necessary to walk down seven steps to get into the building. During the reign of Charles I it was again rebuilt, between the years 1628-30, a period when the classical style of church architecture was just beginning to appear in England. However, the famous aspect of this new building is not so much its architecture as its dedication. It was the only church to be constructed in London during that period, and its dedication was conducted by William Laud, then bishop of London. According to an eyewitness, Laud, who was to administer communion as part of the service, performed an elaborate ritual of bowing, chanting, pronouncement of blessing and curses and the like which aroused considerable amazement and resentment. This consecration later played a significant part in his trial for treason in 1645. Today, however, Laud is commemorated in St Katharine's by a memorial chapel.

Laud's ceremonial dedication may have been offensive to his Reformation-minded audience, but over the centuries St Katharine's has actually been somewhat noteworthy for ceremony. In the Middle Ages morality plays often were held in the churchyard, and later in Elizabethan times it was used for secular dramas. A parish book of 1565 records that certain players 'who for license to play their interludes in the churchyard paid the sum of 27s, 8d'. For many years in more recent days an annual 'flower sermon' was preached on Whit-Monday and was apparently well attended. The congregation all wore flowers, and a large bouquet was placed on the pulpit before the preacher.

Today St Katharine Cree is on the London calendar for the 'Lion Sermon', preached every October 16. This service was endowed by Sir John Gayer, who in 1643 encountered a lion in the Syrian desert and escaped the beast in answer to prayer (a short one, no doubt)! The building is open weekdays only and has been designated as the Guild Church for Finance, Commerce and Industry. ▶Stuart & Commonwealth London **M** Map location, M-12

St Lawrence, Jewry Located on the forecourt of the Guildhall, London's medieval town hall, St Lawrence is the guild church of the Corporation of London and the official place of worship for the city government. The church was first mentioned in 1135 (though it probably dates to Saxon times). It was given by Hugo de Wickenbroke to Balliol College, Oxford, in 1294. After the Great Fire it was rebuilt by Wren in 1671-77. It was gutted during an air raid on 29 December 1940, and then restored by Cecil Brown in 1957.

The term 'Jewry' in the name indicates that St Lawrence's is in the area once known as the Jewish quarter of London. The street called 'Old Jewry', the heart of the ancient ghetto, is just a short way east on Gresham Street. The Jews were expelled from London in 1290 by Edward I, but by then the association had been established.

As the east end of this church is the approach to Guildhall, Wren gave it a more ornate than usual facade, with Corinthian columns supporting a pediment. The tower and steeple (post-war reproduction) are on the west end facing down Gresham Street, and in the triangle created by the front of the church and the side of Guildhall library there is a an attractive pond and fountain. The dignified and spacious interior is designed for large audiences, and there are pews for the Lord Mayor and other city officials. Modern stained glass by Christopher Webb depicts individuals associated in some way with the church, including Sir Thomas More who lived in this parish. The piano was once the property of Sir Thomas Beecham. ▶Restoration London **M** Map location, K-12

St Luke's, Chelsea Chelsea still has the look of a village, especially in the vicinity of St Luke's where there is considerable tree-shaded open ground. Up to the beginning of the nineteenth century Chelsea Old Church (All Saints, Chelsea) served the needs of the small parish. But the development north of Kings Road toward Kensington made a larger church necessary, and St Luke's was authorized by an act of Parliament in 1819. James Savage, the architect, submitted a plan to the Board of Works (which included John Nash, the designer of Regents Park and Regent Street) for a building essentially Gothic in design, with vaulted ceilings within and flying buttresses without. The design passed, not without resistance, and the new building was consecrated in 1824. It was London's (and also England's) first Gothic Revival church.

The outstanding features of the exterior of St Luke's are the flying buttresses already referred to, the porch of five bays and the 142-foot-high tower, which is a pleasant sight from the surrounding open area. Inside, the sixty-foot vaulted nave is the highest of any parish church in London. The chancel is raised, and beyond it is an impressively tall east window. The organ, much of which dates to 1824, is one of London's finest. One of the former organists, John Goss, was the author of the well-known hymn, 'Praise My Soul, the King of Heaven'. Charles Dickens was married to Christine Hogarth here in 1826. The father of Charles Kingsley, author of *Westward Ho*, *Hereward the Wake* and *The Water Babies* was rector at St Luke's, and Charles was curate for a time. ▶ Classical London ◼ Map location, A-8

St Magnus, London Bridge, or St Magnus Martyr St Magnus today is best viewed from Fish Street Hill, the narrow street that runs toward Thames Street from the Monument. This view frames the west end of the church with its tower and large clock and hides the faceless modern block next to it. For centuries (first mention, 1067) this church stood at the north end of London Bridge. After the Great Fire when Wren rebuilt it, 1671-87, the approach to London Bridge ran right past the church tower, and later (after reconstruction due to a fire in 1760) the footpath actually went under the tower. Thus the church was seen to great advantage both from the City and from the bridge.

In the early nineteenth century plans were laid to replace old London Bridge, and the new bridge was built 100 yards south. Upon its completion in 1831 Old London Bridge was demolished, and with it went St Magnus's ancient identity. This is still a parish church, however, and its interior is one of the best in the City, with many fine original furnishings. A good reason for a visit is to see the memorial to the great sixteenth-century Bible translator, Miles Coverdale, once the minister here. It is on the wall to the right of the communion table. ▶ Restoration London ◼ Map location, D-4

St Margaret's, Lothbury This Wren church is at the back of the Bank of England on a short street called Lothbury (hence the name). Lothbury is an extension of Gresham Street, in the heart of London's financial district. Stow says the church is 'upon the water-course of the Walbrook', so there is a possibility that the name 'Lothbury' is connected with the river in some way.

St Margaret's is now a parish church, with a new parish created by the City Churches Reorganization Measure of 1954. It is a good example of how the residential population of the City has shrunk over the centuries, as it combines the former parishes of eight churches as follows: St Stephen's, Coleman Street; St Christopher- le-Stocks; St Bartholomew-by-the-Exchange; St Olave, Jewry; St Martin Pomeroy; St Mildred Poultry; St Mary Colechurch; and, of course, St Margaret's itself.

Because all of these churches (and others nearby as well) have been destroyed in one way or another, the interior of St Margaret's is graced by many of their fine furnishings and memorials. The best of these is the magnificent screen, which came from All Hallows the Great, Upper Thames Street, when that church was demolished in 1894. St Margaret's former graveyard is now a small court with a fountain. In the eighteenth century there were small shops against the front of the church (as at St Peter, Cornhill, today), but these have been removed. ▶ Restoration London **M** Map location, K-13

St Margaret Pattens A medieval church stood here on Eastcheap, one of the City's main market streets, which was rebuilt in 1538. This Tudor structure perished in the Great Fire and was replaced by Wren in 1684-87. The curious term 'Pattens' has an uncertain origin. Stow says the church was so called 'because old time pattens were there usually made and sold'. (Pattens were wooden clogs shod with iron rings for walking above the mud. They were in use well into the nineteenth century and are frequently mentioned in Dickens' novels). However, earlier references than Stow indicate that the name could have been derived from a benefactor named Patynz or Patins.

The soaring tower of St Margaret Pattens is the distinguishing feature of an otherwise plain exterior. The church is bordered on the left (west) side by a small street called Rood Lane, about which Stow tells an interesting story. Apparently when the medieval building was demolished in 1530 a wooden cross was erected on the site, along with a tabernacle where offerings could be made towards the building fund. The lane, formerly called St Margaret Pattens Lane, was renamed after the cross was erected. In May of 1538 the cross and tabernacle were broken up at night 'by people unknown' (this was in the early days of the Reformation, remember). A short time later a disastrous fire was set in the neighbourhood, slowing up the work of reconstruction.

The interior of St Margaret Pattens is richly furnished, including a fine eighteenth-century organ and the Stuart Royal Arms dating from the time of James II. The pattenmakers and basketmakers guilds hold annual services here. When visiting, look for the beadle's pew and punishment bench (north side of the chancel) and the wooden pegs for wigs (west end of Lady Chapel, south wall). St Margaret's is no longer a parish church, but is used as a Christian study centre. ▶ Restoration London **M** Map location, M-13

St Margaret's, Westminster This is the mother church of the City of Westminster and the parish church of the Lower House of Parliament. On special occasions the Commons, led by the Speaker whose pew is directly in front of the lectern, attends services here. It is also a tradition for the bells to be tolled or pealed when the sovereign passes or is nearby. While the original church was probably founded by King Edward the Confessor in the eleventh century, the oldest parts now date to its rebuilding in 1490-1523, placing it within the early part of Henry VIII's reign.

The most obvious feature of this church—its location next to Westminster Abbey—also accounts for the most interesting aspects of its history. The first building on the site is thought to have been erected at about the same time as the Abbey, 1065, by Edward the Confessor. Its purpose seems to have been a dual one: to provide a church for the increasing population in the vicinity and to allow the monks to hold divine services undisturbed by the laity. A second building replaced the original during the reign of Edward III (1327-77), which in turn was replaced by the present building in the time of Henry VII.

The large and impressive stained-glass window at the east end is a particular treasure of St Margaret's. It was made by order of the magistrates in Dort, Holland, as a present to Henry VII on the occasion of the marriage of his son Arthur to Catherine of Aragon. The subject is the Crucifixion of Christ, and Arthur and Catherine are depicted kneeling at the foot of the cross. The window was to have been placed in Henry's new chapel in Westminster Abbey. However, it was not completed when Arthur died, and not long thereafter, in 1509, Henry VII also died. The new king, Henry VIII, himself now married to Catherine, had the window set up in the chapel of the abbot of Waltham near Epping. At the Dissolution it was moved to New Hall, also in Essex, and during the Commonwealth period this place came into the possession of General Monk, who preserved it from destruction. In 1758 the parishioners of St Margaret's bought it for 400 guineas and installed it in its present position.

The association with the Commons was a development of the Puritan movement during the reign of James I. As the Puritans dominated the Lower House, they decided to worship at St Margaret's so as to separate themselves from the high-church ceremonials at Westminster Abbey attended by the House of Lords. The entire House assembled here on Palm Sunday, 17 April 1614. During the turbulent years of the seventeenth century a number of famous Puritan divines preached here, including Dr. John Reynolds (whose proposal at the Hampton Court Conference led to the King James Version of the Bible); John Owen, the chaplain of Oliver Cromwell; and Richard Baxter, author of *Saint's Everlasting Rest*.

St Margaret's has had associations with numerous famous persons, from William Caxton, a member of this church who set up his printing press in 1477 in Almonry and who is buried in the churchyard, to Winston Churchill, who was married here in 1908. Sir Walter Raleigh's decapitated body was buried in front of the altar after his execution in Palace Yard. He is commemorated by a brass memorial near the east door and in a memorial window which also depicts Elizabeth I. Another window commemorates John Milton, with the lines from John Greenleaf Whittier:

The New World honours him whose lofty plan for England's
freedom made her own more sure...

Wenceslaus Hollar, the notable Dutch engraver, is also thought to
have been buried in St Margaret's.

Samuel Pepys, who was married here in 1655, records several visits
to services at St Margaret's, at one time hearing common prayer for
the first time (5 August 1660). Alexander Pope contributed a ten-line
epitaph to the monument of Mrs Elizabeth Corbett which is quoted by
Dr Samuel Johnson in his *Lives of the Poets*. George Whitefield
preached at St Margaret's one Sunday evening in February 1739,
apparently taking the pulpit without official sanction. The sexton
thereupon locked him in, 'to the great confusion of the bewildered
congregation'.

At the restoration of the monarchy in 1660 the remains of twenty-
one prominent persons who had been buried in Westminster Abbey
were disinterred by the rabble and thrown into St Margaret's
churchyard. John Pym, Admiral Robert Blake and Oliver Cromwell's
mother were among this group. An individual who figured in
American history, James Rumsey, who demonstrated his invention of
the steamboat to George Washington in 1784, is also buried in St
Margaret's churchyard. In his memory a curious epitaph by Robert
Herrick ('In memory of the late deceased Virgin mistris Elizabeth
Hereicke') was restored to the church and may be seen on the south
aisle. Unfortunately, the memorial of John Skelton (1460-1529) on
the porch does not remain. Skelton was made 'poet laureate' by both
Oxford and Cambridge, but his witty and barbed satires eventually got
him into trouble with Cardinal Wolsey. He was forced to flee to
Westminster for sanctuary, where he died in poverty. His self-written
epitaph was as follows:

Come, Alecto, lend me thy torch
To find a churchyard in a church porch;
Poverty and poetry this tomb doth enclose:
Therefore, gentlemen, be merry in prose.

▶ Reformation London   **M** Map location, C-7

St Martin-in-the-Fields   This famous church occupies a highly visible
site at the northeast corner of Trafalgar Square and across the street
from the National Gallery. It is probably the one parish church in
London recognized by most tourists. St Martin's has an active
ministry of social welfare. It is also internationally known for classical
music broadcasts of the Academy of St Martin-in-the Fields under the
direction of Neville Marriner.

St Martin-in-the-Fields is at the foot of St Martin's Lane, once a
broad road that ran north from Charing Cross to St Giles Street. It
probably started as a chapel near the village of Charing (or Cheering)
to serve the monks of St Peter's at Westminster on their visits to the

monastery gardens (on the site of the present Covent Garden). By the time of Henry VIII the parish served by St Margaret's, Westminster, had increased in size. The royal court feared possible contagion from the dead bodies that were so often carried past the palace of Westminster for burial at St Margaret's, so a new parish church was built to replace the old chapel of St Martin.

By the eighteenth century the parish of St Giles had grown to over 40,000 people, necessitating a larger building. The present church was designed by the famous James Gibbs, architect of the Radcliffe Camera at Oxford and St Mary-le-Strand. It was finished in 1721. The combination of a classical pedimented portico with stately columns and a soaring clock tower surmounted by a steeple is world famous and has often been imitated, particularly in America.

St Martin-in-the-Fields is a royal church, as the greater part of Buckingham Palace is included in the parish. The names of some of the royal children baptized at the palace may be found in the register. George I was once a churchwarden; in fact, he was the only royal churchwarden in English history! The visitor will see boxes for royalty and the Admiralty in the church. During World War I the Rev. H.R.L. (Dick) Sheppard became vicar after serving on the Western Front. His 'open door' ministry to soldiers passing through Charing Cross Station to and from war service is still affectionately remembered. ▶ Classical London **M** Map location, H-13

St Martin Orgar, Martin Lane See *Towers*.

St Martin-within-Ludgate It is said that in medieval times this church was actually attached to the old Lud Gate, through which traffic streamed westward from St Paul's along Fleet Street and the Strand to Westminster. Its first recorded mention is 1174, and it was rebuilt once in 1437 before being destroyed in the Great Fire. Wren's church was constructed in 1677-87. It is used today as a guild church, with special responsibility for liaison with the Metropolitan Police. It is also the chapel of the Honourable Society of the Knights of the Round Table.

The exterior of St Martin's is not notable except for the slender spire, which Wren designed to contrast with the great dome of St Paul's. It intercepts it perfectly if viewed from about halfway down Fleet Street. The interior was ingeniously constructed to deal with two problems, a sloping site and traffic noise from Ludgate Hill. Wren solved both by creating an aisle on the south (upper, or street) side with a partially enclosed arcade, thus making the body of the church into a square. This minimizes the south-to-north slope and forms a noise buffer next to the street. Of the several fine original furnishings, note the churchwardens' double chair (1690) and the white marble font (1673) encircled by a Greek palindrome (a sentence that reads equally well backwards or forwards). This one is a copy from a font in the church of St Sophia in Istanbul, and the English translation is:

'Cleanse thy sin, not merely thy outward self'. ▶ Restoration London
M Map location, J-18

St Mary Abchurch   The site of St Mary Abchurch is on high ground near
what is considered the most ancient part of London. The first building
dated to around the end of the twelfth century. The present church is
one of Wren's latest, being constructed between the years 1681 and
1686. The appendage to the name is of uncertain origin. Stow says
that 'Abchurch' is derived from 'Upchurch'—that is, up on a rise
above the river. There is also the possibility that the name came from
an early benefactor, someone named Abbe or Abba.

This is a square building faced with red brick (once again exposed
after the bombing) and stone dressing. It is topped by a lantern and
uncomplicated spire. But this very plain outside houses one of the
finest small-church interiors in London. Its unique feature for a Wren
church is the domed ceiling supported by four brick walls. Upon this
ceiling is a painting, executed about 1708, depicting female figures
representing the Christian virtues. This painting, though exposed to
the elements by the bombing, is now much like the original thanks to
architect Godfrey Allen and painter Walter Hoyle.

A majority of the original furnishings of St Mary Abchurch remain,
including carved doorcases, poor boxes, a marvellous font featuring
the four Evangelists, pulpit (with even the original steps), carved
pews— and most magnificent of all, an elegant reredos known by
documentation to have been carved by the masterful Grinling
Gibbons himself). Some fine monuments also remain, of which the
outstanding example is that of Sir Patience Ward, Lord Mayor in
1680.   ▶ Restoration London   **M** Map location, L-7

St Mary Aldermanbury   See *Towers*.

St Mary Aldermary   In olden times, long before Queen Victoria Street
existed as such, there was a thoroughfare called Watling Street,
which ran from the centre of London out to the northwest and was
thought to be an original Roman road. The Church of St Mary
Aldermary stands between Queen Victoria Street and what was once
Watling Street. Its tower (which pre-dates Wren's church by some
sixty-two years) is a prominent landmark on Queen Victoria Street.
The building was first mentioned in 1080 and was rebuilt at least once
before the Great Fire. Wren erected the present structure in 1681-82.

The curious name, typically, is of uncertain origin. Stow says it is
called 'Aldermary' (or 'elder Mary') 'because the same was very old,
and elder than any church of St Marie in the city…' However another
possible source of the name is 'altera' or 'the other' Mary, indicating
that while several churches are dedicated to the mother of our Lord,
this church bears the name of St Mary Magdalene.

Several lord mayors were buried in the medieval church and one,
Sir Henry Keble, was the benefactor of the building constructed in the

early sixteenth century. St Henry had a prominent monument in the church, but Stow tells us that later lord mayors and other wealthy persons were buried in his vault, 'whose bones were unkindly cast out, and his monument pulled down'. In 1835 a crypt measuring 50 x 10 feet and believed to be that of Keble's church was discovered under some old houses on Watling Street.

The rebuilding after the Great Fire was underwritten by one Henry Rogers, and he is supposed to have stipulated that the new building be a faithful copy of the old. Apparently this is why Wren designed it along Gothic instead of classical lines. In the Victorian era St Mary Aldermary was furnished with reredos, altar rails, organ screen, gallery front and pews in the dark wood fashionable during the period, and a screen was put up dividing the lobby from the nave. The ceiling is original from Wren's design but, curiously, is wrought of plaster rather than stone. An unusual object taken from the Keble crypt and now on the north wall of the chancel is a fine monument by Francis Bacon—entirely blank. The unfounded story is that this was placed by a widow for her deceased husband, but the lady married again before she could think of a suitable epitaph. ▶ Restoration London **M** Map location, L-8

St Mary At Hill In the year 1177 a Norman church, 'Sanctee Mariae Hupenhulle', stood on this spot and was attached to the town house of the abbots of Waltham Abbey in Essex. The old church was enlarged in the fifteenth century. After the Great Fire Wren began work in 1672, incorporating the still-standing tower and side walls into the new building. A spire was added in 1695, but this was replaced by a brick tower after 1780. About the phrase 'At Hill' Stow says, 'In this St Marie hill lane is the fair parish church of St Marie, called on the hill, because of the ascent from Billingsgate'.

The interior of this church forms a Greek cross. Wren drew upon the designs of seventeenth-century Dutch churches for his model. This is one of the best interiors in the City, as good as or better than the original despite all the alterations. It is an example of improvement by the Victorians rather than the reverse. The fine box pews and pulpit are the work of a talented nineteenth-century wood carver, William Gibbs Rogers. The lovely gilded reredos, however, is original.

Stow says that Thomas Becket was once a parson in the old church. Its most famous vicar since Wren's rebuilding (from 1892 to 1926) was Prebendary Wilson Carlile. Carlile was the evangelical founder of the Church Army, who often preached in the open air using a trombone to aid in the worship. His trombone is preserved in a glass case in the vestibule. ▶ Restoration London **M** Map location, M-14

St Mary-le-Bow This church is situated prominently on Cheapside, the ancient 'chepe' or main market street of Old London. To be born within the sound of its bells is the mark of a true Cockney. These famous bells play a central role in that favourite childhood story, 'Dick Whittington and his Cat'. Young Dick, who had run away from his master and got as far as Highgate Hill, heard Bow Bells chime the message, 'Turn again, Whittington, thrice Lord Mayor of London!' (The real Dick Whittington actually was mayor four times.) The rest of the story about how the cat made Dick's fortune is legend, but the twelve mighty bells of Bow Church can indeed be heard on Highgate Hill.

Bow Church was probably first built during the reign of William the Conqueror (1066-87). It was rebuilt by Wren after the Great Fire, 1670-83. In May of 1941 it was burnt out by incendiary bombs. It was then restored by Laurence King in 1956-64. The 'Bow' in the name refers to the stone bows or arches which the Normans used for a foundation. However, it was first called 'St Mary Newchurch', meaning either (or both) that it replaced a Saxon structure or was being distinguished from the older St Mary Aldermary.

Bow Church has had more than its share of violence over its life of at least 900 years. During Norman times a hurricane-force wind lifted the roof off and deposited it in the street, driving the rafters deep into the ground and killing several people. A hundred years later (in 1196) a murderer took refuge in the tower and was subsequently smoked out. The tower itself collapsed in 1271. In 1284 a certain Laurence Duckett wounded one Ralph Crepin in a fight over a woman and took sanctuary in the steeple. Friends of Crepin violated the sanctuary and killed Duckett, leaving his body to appear a suicide. They in turn were discovered and executed, and the building had to be purged. In 1331 a temporary grandstand built at the front of the church, in which the wife of Edward III was viewing a tournament, collapsed. And, as already mentioned, Bow Church was a victim both of the Great Fire and the blitz.

The tower and steeple of Bow Church, together with its bells, are justly famous. The lofty pre-Fire tower had lanterns on all sides and in the centre to illuminate Cheapside. Wren dismantled what was left of the old tower and rebuilt it on a line with the other buildings along Cheapside, connecting it to the nave with a vestibule. He topped it with a steeple that is one of his masterpieces and the most elaborate in the City. It took seven years to build, and as a result Bow Church is his most expensive. After the blitz the tower and steeple again had to be taken down to strengthen the foundation, but it is once more the outstanding landmark of Cheapside.

The other celebrated feature of Bow Church is the Norman crypt, rediscovered by Wren and rebuilt after World War II. Here one can see the stone 'bows' upon which the church rests and which make St Mary-le-Bow, in one sense, the oldest parish church still existing in London. From medieval times right up the present day a church judicial body, called the Court of Arches, has met in the crypt of Bow church to decide cases of ecclesiastical law and to confirm the election of bishops. ▶ Restoration London **M** Map location, L-9

St Mary-le-Strand This is one of two churches (St Clement Danes is the other) located on islands in the centre of the Strand, the wide street that was once the main road between Old London and Westminster. There has been a church on this site since 1147 or earlier, with a certain interruption as we shall see. It is now used for recitals and exhibitions. In 1984 a slide presentation of 'Our Christian Heritage' was shown here several times a day.

When the powerful duke of Somerset, uncle of the young King Edward VI, built his riverside mansion, the old church that stood on the site was simply done away with, with no compensation to the parishioners. For the next 174 years there was no place of worship in the area at all. The present building was consecrated in 1723. Architect James Gibbs made excellent use of its prominent location, combining a rounded porch on the west end facing the Strand with a highly creative steeple. So attractive was the completed building that when Gibbs was asked to compete for the contract for St Martin-in-the-Fields, he took the committee to see St Mary-le-Strand and immediately won their approval. ▶ Classical London **M** Map location, H-14

St Mary Somerset, Upper Than. 2s Street See *Towers*

St Mary Woolnoth This church and its ancestors have stood at the heart of London's commercial and financial district since Saxon times. It is in the very shadow of the Royal Exchange, at the junction of King William and Lombard Streets, and just across from Mansion House, the lord mayor's residence. The name 'Woolnoth' is of uncertain origin. It may be related to the wool trade, so important in London's commerce in early times. Indeed, there was another church where Mansion House now stands called St Mary Wool Church. But it is also possible that the origin is 'Wulfnoth', the name of some Saxon benefactor.

The present building was built during 1716-27 to a design by Nicholas Hawksmoor, Wren's pupil and associate. It is unique among the London churches of the classical period in combining Renaissance forms—Corinthian columns, balustraded turrets, and so on—with a square-set geometric front emphasized by horizontal grooves in the facade. The unusual tower and twin turrets have been much admired (and criticized). It is the only church in Old London to have come through the bombing entirely unscathed.

St Mary Woolnoth's most famous association is with John Newton, rector from 1779 to shortly before his death in 1808. On the north wall is a simple tablet with the following inscription:

John Newton, clerk, once an infidel and libertine, a servant of slaves in Africa, was, by the rich mercy of our Lord and Saviour

Jesus Christ, preserved, restored, pardoned, and appointed to preach the faith he had long laboured to destroy.

Another notable person connected with this church was Claudius Buchanan, pioneer Anglican missionary to India. An inscription near the pulpit tells of his conversion here. Each year the famous 'Spital Sermon' is preached in St Mary Woolnoth (now a guild church). The tradition of this annual sermon was begun at the church of St Mary Spital (which was related to the old Hospital of St Mary Spital), hence the name. ▶ Classical London **M** Map location, L-11

St Marylebone Parish Church The peculiar name of this church, and the main road that it faces, has an interesting history. The original church was dedicated to St John the Evangelist, later changed to St Mary. The nearby brook was called Tyburn, from the name of the village where Marble Arch is now located. But when 'Tyburn' became synonymous with 'execution' the brook was simply called the Bourne. Thus the church became 'St Mary at Bourne' or 'by the Bourne', and eventually 'St Marylebone'.

The first St Marylebone, however, was not in the present location but somewhere on the old road to Tyburn near where Marylebone Lane comes into Oxford Street. Second and third churches, located to the north on the High Street, were built in 1400 and 1740 respectively. The present building, placed still farther north on Marylebone Road and designed in classical style by architect Thomas Hardwick, was consecrated in 1817. It is a pleasant landmark on busy Marylebone High Road. The gate to Regents Park across the road was designed by John Nash to allign with the portico and its circular tower.

The celebrated marriage of Robert Browning and Elizabeth Barrett took place secretly in the present church in 1846. In 1946 a Browning Chapel was created at the west end. Charles Dickens, whose son was baptized here, made St Marylebone the place of Mr. Domby's marriage to Edith Granger in *Domby & Son*. In the old churchyard on Marylebone Lane, mentioned earlier, are buried the great hymnwriter Charles Wesley (died 1788) and his son Samuel Wesley (died 1837). An obelisk in their honour may be seen in the present garden of rest. Here, too, is the grave of James Gibbs, architect of St Mary-le-Strand and St Martin-in-the-Fields. ▶ Classical London **M** Map location, E-5

St Michael's, Cornhill There are records which show that this church was given by a priest named Alnothus or Alnod to the Abbey of Evesham in the year 1055, eleven years before the Norman Conquest. Thus (along with St Peter, Cornhill) it is unique in having a *proven* Saxon foundation, as records from Saxon days are quite rare. It was rebuilt in the fifteenth century and a spire was added, but that church was destroyed in the Great Fire. Wren's building dates from 1670-77 but he left the earlier tower, which was replaced in 1722.

The street called Cornhill, where the church is located, derives its name from the medieval grain market which was held here. The high ground all around this area was part of the old Roman city of Londinium, and it is not unusual for Roman structures to be found when excavation is done for a new building. St Michael's is pretty well eclipsed by modern buildings, and only the neo-Gothic doorway by the Victorian architect Sir George Gilbert Scott can be seen from Cornhill.

At the back of the church, however, there is a nice green that was once the old churchyard and originally was surrounded by cloisters. Above the church soars a very grand tower, built in the Gothic style with carved pinnacles, sculptured heads, and so on. Not much of the interior is original, but note the fine carved-wood pelican (1775), the organ (eighteenth century) and the carved pulpit, lectern and bench-ends by W. Gibbs Rogers. Monuments of three of the ancestors of the poet William Cowper may be seen near the southwest door of the vestibule. ▶ Restoration London ▪ Map location, L-12

St Michael's, Paternoster Royal The earliest mention of this church was 1219. A new building was constructed in 1409 with money provided by the famous merchant and lord mayor Richard Whittington, associated by legend with St Mary-le-Bow. Wren rebuilt it between 1686 and 1689, and the steeple was completed in 1713. In 1944 it was blasted by a flying bomb, and its latest reconstruction took place in 1968.

'Paternoster' and 'Royal' are associations with the rosary-maker and vintner trades which flourished near here in early times. Everyone recognizes 'Paternoster' or 'Our Father' as the opening words of the Lord's Prayer used in the rosary. 'Royal' is actually derived from the name of the town of La Reole near Bordeaux where much of the London wine was obtained.

This church, not far from the banks of the Thames, was next to the estate of the fabled Dick Whittington, as already mentioned. In addition to providing funds for the rebuilding of the church, this good man founded a 'college' or religious community, together with an almshouse, 'to provide for such pouer persons which grevous penuere and cruel fortune have oppressed, and be not of power to get their lyving either by craft or by any other bodily labour'. Members of the community were required by Whittington's will to pray daily for his soul and that of his wife. Whittington's sumptuous memorial was destroyed during the Reformation in the sixteenth century. College Street takes its name from the aforementioned college.

The restored Wren building has a simple exterior with a pleasant tower and steeple on one corner. It is set back in a little garden. Inside, the altar-piece, lectern, pulpit and door cases are the original carved wood, and there is a fine candelabrum which predates the building (1644). Note the modern stained glass by John Hayward on the south side. The window on the west end depicts young Dick Whittington with his indomitable cat and, above, London with streets of gold surmounted by the lord mayor's seal. ▶ Restoration London **M** Map location, L-13

St Nicholas, Cole Abbey (Cole Abbey Presbyterian Church)

Located on a rise above Queen Victoria Street, this church reminds one of a lighthouse, with a trumpet-shaped spire, porthole-like windows and balcony resembling a crow's nest. It first appears in recorded history in 1144 in a letter of Pope Lucius II. After the Great Fire it was one of Wren's first restorations, 1671-77. In 1941 it was burnt out by fire bombs. It was restored in 1962 along the lines of Wren's design.

'Cole Abbey' in the name is of uncertain origin. Stow says, 'it hath been called of many Golden Abbey, of some, Gold Abbey, or Cold Bey, and so hath the most ancient writings, as standing in a cold place, as Cold harbour, and such like'. He also adds the note, 'But I could never learne the cause why it should be so called, and therefore I will let it passe'. In late Victorian times it was nicknamed 'Coal-hole Abbey' due to a nearby railway tunnel vent which emitted black smoke.

We have already alluded to the lighthouse-like appearance of St Nicholas, Cole Abbey. On the top of this church is a ship weathervane, a reminder of its age-old association with the sea and seamen. Actually it was not deep-sea sailors so much as fishermen who were ministered to by the old church. Before Billingsgate Fish Market was built, the London fish market was nearby. The fisher- folk worshipped here, and many were buried in and around the old building. The name, as Stow points out, quite possibly alludes to a place of shelter from the sea.

The very plain and completely open interior of the restored church is enriched by the original Wren pulpit, altar rails and font. Original carving may also be seen on the three west doorways, the screen at the west end and above the south doorway. The parish of St Nicholas was particularly hard hit during the Great Plague of 1665. Of the 125 parishioners, ninety-one perished. In 1737, during the Evangelical Revival, George Whitefield preached here. Now it is a Presbyterian Church associated with the Free Church of Scotland. ▶ Restoration London **M** Map location, L-14

St Olave's, Hart Street

This venerable old church is best known for its associations with the Norwegians from whom it derives its name and also with the seventeenth-century naval official and man- about-town, Samuel Pepys, whose *Diary* reveals his fondness for St Olave's, his parish church. The crypt dates back to 1250 and is the oldest part of the building. Otherwise the present church was built in 1450. Having escaped the Great Fire with the help of Pepys and Admiral Pen, it suffered serious bomb damage during the blitz in 1941; the roof, when it fell in, destroyed the clerestory and most of the walls. However, it has been beautifully restored by architect Ernest Glanfield. The restoration stone was laid in 1951 by King Haakon of Norway.

The seventeenth century appears to be the period when a number of interesting persons were members of this parish, and their monuments can be seen today in the church. Above the vestry door is a monument to Sir James Deane, his three wives and his children. He was a merchant adventurer who made a great fortune and was very generous in his charity. Near this in the east wall is a monument to Dr William Turner, who died in 1614, both an eminent herbalist and naturalist and an outspoken Reformer who was imprisoned by the infamous Bishop Gardiner. The monument to Sir John Minnes, vice-admiral to Charles I and governor of Dover Castle under Charles II, has disappeared. This brave and witty man is the author of those famous lines:

> For he that fights and runs away,
> May live to fight another day.

Samuel Pepys himself is remembered by both a monument in the south aisle and a tablet on the outside of the church. Pepys was Secretary of the Navy, whose office was nearby on Seething Lane. The Navy Office had its own pew in a gallery which connected with the churchyard by an outside stairway. The tablet is affixed to the outside wall near this stairway, and the monument inside the church covers the blocked doorway to this gallery. Pepys honoured his wife Elizabeth, a buxom beauty of French extraction who died in 1669, with a bust located in the northeast corner. Pepys died in 1703 but had no monument until 1884.

It is recorded in the parish register that 326 plague victims of 1665 were buried in St Olave's churchyard. However, the elaborate churchyard gate with its skulls and spikes was erected in 1658, some seven years before. Charles Dickens in the *Uncommercial Traveller* immortalizes this churchyard and gate with a lengthy essay entitled 'The City of the Absent.' He says:

> One of my best beloved churchyards, I call the churchyard of Saint Ghastly Grim... The gate is ornamented with skulls and cross-bones, larger than life, wrought in stone.

As any visitor to St Olave's can see, nothing has changed. ▶ Medieval London **M** Map location, M-15

St Olave's, Old Jewry See *Towers*.

St Pancras New Church This church on Euston Road, across from the railway station, is the most Greek of all the neo-classical churches in the West End, having been designed after the temple of the

Erectheum on the Acropolis in Athens. Architect William Inwood's son, Henry, actually made a trip to Greece to make drawings used in the church's plans. The tower, 156-feet high, is modelled after the Temple of the Winds at Athens. At the east end are projecting porticos with large female figures supporting the entablature, also in imitation of the Erectheum. These porticos are entrances to the crypt. The portico at the west end facing the street is graced by six Ionic columns, behind which are the three entrance doors. St Pancras (which is the second church by this name in the area) was consecrated in 1822. ▶ Classical London **M** Map location, G-4

St Pancras Old Church Old St Pancras is one of those curious London churches, like St Sepulchre's, that belongs to all periods of history, though the outside appearance today is Gothic Revival. It is very, very old; there is some evidence that it goes back to Roman times. The church stands on what used to be a hillock overlooking the River Fleet, and the site is thought to have once been a pagan shrine. Today, however, the old church grounds lie between busy Pancras Road and the railroad right of way.

The reason that St Pancras Old Church belongs to all periods is that it was never *completely* destroyed and rebuilt. Thus one can find Norman work (north wall and north and south doors), Early English (part of a lancet window), thirteenth and fifteenth-century objects (piscina, or a shallow stone basin in the wall; sedile, or a recessed stone seat), a gallery with eighteenth-century scroll work, and the nineteenth-century tower and walls already mentioned. The oldest object in the church is an altar-stone found under the tower during the partial rebuilding in 1847-48. Five crosses cut into it lead historians to believe it dates from the sixth century!

In very early times this was the village church of St Pancras. The city was then quite a distance away to the southeast. By the eighteenth century the area had become a kind of desolate wilderness on the edge of the growing metropolis. An observer of 1777 describes it as 'a rural place, in some parts entirely covered with docks and nettles, enclosed only by a low hand-rail, and commanding extensive views of open country in every direction'. The new St Pancras was built in 1822, and the old church became a chapel of ease to it. It was restored in the Norman style in 1847-48 and again made a parish church in 1863.

Old St Pancras still retains a kind of rural aspect. Like a village church it is surrounded by an ancient churchyard, now a public garden. A great many illustrious persons are buried here and not a few notorious ones. The most prominent monument is that which was provided by Sir John Soane, founder of the Soane Museum, for his wife. The interior of Old St Pancras, also not unlike a country parish church, possesses a number of monuments from the sixteenth and seventeenth centuries. In these days the building is kept locked for fear of vandalism, but may be seen during services on Wednesday and Sunday mornings. **M** Map location, G-5

St Paul's Cathedral St Paul's Cathedral is the most prominent edifice in Old London, and one of the world's great city churches. It is a landmark that symbolizes London, along with Tower Bridge, to millions around the world. The soaring beauty of its interior is viewed by hundreds of thousands of visitors each year, not to mention the vast television audience who watched the wedding of Prince Charles and Princess Diana in July 1981. Its presence atop Ludgate Hill testifies to the central place occupied by the Christian faith in London's long history. But the building itself is a monument to one man, Sir Christopher Wren.

Christopher Wren was first consulted on the restoration of St Paul's when the old building was still standing. John Evelyn, who was one of the commissioners, records in his diary on 27 August 1666, that Wren 'persisted that it required a new foundation' and proposed also a 'noble cupola' in place of the tower. However the Great Fire, which began on 2 September, reduced the old cathedral to a ruin, and Wren quickly perceived that not only a new foundation but an entirely new building was needed.

He had previously proposed a combination of Gothic and classical styles, intending to carry the Renaissance influence even further than his predecessor, Inigo Jones. With this new opportunity before him, his first plan for the magnificent new church was totally classical, in the shape of a Greek cross with a great dome in the centre. The king approved, but the commissioners could not agree and eventually vetoed the plan. A second design was then submitted, in the shape of a Latin cross with a longer nave on the west side and shorter quire on the east. Again the commissioners were divided, but the king settled the matter by giving a warrant of approval and considerable freedom to the great architect. A model of the first bulding plan may be seen in the crypt of the present cathedral.

Demolition of the massive ruins was necessary before any work on the new cathedral could commence. The pillars, 200-feet high, which once supported the tower and spire of Old St Paul's, posed a particular problem. At first Wren tried small charges of gunpowder, which worked better than pickaxes but proved to be somewhat hazardous to the surroundings. The method that finally succeeded was a variation of the ancient battering ram. In excavating the site for the new foundation, Wren was able to learn much about what had previously existed on the site. While there were Roman graves, he exploded the myth that a Temple of Diana once stood here.

Once the mountain of rubble from the old cathedral had been cleared (much of it dumped in the Moorfields to the north of the city), Wren himself took charge of the surveying. He determined where the new dome would stand by laying out a circle, marking the exact centre with a piece of old tombstone that a workman brought him. Observers were struck by the fact that one word could be clearly seen on the stone—*Resurgam*—'I shall rise again.' It was a prophecy that now had a double meaning!

Construction on the new cathedral began in November 1673 and continued until 1708, when the last stone was laid. The task of decorating the interior went on for another decade or so. By 1723, the year of Wren's death, the money spent on the new building amounted to £748,000, most of which came from a tax on seaborne coal entering London. After Queen Anne's death in 1714 Wren had much less influence, and various alterations were made despite his objections. However, he had the satisfaction of seeing the great church completed largely according to his design; as an old man, he came every Saturday to view his handiwork. A tablet above his simple grave in the crypt reads, *Si monumentum requiris, circumspice* ('If you seek his monument, look around you').

The visitor entering St Paul's for the first time is likely to be drawn to the centre under the great dome. Everywhere—above to the painting of Sir John Thornhill depicting the life of St Paul, eastward to the magnificent quire with wood carving done by the masterful Grinling Gibbons, beyond that to the high altar canopied by a splendid modern baldachino, westward to the spacious nave, and northward and southward to the aisles with their richly decorated bays—the interior is fully deserving of its position as the cathedral of England's capital city.

St Paul's has tended to be the last resting place of England's famous military heroes. Outstanding among these are the duke of Wellington and Admiral Lord Nelson, who are both honoured by impressive monuments as well as splendid tombs in the crypt. The apse at the eastern extremity of the cathedral is a memorial chapel dedicated to the 28,000 Americans based in Britain who lost their lives in World War II. Of particular interest among the military monuments is that of General Charles George Gordon in the north aisle. Visitors will also wish to see the effigy of Dr John Donne in the south quire aisle, Holman Hunt's painting of Christ ('The Light Of the World') in the south aisle of the nave, and the memorial to John Wyclif near the duke of Wellington's tomb on the north side of the crypt.

▶ Restoration London **M** Map location, L-15

St Paul's, Covent Garden
This church was built by Inigo Jones in 1633 and consecrated in 1638. It was destroyed by fire in 1795 except for the walls, portico and southeast chapel, but was rebuilt on the plan and in the proportions of the original. It was the first formally Classical building in England, that is, the first to have a row of columns across the front. It appears in a print by Hogarth entitled 'Morning', indicating that many of the homeless inhabitants of London gathered here in a makeshift shelter called 'Tom King's

Coffee House'. The portico gained its greatest fame, however, when it figured in the opening scene of George Bernard Shaw's play *Pygmalion*. Later, a stage representation of it was seen by millions around the world in the musical and film adaptation of *My Fair Lady*.

Covent Garden, once the vegetable gardens of Westminster Abbey, was in the seventeenth century the property of the earl of Bedford. His plan was to create a piazza with the church as the focal point. Toward that end, he engaged architect Inigo Jones as builder. Apparently the earl had second thoughts about the cost of his project, and he told Jones that the new chapel should not be 'much better than a barn'. The architect replied, 'Well, then, you shall have the handsomest barn in England'.

In the early days of St Paul's, Covent Garden, it had a burying ground like a country church. Here were laid to rest a great many persons famous in the world of the theatre, the arts, music and literature. These included Sir Henry Herbert, master of the revels under Charles I; Samuel Butler, author of *Hudibras*; Sir Peter Lely, the painter; William Wycherley, the dramatist; and Grinling Gibbons, sculptor and woodcarver. Some later associations are the great watercolour artist, J.M.W.Turner, who was baptized here on 29 August 1773; W.S.Gilbert of musical-comedy fame, who was also baptized here, on 11 January 1837; and the great Victorian actress Ellen Terry, friend of Charles Dickens, whose ashes are in a casket on the south wall. Other more modern theatre personalities are commemorated on a screen at the west end of the church.

For many years Covent Garden was the site of the wholesale fruit, vegetable and flower market. In Edwardian times, flower girls like Eliza Dolittle sold their wares from the steps of St Paul's. The wholesale market has now moved outside London, and its picturesque building near the church is now a museum of London Transport, surrounded by restaurants and shops. The church is still used for worship services and as the headquarters of the Actors' Church Union. ▶ Stuart & Commonwealth London **M** Map location, H-15

St Peter's, Cornhill St Peter's shares with its neighbour, St Michael's, the distinction of having a recorded foundation from before the Norman Conquest, in this case 1040. But St Peter's boasts an even greater antiquity. A brass plate in the vestry (dating from the time of Henry IV, 1399-1415) claims a foundation in AD179 by a mythical King Lucius! Whatever building was here in 1666 perished in the Great Fire, and the present Wren building dates from 1677-87.

The street side of St Peter's is hidden by shops, with only the doorway showing, a feature common in the nineteenth century but unique to this church today. However, there is a pleasant little churchyard in the back from which the south side of the building can be viewed, and the east side can be seen from Gracechurch Street. In medieval times this church had a number of chantries, and it was also used as a sanctuary for lawbreakers. There was a grammar school at St Peter's from 1425 to 1666. A gilded statue of St Peter is on the churchyard gate.

St Peter's, Cornhill, is the only church in the City to possess a Wren chancel screen in its original setting. The reredos is also from the time of Wren's rebuilding. The organ dates from 1681, though considerably altered, and has the keyboard upon which Mendelssohn played in 1840 and declared it the 'finest in London.' His autograph may be seen in the vestry. Also in the vestry is a seventeenth-century long wooden table used by the Puritans for holy communion. The interior is somewhat dark due to stained glass left from the nineteenth century. ▶Restoration London ▪M Map location, L-16

St Peter-ad-Vincula (St Peter in Chains)

The first chapel on this site was built during the reign of Henry I (1100-35). A major fire in 1512 destroyed the old building, and the oldest parts of the present chapel therefore date from the sixteenth century. As the Tower of London was at first a residence of the sovereigns, the first chapel probably had stalls for the royal family (though their normal place of worship would have been the Chapel of St John the Evangelist in the White Tower.) However, as the Tower from earliest times was a prison for persons accused of offences against the crown, St Peter-ad-Vincula came to be used by the warders and soldiers on duty and their families. It also became the burial place of a number of the more important prisoners who paid the extreme penalty. The site of the block is only a few yards from its door.

The history of executions at the Tower is closely linked to the history of England itself and, in particular, of the English Reformation. Most of those who died on the block were famous, and some were of noble or royal blood. Some were truly guilty, others merely the unfortunate victims of circumstance. In several cases the facts are still a mystery. As Carlyle says, 'In this little Golgotha are interred mighty secrets now never to be solved; for half the crimes of our English monarchs were wrought out on the little plot outside the church-door of St Peter-ad-Vincula'.

The roster of execution victims from the Reformation period interred in St Peter's includes:

Anne Boleyn, second queen of Henry VIII (1536);
Margaret, Countess of Salisbury;
Catherine Howard, fifth queen of Henry VIII (1542);
Sir Thomas More;
Bishop John Fisher;
Thomas Cromwell, the Earl of Essex;
(all of whom were put to death under Henry VIII);
Thomas, Lord Seymour of Dudley, the Lord Admiral;
Seymour, the Protector Somerset
(both of whom died during the reign of Edward VI);

Lady Jane Grey;
Earl of Essex;
John Dudley, earl of Warwick and duke of Northumberland
(who were executed under Mary I).

As St Peter-ad-Vincula was not affected by the Great Fire and not
seriously damaged by the bombing, a number of fine monuments to
various officers of the Tower have survived from the sixteenth and
seventeenth centuries. A comparison with an old print of 1547
indicates that at that time the building had battlements and the porch
was on the south side. But despite various changes and inevitable
modernization, this royal chapel has, in a small way, much in
common with Westminster Abbey as a church of great historic
interest. ▶ Reformation London **M** Map location, M-16

St Peter's, Vere Street This is an excellent surviving example of an
eighteenth-century estate church—that is, a chapel built to
accommodate residents of the new homes developing around
Cavendish Square. It was commissioned by Edward Harley, earl of
Oxford, and completed in 1724. The architect was James Gibbs, who
was at the same time working on St Martin-in-the-Fields and was able
to use some of the same construction crew.

Outside, St Peter's is a plain brick building with quaint double
cupolas topped by a dome, all set on top of a square tower. The
original clocks still grace the tower. A Tuscan-style portico is the
approach to the main entrance off Vere Street. Inside, the visitor sees
a beautiful east window of Christ and the Woman at the Well,
executed by the Pre-Raphaelite artist Sir Edward Burne-Jones (1833-
98). A gallery runs around three sides, supported by columns, and
there is a fine curved ceiling.

The setting of this church today, just a few steps off Oxford Street,
is one of modern department stores and office blocks, to which it is a
pleasant contrast. St Peter's, Vere Street, is now a chapel of ease to
All Souls, Langham Place, and the facilities house the London
Institute for Contemporary Christianity.

Lectures by well-known scholars are usually announced on a large
chalkboard at the entrance. ▶ Classical London **M** Map location, E-6

St Sepulchre without Newgate This church defies category, having
been restored and rebuilt numerous times while still retaining some of
its medieval features. It has been known as 'St Sepulchre's' since
before Stow's day, but was originally dedicated to St Edmund, the
martyr king of East Anglia. It stood just outside what was called the
'Chamberlain Gate' in earliest times and was called variously 'St
Sepulchre's by Chamberlain Gate' or 'St Sepulchre's in the Bayly'.
The association with the city gate stuck when its name was changed
to Newgate. The *official* name, however, is The Church of the Holy
Sepulchre Without Newgate. It alludes to the Church of the Holy

Sepulchre in Jerusalem and undoubtedly had associations with the Crusaders, who perhaps thought of themselves as linking London and Jerusalem through their exploits.

This, the largest parish church in the City, has had a remarkable number of connections with famous people and events over the centuries: the Saxons, the Crusaders, the Reformation, Elizabeth I, the Virginia Colony, the condemned inmates of Newgate Prison, military units of London and some of London's finest musicians. While the association with the Saxons is a bit vague, the link with the Crusaders is more tangible in that it is located in approximately the same spot in relation to the walled city of London as the Church of the Holy Sepulchre is to the walled city of Jerusalem. There is evidence that some of the Crusaders departed from here and that their hostelry was an ancient inn on Snow Hill nearby, the Saracen's Head, which lasted well into the nineteenth century.

During the reigns of either Henry VI or Edward IV (that is, between 1422 and 1483), a member of the wealthy Popham family financed a reconstruction of the twelfth-century building. At this time a beautiful chapel was added on the south side as well as the porch which remains today, the original fan vaulting still intact. A remnant of an Easter Sepulchre with carved canopy on the north wall dates to the fifteenth century as well.

On the left side, as one enters the nave through the glass doors, there is a framed roster of vicars and rectors of the church since 1249. Here may be seen the name of John Rogers, who worked with Tyndale in translating the Scriptures and was himself the producer of the Matthew Bible. Upon the accession of Mary in 1553 he boldly spoke out against a return to Roman Catholicism, for which he was arrested. Ultimately he was condemned to death and burned at Smithfield, the first Protestant martyr of many during Mary's reign.

Queen Elizabeth's Latin secretary and tutor, Roger Ascham, a widely recognized scholar and author, is buried in the Easter Chapel. Somewhere in the southeast corner of the church lie the remains of Captain John Smith, one of history's most colourful soldiers of fortune. His leadership of the Virginia Colony, founded in 1607, is commemorated by a brass plate and also a memorial window on the south side. Smith's success in Virginia resulted from his friendship with the native tribespeople through the intercession of Princess Pocahontas. (His statue may also be seen in the court next to Bow Church.)

The seventeenth century brought to St Sepulchre's a great treasure worthy of a 'musician's church', namely a fine organ built by Renatus Harris in 1670. According to tradition, both Handel and Mendelssohn played it, and both Samuel Wesleys certainly did, as well as the famous Sir Henry Wood, founder of the Promenade Concerts. The organ originally stood in what is now the Musicians' Chapel, but was moved in 1878 and again in 1932, when it was rebuilt. Everything in the Musicians' Chapel was given either by or in memory of London musicians, and the Musicians' Book of Remembrance contains hundreds of their names.

St Sepulchre's was for centuries cheek-by-jowel with the city prison, which at first was in the wall at Newgate and later (after 1774) a separate building. The site is now occupied by Old Bailey, the Central Criminal Court. In early times condemned prisoners were taken by cart to Tyburn for hanging, passing the church on the way. While the bells pealed, they were given a nosegay of flowers, and the sexton would ring a handbell and exhort the crowd to pray for the man. Concern for the spiritual welfare of these doomed persons motivated Robert Dowe in 1602 to give a fund to establish what seems now a quaint custom. The sexton went early to the cell of the condemned prisoner, rang a handbell, and recited a message as follows:

> Examine well yourself, in time repent,
> That you may not to eternal flames be sent.

The handbell used for this purpose may be seen in a glass case on the south aisle. Later, when hangings took place at Newgate Prison, the church bells tolled the moment of executions at 8.00 a.m.

Like several other London churches, St Sepulchre's honours certain of London's military units. In the north aisle is the war memorial of the 6th Battalion City of London Rifles, with a book of remembrance containing 1,329 names. On the south aisle is the regimental chapel of the Royal Fusiliers, City of London Regiment, with rolls of honour, memorial book and the colours of the various battalions. Several livery companies dating from medieval times have yearly services in St Sepulchre's. Also, the choir stalls are used throughout the year by many fine singing groups from colleges, academies and schools of music. **M** Map location, J-19

St Stephen's, Walbrook The name 'Walbrook' attached to the name of this church indicates that it was built on the bank of a river. In early times the Walbrook entered London under the walls where the Barbican and the Museum of London now stand, meandered through the old city, and emptied into the Thames where Walbrook Street runs into Thames Street. The original church (first mentioned about 1096) was built on the west bank, but in 1439 it was rebuilt across the stream. After the Great Fire, Wren's reconstruction, completed in 1679, was also on the east bank. This building was burnt out in May 1941, and restored by Godfrey Allen in 1954. Extensive work was again done in the late 1980s.

St Stephen's is said to be one of Wren's masterpieces, the construction of which he personally supervised. Out of a simple rectangle he created a cruciform using Corinthian columns, eight of which support a magnificent dome weighing over fifty tons. Light

St Stephen, Walbrook.

comes from a cupola atop the dome as well as from the windows. This dome is said to be the first of its kind built in England and the prototype for St Paul's. Some fine furnishings from Wren's time include an organ gallery and case, pulpit and reredos. Under the dome is a massive Henry Moore altar of rough-hewn stone. Look for the unusually beautiful octagonal font cover and the painting by Benjamin West of the stoning of St Stephen, which hangs on the north wall. ▶ Restoration London   M Map location, L-17

St Vedast's, Foster Lane   A nice tree-framed view of this church may be had from the garden at the east end of St Paul's. It was first mentioned in 1170, and Wren's church dates from 1695-1700. This building was burnt out in December 1940 and restored in 1962. Foster Lane, the little street on which the building stands and which identifies it, has a curious etymology growing out of the original name of the church, 'St Vedast-alias-Foster'. This name indicates that 'Foster' is actually the English equivalent of 'Vedast', which came about as follows: Vedast to Vaast, then Vastes, Fastre, Fauster and finally Foster.

The Great Fire left the walls of the old church standing, and Wren incorporated these into the present building. His simple yet elegant steeple, the vertical lines of which pleasantly contrast with the nearby dome of St Paul's, fortunately escaped the bombing. The plain

177

rectangular interior is enlivened by a flat ceiling richly decorated with
gold and silver paint in wreaths and rectangles. Some fine furnishings,
all of which came from other churches, include an eighteenth-
century organ cover, a fine octagonal pulpit, a carved wooden font
and cover, and an attractive altarpiece and altar table. The modern
stained glass in the east window features scenes from the life of St
Vedast. ▶ Restoration London **M** Map location, K-16

St Vedast, Foster Lane, rebuilt after
the Great Fire, still has its original walls.

Sanctuary In medieval times Westminster was a sanctuary for debtors and
others in trouble with the law. The street leading into Parliament
Square is still called Broad Sanctuary. ▶ Medieval London

Savoy Chapel (Queen's Chapel of the Savoy) This chapel, located
just off the Strand and not far from the Savoy Hotel, is historically

very ancient, though most of the present building and its furnishings date to the period following a fire in 1864. It serves a small area of about five surrounding acres, which is known as the Precinct of the Savoy. This area was at one time occupied by the Savoy Manor, a grand residence on the riverfront originally owned by Peter of Savoy (an uncle of the queen) in the thirteenth century. It became associated with the House of Lancaster by being next owned by Edmund, first earl of Lancaster, brother of King Edward I. Eventually the Duchy of Lancaster was united with the crown when Henry Bolingbroke, duke of Lancaster, became King Henry IV in 1399. Thus it is a chapel of the present sovereign, Queen Elizabeth II (though not a royal chapel), through her right of the Duchy of Lancaster.

In the fourteenth century Henry, first duke of Lancaster, built a fine palace on the property, which was used by his son-in-law John of Gaunt, son of Edward III and the patron of John Wyclif and Geoffrey Chaucer (see Medieval London). During the Peasants' Revolt in 1381 the palace was plundered and burned, and for a long time it lay abandoned. In the late fifteenth century Henry VII provided in his will for a hostel for 100 poor men to be built on the site. This was quite a noble undertaking, with a splendid hall longer than Westminster Hall, and including three chapels, dedicated to St John, St Catherine and Our Lady. St John's Chapel, probably consecrated in 1515, was the forerunner of the present Savoy Chapel.

When the Hospital of the Savoy ceased to function after nearly two centuries and the buildings were put to other uses, the Savoy Chapel continued under various administrations. It remained even when the old buildings were cleared away in 1820-21. The rebuilt chapel to be seen today survived the bombing, all except for some of the windows. It is entered off Savoy Street, which is on the river side of a set of buildings that face the Strand (including the Savoy Hotel). The interior is very attractively furnished, and there are numerous reminders of its association with the Lancastrians and the royal family, as well as the Royal Victorian Order of which it is the official chapel. The Savoy Chapel is noted for its music; there is a full choir of men and boys each Sunday except for August and September. The service is conducted 'fully in the tradition of the Prayer Book and untouched by modern revisions'. ▶ Medieval London ▪ Map location, H-16

Sawtrey, William (died 1401) Sawtrey was the first to be tried under the heresy law (*De Haeretico Comburendo*) passed by Parliament against the Lollards after Wyclif's day. He was attached to St Osyth's, London, at the time and was charged by Archbishop Arundel with refusing to adore the cross, holding that money spent on pilgrimages should be given to the poor, rejecting transubstantiation, and so on. He made a spirited defence, even appealing to Parliament and the king on the grounds that his views were supported by the New Testament and St Augustine. However, he was condemned and burnt in chains at Smithfield. ▶ Medieval London

Sayers, Dorothy Leigh (1893-1957)

Dorothy Sayers, like G.K. Chesterton, is best known for a popular series of murder mysteries, still avidly read today. These are the Lord Peter Wimsey stories, which include such catchy titles as *Whose Body?*, *Five Red Herrings*, *Clouds of Witness* and *The Unpleasantness at the Bellona Club*.

However, Sayers was a Christian scholar and writer of great ability, producing one of the finest English translations of Dante's *Divine Comedy* ever done, with notes illuminating the Christian meaning; a series of radio plays on the life of Christ, *A Man Born to Be King* (1941); a superb apologetic work entitled *The Mind of the Maker*; and a number of other works, most still in print.

Dorothy Sayers was born in an Essex vicarage and was educated at Oxford. Her first work, a book of poetry called *Op I*, was published by Blackwells bookstore at Oxford. Her first literary success, the Peter Wimsey series, began in 1923. During World War II she resided at Oxford and was acquainted with C.S.Lewis, J.R.R. Tolkien, Charles Williams and Owen Barfield. However, from 1929 until her death in 1957 she maintained a house at Witham, Essex, from which she commuted into London and the B.B.C. This house now is the headquarters of the Dorothy Sayers Society. Her ashes, however, rest beneath the tower of St Anne's, Soho, near the Theatreland to which she contributed so much. ▶ Twentieth-century London **M** St Anne's, Soho (ruin), F-3

Shakespeare, William (1564-1616)

There is no greater name in the literature of the English language (or in any language, for that matter) than William Shakespeare. Shakespeare crowns the glories of the Elizabethan Age by bringing English—which had been developing over a period of some thousand years—to a peak of poetic perfection. Moreover, Shakespeare was but the brightest diamond in a whole crown of sparkling literary jewels that came into being especially after the defeat of the Spanish Armada. These posterity will always identify with the triumphant later years of Good Queen Bess. During a span of some thirty years (actually overlapping into the reign of James I), London saw more great poets and dramatists than the combined populations of Great Britain and America have managed to produce in the last hundred years.

Shakespeare and his great contemporaries Edmund Spenser, Sir Philip Sydney, Christopher Marlowe, Sir Walter Raleigh and Ben Jonson, appear to be the flowering of the Renaissance in England. They were to England what Boccaccio, Petrarch and Dante were to Italy a century or so earlier, artists who shrewdly observed human life, with its comedy and tragedy, and painted the scenes with language—language which remains unsurpassed for its beauty and vitality. As

Classical Humanists they were educated men in the finest sense of that word: educated in Greek and Latin literature (which they read in the original), ancient history, English history, chivalry and heraldry, and, of course, the Bible. Some of them may have been devout Christians personally, but unlike Donne and Herbert and Crashaw of the next generation, the gospel or personal holiness was not the primary concern of their writing.

From a Christian standpoint, however, the important thing about Shakespeare's great dramas is that they *assume the same kind of reality* that the Bible assumes. In them, the natural world is one of created order:

> The heavens themselves, the planets, and this centre
> Observe degree, priority and place
> Insisture, course, proportion, season, form,
> Office, and custom, in all line of order.

Man himself is the noblest work of nature:

> What a piece of work is a man!
> how noble in reason! how infinite in faculty!
> in form and moving how express and admirable!
> in action how like an angel! in apprehension
> how like a god! the beauty of the world!
> the paragon of animals!

While man is neither a god nor an angel, he alone in nature has the propensity for evil—sometimes an evil that is the outgrowth of some personal flaw, like an overpowering ambition (as Macbeth), or other (and rarer) times an evil that seems to be expressed for the sheer pleasure of it (as Iago in *Othello*). Good men and women are not gods or angels either, but merely individuals who, though flawed and human, are constant in their loyalty and love (as Mercutio in *Romeo & Juliet*). The noblest human trait of all, in fact, is that of mercy—the love of the New Testament gospel:

> Mercy...
> 'Tis mightiest in the mightiest: it becomes
> The throned monarch better than his crown;
> His sceptre shows the force of temporal power,
> The attribute to awe and majesty,
> Wherein doth sit the dread and fear of kings;
> But mercy is above this sceptred sway,
> It is enthroned in the heart of kings,
> It is an attribute to God himself,
> And earthly power doth then show likest God's
> When mercy seasons justice.

▶ Elizabethan London ◼ Monument & memorial window, Southwark Cathedral, D-6 Painting, engraving, plaster castings of effigies, National Portrait Gallery, H-9

Sheppard, H.R.L. 'Dick' (1880-1937) London clergyman from 1907 to 1926 and vicar of St Martin-in-the-Fields from 1914 onward. He was greatly gifted in reaching out to non-churched people and through his ministry St Martin-in-the-Fields became nationally famous. During World War I he gave much of his time to servicemen. He was one of the first churchmen to recognize the possibilities of radio, as a result of which grew the Academy of St Martin-in-the-Fields. After the war he became an ardent pacifist. ▶ Twentieth-century London M Map location of St Martin-in-the-Fields, H-13

Simon Zelotes (Simon the Zealot) In *Foxe's Book of Martyrs* we read, 'Simon, surnamed Zelotes, preached the Gospel in Mauritania, Africa, and even in Britain, in which latter country he was crucified, AD74.' If St Simon reached Britain, he would have been the only one of the apostles to do so, and of course he could well have visited or even landed at the port of Londinium. However, there is no other evidence, and he is not mentioned in Bede's *History of the English Church*. St Alban is the first Christian martyr in Britain whom we know anything about. ▶ Roman London

Solemn League & Covenant An agreement by the English and Scottish parliaments in 1644 to adopt the Reformed or Presbyterian form of worship and doctrine throughout the British Isles. The representives of the English parliament met in St Margaret's, Westminster.
▶ Stuart & Commonwealth London M St Margaret's, Westminster, C-7

Southwark Cathedral (St Saviour's) The beginnings of this ancient church are unknown, as the Saxons kept few records. But a popular legend told to Stow by the last prior, Bartholomew Linsted, links it with an early London Bridge. According to the story, a ferryman named Audrey once lived on the site of the cathedral. The old man thought to cheat his servants by pretending to be dead, assuming that they would fast in mourning. Instead, they had a party. When Audrey sprang up and attacked his apprentice, the younger man slew him. Mary Audrey, the gentle daughter, gave her inheritance to found a nunnery on the spot, dedicated to the Virgin, which later subsisted by the profits from the ferry. Between 852 and 862 St Swithen, Bishop of Winchester, changed it to an Augustinian monastery, called St Mary Overie (or St Mary Over the Water), whose monks supposedly built a wooden bridge.

In the year 1106 a church building was erected by the Priory of St Mary Overie. This was destroyed by fire and replaced in 1207 by an edifice of stone. The choir and Lady Chapel of the present church are survivals from this date. In medieval times St Mary Overie was the scene of many elaborate religious ceremonials, processions and various events involving royalty. In 1406 Edmund Holland, earl of Kent, was married to Lucia, eldest daughter of Barnaby, lord of Milan. King Henry IV himself 'gave away' the bride and conducted her to the marriage banquet at Westminster Palace. Eighteen years later, in 1424, James I of Scotland was wedded here to the golden-haired beauty Jane Beaufort, daughter of the earl of Somerset.

The name of 'St Saviour' was attached to St Mary Overie during Reformation times. The priory was dissolved in 1539, and St Mary's was purchased by the members of two nearby parishes and joined with a separate priory church called St Saviour's, whose name it acquired. During the reign of Mary Tudor the retro-choir was used as a consistorial court, presided over by Bishops Gardiner and Bonner. Here John Rogers and Bishop Hooper were condemned as heretics and sentenced to the stake, as were Bradford, Ferrar, Saunders and Taylor.

As might be suspected from its location near the old Globe Theatre, St Saviour's has associations with Chaucer and Shakespeare, as well as other famous literary figures. Shakespeare is commemorated by a memorial window as well as an alabaster monument. John Gower, the friend of Chaucer and a substantial benefactor to this church, is buried here; as is Edmund Shakespeare, brother of the bard; the dramatists Fletcher and Massinger; and Lawrence Fletcher, a joint lessee of the Globe Theatre with Shakespeare and Richard Burbage. John Harvard, founder of the university that bears his name, was baptized in St Saviour's on 29 November 1607. A beautiful chapel is dedicated to him. The famous divine Launcelot Andrewes, one of the translators of the King James Version of the Bible, is commemorated by a fine tomb in the south aisle.

St Saviour's became the seat of a bishop in 1905, hence the present name of Southwark Cathedral. It has undergone a number of alterations and repairs over the centuries: the famous Lady Chapel became a bakery in the seventeenth century and has been restored twice, the stone nave vault collapsed in 1469 and was rebuilt then and again in 1890. A railway bridge was built nearby in the nineteenth century, and during World War II it received considerable war damage, requiring a recent restoration. Yet St Saviour's is still today one of London's great medieval treasures, with a near-perfect Early English Lady Chapel, a choir and retro-choir that are among the earliest Gothic work in London, and numerous monuments and famous associations. ▶ Medieval London **M** Map location, D-6

Spanish & Portuguese Synagogue Located on a short street called Bevis Marks near the old Aldgate, this is the oldest synagogue in London (or in all of England, for that matter). It was moved to this location from Creechurch Lane in 1701. Its name may allude to the great exodus of Jews from Spain and Portugal during the Inquisition of 1492 and thereafter.

Speaker's Corner The north-eastern corner of Hyde Park near Marble Arch is where Londoners practise free speech in the open air, generally on Sunday afternoons. On a fine day in summer there will be some ten to twenty speakers mounted on portable platforms and haranguing the crowds on numerous subjects, but mainly politics and religion. There are eccentrics, radicals of every hue, exhibitionists, the inevitable Communists, and often some very gifted gospel preachers. In fact, it is not unusual for Christian speakers to outnumber all the others. This is the modern-day version of Paul's Cross, and it is well worth an hour to hear some of these Bible veterans defending Christian truth in the face of incredible invective and abuse. ▶ Twentieth-century London **M** Map location, E-7

Spurgeon, Charles (1834-92) The most successful preacher, evangelist and theologian in Victorian London by any standards was Charles Haddon Spurgeon. During a ministry of thirty-eight years he built up a congregation of 6,000, and it is estimated that over 14,000 new members were added to the church during this time. Spurgeon regularly preached in his Metropolitan Tabernacle to an audience of 5,000, and is said to have had an amazing ability to remember names of his members. He had a library numbering some 12,000 volumes, and he not only read a half-dozen substantial books a week, but also remembered what he had read and where. Spurgeon's sermons were originally published in fifty-six volumes, and these as well as numerous works by and about him are still being published and widely read.

Spurgeon, whose father and grandfather were both Nonconformist ministers, was called to the New Park Street Baptist Chapel, Southwark, in 1859. Soon overflowing crowds necessitated the building of the huge Metropolitan Tabernacle, on the site of which the third chapel of that name survives today (see Places and Monuments). His immense popularity and unconventional methods, such as preaching in Surrey Music Hall while his tabernacle was being prepared, led to much attention from the press and a great deal of harsh criticism. Undaunted by criticism, Spurgeon was a pioneer throughout his lifetime, establishing a famous pastors' training school now known as 'Spurgeon's College', temperance and clothing societies, an orphanage (still in existence), a mission and a colporterage association. He also helped to found the London Baptist Association.

Here is a description of Spurgeon by the London diarist Charles Greville:

> I am just come from hearing the celebrated Mr Spurgeon preach in the Music Hall of the Surrey Gardens. It was quite full; he told us from the pulpit that 9,000 people were present. The service was like the Presbyterian: Psalms, prayers, expounding a Psalm, and a sermon. He is certainly very remarkable, and undeniably a fine character; not remarkable in person, in face rather resembling a smaller Macaulay, a very clear and powerful voice,

which was heard through the whole hall; a manner natural, impassioned, and without affectation or extravagance; wonderful fluency and command of language, abounding in illustration, and very often of a familiar kind, but without anything either ridiculous or irreverent. He gave me an impression of his earnestness and his sincerity; speaking without book or notes, yet his discourse was evidently very care- fully prepared. The text was "Cleanse me from my secret sins"… He preached for about three-quarters of an hour, and to judge of the handkerchiefs and the audible sobs, with great effect.'

▶ Victorian London   **M** Portrait, National Portrait Gallery, H-9   Map location of Metropolitan Tabernacle, D-2

Stoke Poges Church and Churchyard   Country church and churchyard made famous by Thomas Gray's *Elegy*.   **M** Map location, N-1

Stow, John (1525-1605)   Stow, who was a tailor by trade, was recognized in his day as an accomplished antiquarian and historian, and published several works that were much appreciated by learned people, including the scholarly archbishop Matthew Parker. However, his name has come down to us through his one surviving book, the *Survey of London*. Stow's hobby consisted of minutely observing the London of his times during the reign of Queen Elizabeth and writing details of every church and public building, every square and street and alley. His laborious and exacting *Survey* was produced, literally, in his spare time. Born in 1525 in the parish of St Michael's, Cornhill, he lived and worked most of his days in a house near Aldgate Pump.

Near the end of Stow's life King James I was made aware that the distinguished old man was in financial need, but James merely authorized him to collect 'voluntary contributions and kind gratuities'—in other words, to beg. He died in poverty in 1605. Later his widow had a terra cotta monument placed over his grave in St Andrew Undershaft, where it may be seen to this day. It portrays him seated, feather pen in hand, with a book before him, and though squat and stiff it is said to be a good likeness. Each year a ceremony of replacing the pen is held by the Corporation of London, and the old pen is given to the author of the best essay on the City.   ▶ Elizabethan London   **M** Monument, St Andrew Undershaft, M-5

Tate Gallery   The Tate Gallery is located on Millbank facing the Thames between Lambeth and Vauxhall Bridges. There are sixty-two rooms featuring works of British artists from the sixteenth century to the present day. Of particular interest to Christian viewers are the following:

Room 6 - Painters of the Exotic and the Sublime   Room 7 - Blake and

followers   Room 15 - The Pre-Raphaelites   Room 16 - High
Victorian Painting

There is a good-sized shop where one can buy books about artists and
their works, prints, slides and so on. A self-service restaurant is in the
basement.
M Map location, C-8

Taylor, J. Hudson (1832-1905)   The famous founder of the China Inland
Mission established a missionary training base at Newington Green
which was used by the China Inland Mission (now Overseas
Missionary Fellowship) until after World War II. The entry arch with
the words 'Trust In God' may still be seen (one of the few structures in
the area to escape the bombing), as can panels of Chinese characters
on the main building.

Temple Church   During the Crusades, many churches were built by the
Knights Templar and Knights Hospitaller, often 'in the round' to
imitate the Church of the Holy Sepulchre in Jerusalem. Temple
Church is the most historically prominent of all the round churches
in Europe, of which there are four in England. It unites the round
arches of Norman architecture with the Gothic pointed arches in
Early English style in one building, and has the only Norman doorway
in London. It is a magnificent monument to the best ideals of the
Crusades and is a visible link with that most interesting (and tragic)
period in church history.

Under 'The Crusades and London' the story is told of how the
Templars moved to this plot of ground by the Thames in 1161 and
built a place of worship. This consisted of a round nave (the one seen
today) on the west and a rectangular chancel on the east. Note the
inscription above the entrance door telling about the dedication by
Heraclius, the patriarch of the Church of the Holy Sepulchre. The
chancel was later enlarged in Early English style and was consecrated
in 1240 in the presence of King Henry III.

Looking at the present-day Temple Church from the pleasant
courtyard on the south side, the Norman nave on the left and the
Early English chancel on the right, it is difficult to imagine the many
stages of renovation and restoration that this ancient structure has
undergone, leaving it at last very much like the original. During the
reign of Charles II, as part of a 'beautification' plan, formal pews were
installed and the walls were covered with oak wainscoting to a height
of eight feet. The arches where the nave and chancel join were filled
with a screen and ornate organ gallery furnished by Christopher
Wren, creating two churches. An enormous screen in the classic style
was built at the east end of the chancel. In the round church a large
pulpit and sounding board were erected in the centre under the dome.
In the eighteenth century there were liberal applications of
whitewash, paint and gilt. Finally, at the end of the nineteenth

century, removal of this embellishment was begun. The nave roof was destroyed during an air raid in 1941, but the work of restoring Temple Church to its original state was completed after World War II.

Various striking reminders of the days of the Knights Templar are evident in Temple Church. On the floor of the round church are the remains of several recumbent figures in mail dating from the thirteenth century or possibly before. At one time there were eight, not representing members of the Order itself but generous 'associates'. These included the rather notorious Geoffrey de Magnaville in the cylindrical helmet; the warrior and statesman William Marshall, Protector of England during the minority of King Henry III; William Marshall the younger, one of the leaders of the barons who forced King John to sign the Magna Carta; Gilbert Marshall, Earl of Pembroke; and the praying figure of Robert Lord de Ros, another of the Magna Carta barons. The rest of the figures are unknown.

Another relic of Crusader days is the fine sculpture of a bishop in a recess in the south aisle wall. His identity is uncertain. Also in the wall by the south aisle is an early double piscina (drain where the chalice was cleansed). Evidence that the Crusader brotherhood was an order of almost unbelievable strictness may be seen by the door in the northwest corner, which opens into the tiny penitential cell. Disobedient members were confined here in chains with no room to lie down. One brother, Walter le Bacheler, knight and Grand Preceptor of Ireland, was actually starved to death here.

Oliver Goldsmith, friend of Samuel Johnson and author of *The Vicar of Wakefield* and *Deserted Village*, was buried in Temple Church in 1774, but his monument perished in the bombing. Likewise the monument of the famous sixteenth-century divine, Richard Hooker, author of the *Laws of Ecclesiastical Polity*, who died in 1600.

Today Temple Church is the private chapel for the lawyers of the Temple, and it is not under the jurisdiction of the bishop of London. It also has a tradition of fine music and has had the distinction of several outstanding organists. Its choir has become known throughout the world through recordings. ▶ Medieval London
M Map location, J-20

Thirty-Nine Articles The doctrinal statement of the Church of England and, officially, what Anglicans believe. The Thirty-Nine Articles were forged during the Reformation period, beginning in 1536 under Henry VIII with Ten Articles, revised to Forty-Two Articles under Edward VI, revised in 1563 under Elizabeth I to thirty-eight and finally, in 1571, to thirty-nine. Thomas Cranmer and Nicholas Ridley played significant parts in their development. Matthew Parker guided their final shape under Elizabeth. ▶ Elizabethan London

Thompson, Francis (1859-1907) Francis Thompson is remembered today almost solely for his great allegorical poem of God's pursuit of an individual soul, 'The Hound of Heaven'. Its opening lines are as follows:

I fled Him down the nights and down the days,
I fled Him, down the arches of the years;
I fled Him, down the labyrinthine ways
Of my own mind; and in the midst of tears
I hid from Him; and under running laughter.

The poet was educated for the Roman Catholic priesthood, switched to medicine and, failing at that, moved to London where he became a vagrant and opium addict. He was rescued by Wilfred and Alice Meynell, who cared for him the rest of his short life and to whom his first volume, *Poems*, was dedicated in 1893 (in which 'The Hound of Heaven' appears). His second collection, *Sister Songs*, was published in 1895. ▶ Victorian London ◼ Sketch, plaster cast of life-mask, National Portrait Gallery, H-9

Toleration Act of 1689   In the first year of the reign of William and Mary, following the 'Glorious Revolution' and the flight of James II, Parliament passed a Toleration Act, giving relief to Nonconformist bodies. Such groups as Baptists and Congregationalists, though required to register as Nonconformists, were permitted to have their own places of worship and their own pastors and teachers (provided these were willing to accept the Thirty-nine Articles and take certain oaths of loyalty). Catholics were also included under this act, though all Nonconformists were still subject to restrictions and debarred from public office. ▶ Restoration London

Towers, Ruins and Gardens   Here and there scattered about Old London are a number of towers formerly of churches that have now disappeared, along with some other ruins or sites of ruins that have been made into public gardens. These landmarks happily have been left to remind us of the ancient city that once had more than 100 churches within its walls. Try to keep an eye out for the following:

All Hallows, Staining, M-3. The original medieval building fell down in 1671, was rebuilt, and the later church demolished in 1870 except for the tower.

Christ Church, Newgate Street, J-2. Wren built one his most expensive churches here on the site of the chancel of the old Franciscan friary church, 1677-91. The buildings of the friary were used for Christ's Hospital, a famous foundling school for boys (Bluecoat Boys) which continued on this site until 1902. In 1940 the church was gutted by incendiaries, but the beautiful steeple was spared and later restored by Lord Mottistone in 1960. The ruined walls and burial ground are now laid out as a garden.

St Alban, Wood Street, K-6. The church here was probably founded in Saxon times, may have been rebuilt by Inigo Jones in 1633-34, then was partly rebuilt by Wren after the Great Fire. All but the tower was removed after destruction in the bombing.

St Augustine with St Faith's, L-2. Wren built this church east of St Paul's with a slender spire similar to St Martin-within-Ludgate to act as a foil to the broad dome of the cathedral. The church was destroyed in the bombing but the spire has been restored (in fibre-glass) to its original shape. The modern St Paul's Choir School has replaced the church.

St Alphage, London Wall, K-7. An early church was built against the wall itself, but the original of this tower was a fourteenth-century priory church. The chancel was rebuilt in 1777, then all but the medieval tower was demolished in 1924.

St Dunstan's-in-the-East, M-8. The original church on this site was dedicated in Saxon times. It was partly burned in 1666 and repaired by Wren, who built its famous steeple with a spire set on flying buttresses ('crown spire'). It was rebuilt again in the nineteenth century. Burnt out by incendiaries in 1941, the steeple and walls have been preserved and the site laid out as a public garden. The weathered Portland stone of the ruins is said to be especially beautiful in the evening.

St Mary Somerset. Only the tower remains.

St Martin Orgar, Martin Lane, D-5. The first church was burned in the Great Fire but not completely destroyed. The parish was united with St Clement, Eastcheap, and the ruins patched up and used by a French Protestant congregation until demolished in 1820. The old tower stood until 1851 and then it too was pulled down. But oddly enough it was replaced by a new and loftier tower which stands today. The churchyard also remains.

St Mary Somerset, Upper Thames Street, L-10. This Wren church was pulled down in 1871 except for the tower with its elegant crown of tall obelisks and urns. The ornaments were removed for safety during the blitz but have been carefully restored by the City Corporation.

St Mary Aldermanbury, K-14. The site of this Wren church dedicated to the Virgin (Aldermanbury, the name of the street, means 'court of the alderman') has been laid out as a public garden. After the bombing the stones were numbered and shipped to the campus of Westminster College, Fulton, Missouri, where the church was reconstructed as faithfully as possible to the original plan. It stands as a memorial to Winston Churchill and the wartime co-operation between the United States and Great Britain. It was here, in March 1946, that Churchill made his famous 'Iron Curtain' speech.

St Olave, Old Jewry, K-15. The Wren church that stood here was demolished in 1887-88 except for the tower, which was converted into an entrance to offices and a house, the rectory of St Margaret Lothbury. The buildings were destroyed in World War II, exposing some medieval portions of the pre-Wren church wall. The tower and churchyard remain.

The Tower of London   The Chapel of St John the Evangelist in the White Tower and the Chapel Royal of St Peter-ad-Vincula on Tower Green, while both part of the Tower of London, appear separately under the heading of Churches and Chapels. But something needs to be said about the role of the Tower of London in general in the history of Christian London.

The Tower of London, London's most important historical treasure after Westminster Abbey, is a typical medieval fortress consisting of a central tower or 'keep' (the White Tower), inner and outer defensive walls and battlements, and a moat (now dry) crossed by a single drawbridge. Its fame arises from its strategic location at the southeast corner of the old City of London and from its use as a royal prison (it also served as a royal residence up until Tudor times). Stories growing out of its long and romantic history are inexhaustible; the yeoman warders never tire of telling about the murder of King Henry VI in the Wakefield Tower, of the two little princes done away with in the Bloody Tower by assassins hired by Richard III, of the tragic execution of Lady Jane Grey, and of Sir Walter Raleigh's long imprisonment, during which he wrote a *History of the World*.

Since the days of Wyclif the Tower has played a grim part in Christian history, as the laws against heretics and the shifting religious positions of the monarchs during the Reformation brought many dissenting churchmen and not a few laymen here. Some of the

more famous include the Lollard Sir John Oldcastle, Bishop John Fisher, Sir Thomas More, Bishops Nicholas Ridley and Hugh Latimer, Archbishop Thomas Cranmer, Archbishop William Laud, the Puritan divine Richard Baxter and the Quaker William Penn (who wrote a book, *No Cross, No Crown*, within its walls). Untold numbers of Lollards, monks from the dissolved monasteries, Jesuits, and Nonconforming Christians of all sorts, suffered in the Tower over the centuries, and many gave up their lives on Tower Hill nearby.
▶ Medieval London   **M** Map location, M-19

Tyburn   A village on the banks of a brook of the same name, it became a place of execution as early as the fourteenth century. At first elm trees in the district served as hanging trees, but later a gallows was erected roughly on the same site now occupied by Marble Arch. Here, in addition to innumerable highwaymen, murderers and traitors, perished the abbot and monks of the Carthusian monastery replaced by Charterhouse and a great many Catholic priests up to 1688. Tyburn is depicted in a painting of Catholic martyrs in Brompton Oratory.   **M** Map location of Marble Arch, E-7   Map location of Brompton Oratory, A-1

Tyler, Wat (died 1381)   Leader of the Peasant's Revolt of 1381. The mobs did great damage to many London churches as well as to Lambeth Palace, Savoy Palace and other buildings associated with the established church. Tyler was stabbed to death by the Lord Mayor and his men.   ▶ Medieval London

Tyndale, William (?1494-1536)   William Tyndale, who in some ways ranks next in importance to Henry VIII himself as a prime mover of the English Reformation, was a gifted scholar in languages at Oxford when he discovered Erasmus's Greek New Testament. This discovery redirected his life; he became proficient in his knowledge of the Bible and began to give lectures. Before long he met opposition from the religious authorities. He moved to Cambridge, where there was considerable underground interest in the Lutheran Reformation, but was driven by the threat of arrest to the west of England. Here he became a tutor in the house of Sir John Walsh in the tiny Cotswold village of Little Sodbury. His famous words spoken to an arrogant prelate expressed his dangerous plan: 'If God spare my life, I shall cause the boy that driveth the plow to know more of the Bible than thou dost!'

Through a friend of Sir John Walsh, Tyndale secured a preaching post at St Dunstan's-in-the-West, London, and a rich merchant, Humphrey Monmouth, who heard him there allowed him to work in his home. For six months Tyndale, assisted by his Cambridge friend John Frith, worked on New Testament translation in London. But again persecution caught up with him, and in 1524 he fled England to spend the last twelve years of his life in Europe. He first went to

Hamburg, then to Wittenberg to confer with Luther, then to Cologne, where printing was finally commenced on the first edition of his New Testament. He was followed here by an English spy who notified the religious authorities, and Tyndale barely escaped to Worms with his unfinished sheets. In Worms the first completed New Testaments, around 6,000, came off the press by the end of 1525.

In order to get the books back into England Tyndale enlisted the help of several sympathetic merchants, and the New Testaments were packed into barrels, sacks and crates and hidden by other

William Tyndale was the great Bible translator of Reformation times. His work underlies the Authorized (King James) Version.

merchandise. In four years 15,000 copies were circulating all over Great Britain. In desperation, the bishop of London engaged an agent named Packington to buy all the remaining copies to burn at Paul's Cross. But this plan backfired as Packington went straight to Tyndale who recognized it as an excellent opportunity to finance a new edition. A deal was struck, and as John Foxe says in the *Book of Martyrs*, 'the bishop of London had the books, Packington had the thanks and Tyndale had the money'.

Tyndale moved to Marburg then to Antwerp, for a time escaping the spies of Cardinal Wolsey who were hunting for him throughout Europe. He completed the translation of the first five books of the Old Testament, and a number of papers and tracts. During his stay in Antwerp he had a special copy of his New Testament printed on vellum and illuminated, and sent this as a gift to Queen Anne Boleyn. It was this that she later carried with her and read while awaiting execution in the Tower of London (it may be seen in the British Library). Eventually, in 1535, Tyndale was trapped by a spy named Henry Philips who had gained his confidence. For sixteen months he was confined in the dungeon of Vilvorde Castle. On 6 October 1536, he was strangled and burned, his last words being a prayer, 'Lord, open the king of England's eyes.' ▶ Reformation London **M** Statue, Victoria Embankment Gardens, C-9 Medallion, Westminster Abbey, C-10 Alleged likeness, National Portrait Gallery, H-9 Small face in stone at entrance to St Dunstan's-in-the-West (J-14) said to be likeness Anne Boleyn's copy of Tyndale Bible in British Library, H-1

Victoria & Albert Museum The Victoria & Albert, located in South Kensington, is one of the largest collections of applied art in the world. It started in 1852 as the Museum of Manufactures founded by Prince Albert, with the object of providing models which craftsmen could study and use to improve the decorative design of manufactured items. It became part of the South Kensington Museum in 1857 and was given its present name by Queen Victoria in 1899 when she laid the foundation stone for the Museum's extension.

The Victoria & Albert contains every kind of applied art imaginable: ceramics, furniture, woodwork, musical instruments, textiles, clothing, glass... and includes also prints, drawings and paintings. Of particular interest to Christians are a wealth of objects from the late Roman period and the Middle Ages related to the church and Christian worship—altar furniture, reliquaries, candlesticks, stained glass, book covers, statuettes and so forth. Many of the Renaissance items also have Christian significance, including Room 48 which contains seven of ten cartoons by Raphael designed as patterns for tapestries woven in Brussels for the Sistine Chapel (1515-16).

See in particular:

Room 43 - Decorative Art From Early Christian to Gothic

Rooms 22-24 - Gothic Art of Italy, England, France, Germany
Rooms 11-20 - Renaissance Italy
Rooms 26-27 - Renaissance Northern Europe
Room 21 - The High Renaissance
M Map location A-9

Walls and Gates of Old London   The walls and especially the gates of
Old London were popular places for churches and chapels, as they
were close to main thoroughfares where great crowds passed
continually. The medieval walls, which generally were built on
Roman foundations, began at the Tower on the banks of the Thames
east of the City. They described a semi-circle around to the Thames
west of the City where a fortification called Bayard's Castle stood.

There were seven gates: Aldgate, Bishopsgate, Moorgate,
Cripplegate, Newgate, Aldersgate and Ludgate. There was also a gate
at the northern approach to London Bridge. Today the physical walls
with their gates and bastions have virtually disap- peared. But
churches remain on the sites of six of the gates, and another stands on
the line of the old wall.   All Hallows, London Wall, M-2   St Botolph,
Aldersgate, K-10   St Botolph, Aldgate, M- 6   St Botolph, Bishopsgate,
M-7   St Giles, Cripplegate, K-11   St Martin-within-Ludgate, J-18   St
Sepulchre-without-Newgate, J-19   ▶ Medieval London

Walton, Izaak (1593-1683)   One of the most beloved figures of English
literature is Izaak Walton, author of *The Compleat Angler, or the
Contemplative Man's Recreation*, first published in 1653. He is also the
author of biographies of John Donne and the saintly George Herbert,
among others. As the title suggests, Walton's immortal book is not
only a manual on how to fish but also an expression of delight in the
natural good things that God has given. Walton loves everything
connected with the country and its rivers and streams, including the
unaffected country people and the good food, drink and
companionship of snug country inns.

Izaak Walton lived in London near Chancery Lane for a time, and
was acquainted with the poet Ben Jonson and also was a close friend
of John Donne. He was on the vestry board of St Dunstan's-in-the-
West, a fact noted by a plaque near the entrance of that church. He
was married to the sister of Bishop Ken, the hymn writer. In the early
seventeenth century the countryside was still hard by the walls of
London, and Walton used to fish in the River Lea which ran through
the fields near present day Tottenham Court Road.   ▶ Stuart &
Commonwealth London   M Portrait, National Portrait Gallery, H-9
Mentioned in entrance to St Dunstan's-in-the-West, J-14

Wars of the Roses and the Reformation   In the fourteenth century one
of England's kings, Edward III, reigned from 1327 to 1377, an
extraordinarily long time. His eldest son and heir apparent, Edward,
known as the 'Black Prince', died before his father, and thus when

Edward III died there was no clear successor to the throne. Parliament solved this problem by declaring the Black Prince's twelve-year-old son as King Richard II. But this move was disputed by other members of Edward III's family. Thus between 1377 and the succession of Henry VII in 1485 the line of royal descent was often under dispute, and the right to the throne was claimed by various candidates who were in the line of one or another of Edward III's four sons.

After some twenty years on the throne, Richard II had become exceedingly unpopular and was deposed by his cousin Henry of the House of Lancaster, son of John of Gaunt, Edward III's third son. The crown then remained in the hands of the Lancasters for three generations of kings—Henry IV, Henry V and Henry VI. But in 1461, after a long period of strife, Edward of the House of York, a descendant of Edward III's fourth son Edmund, seized the throne and was crowned Edward IV. For twenty-four years after this there were periods of bloody civil war, fought mainly by the nobles and their armed knights. These are popularly known as the 'Wars of the Roses': the emblem of the House of Lancaster was a red rose, and the emblem of the House of York was a white rose. Eight out of ten of Shakespeare's English historical plays deal with the dramatic events of this troubled period between 1377 and 1485.

Finally Henry Tudor, earl of Richmond, a Lancastrian who had descended through a daughter of John of Gaunt, ended this tragic conflict by slaying the Yorkist usurper, Richard III, at the Battle of Bosworth Field. As Henry VII he began a long period of peace and prosperity and was succeeded by his second son, Henry VIII. It is not difficult for anyone to understand how Henry VIII, being thoroughly familiar with the history of his own succession, would view with the greatest alarm the possibility of his dying without a male heir and plunging England once again into a period of disputed succession.

▶ Reformation London

Watts, Isaac (1674-1748)

Isaac Watts is known as the founder of modern English hymnology, so called because he was the first to compose divine poetry specifically to be sung. Prior to his time only the Psalms were sung in Protestant churches. Watts also used the Psalms as a basis for Christian hymns in his *The Psalms of David Imitated in the Language of the New Testament* (1719), which included two of his most famous works, 'Oh God Our Help in Ages Past' (Psalm 90) and 'Jesus Shall Reign' (Psalm 72).

His first collection of hymns, published in 1707, was called *Hymns and Spiritual Songs*, and contained his best-known composition, 'When I Survey the Wondrous Cross'. *Divine and Moral Songs For the Use of Children* appeared in 1720, making him the first to publish children's hymns. Other works included *Horae Lyracae*, a book of Christian poems. He also wrote on logic, astronomy, theology, geography, English grammar and education. In addition,

Watts was one of the best preachers of his time, and he produced three volumes of discourses.

Watts was in frail health all his life and never married. He was educated in a dissenter's academy at Stoke Newington just north of London, and he eventually became pastor of a Congregational church on Mark Lane off Fenchurch Street. From 1712 until his death he lived at the country mansion of St Thomas and Lady Abney, and here most of his works were written. He was buried in Bunhill Fields and a medallion with his likeness was placed in Westminster Abbey. In 1845 an imposing monument was erected in his memory in Abney Park Cemetery on the site of Abney House. Dr Samuel Johnson said of him, 'Such he was, as every Christian church would rejoice to have adopted'. ▶ Classical Lon- don M Portraits, National Portrait Gallery, H-9 Sarcophagus, Bunhill Fields, K- I Medallion, Westminster Abbey, C-10 Monument, Abney Park Cemetery

Wesley, Charles (1708-88)   Charles was the younger brother of John Wesley, the eighteenth child and youngest boy of Samuel and Susanna Wesley. He was educated at the Westminster School, London, and was the founder of the Holy Club at Oxford, though John took the leadership. He joined John on the unfruitful missionary journey to Georgia and was also deeply impressed by the spiritual qualities of the Moravian believers. In 1738, three days before his brother John's conversion, he was lying ill in the house of a friend on Little Britain, London, and was reading Luther's commentary on Galatians. In his words, 'I now found myself at peace with God, and rejoiced in hope of loving Christ'.

Charles quickly threw himself into evangelistic endeavours, preaching in houses, prisons, churches until the doors were closed to him, and eventually in the open air. His impact was hardly less powerful than John's, but he did not engage in extensive travel. He married and made his home in Bristol near the New Room (as the Methodist Chapel was called) until 1771, when he moved to London. He died in 1788, and is buried in the old graveyard of St Marylebone Church, where his monument may be seen today.

The fame of Charles Wesley, however, rests not so much on his preaching as upon his hymns. Altogether, he wrote some 7,270 such compositions, making him the most prolific by far of all English hymnwriters. A significant number are widely known and sung today, including:

Hark, the Herald Angels Sing
O, For a Thousand Tongues
Christ the Lord Is Risen Today
Jesu Lover of My Soul
And Can It Be
Love Divine, All Loves Excelling
Soldiers of Christ Arise

▶ Classical London   **M** Medallion, Westminster Abbey, C-10   Monument, Old St Marylebone Churchyard, E-8   Plaque describing conversion on a building in Little Britain Plaque mentioning conversion on Aldersgate Street entrance to Postman's Park next to St Botolph, Aldersgate, K-10   His organ may be seen in Wesley's Chapel, K-16

Wesley, John (1703-91)   John Wesley was the founder of the Methodist church (though he thought of himself as a disenfranchized Anglican clergyman). He possibly had a greater influence upon England's social and spiritual life than any other person of the eighteenth century. At Oxford University he was a leader of a group of Christian activists called the 'Holy Club', and shortly after graduation he made a brief missionary journey to Georgia. But despite his intentions to serve God as a Christian minister, Wesley felt his life to be devoid of spiritual power. On the voyage to Georgia he met a company of German Moravians and was impressed by their example of faith. Through a Moravian friend in London, Wesley went 'most unwillingly' to a meeting in a house on Aldersgate Street on 24 May 1738. Here, he relates in his world-famous *Journal*, his heart was 'strangely warmed' as he listened to a reading from Luther's preface to Romans. This experience marks the beginning of his career as an evangelist.

Wesley visited the Moravian settlement in Germany and its leader, Count Zinzendorf, and returned to England convinced that God had given him a commission to evangelize Great Britain. At the suggestion of George Whitefield, he took to open-air preaching at the Kingswood mining area near Bristol in April 1739. He continued in this practice until just a few days before he died, travelling some 5,000 miles a year over unpaved roads and facing every kind of hardship and peril, including mob violence. The net result of his work was a mighty wave of conversions—in all levels of society but primarily among the working classes—and the establishment of hundreds of Methodist chapels. The changed lives of the converts made a powerful impact upon British society through a decrease in both crime and drunkenness and the practical application of Christian charity to relieve poverty and suffering.

Although born and raised in Epworth, Lincolnshire, where his father had been rector of the parish church, John Wesley was educated at the Charterhouse School and, later, made London the base for his preaching journeys. It was often his practice to follow a triangle in these journeys, with Bristol on the west and Newcastle in the north as the other two angles. Chapels and a headquarters for training preachers were eventually established in all three cities.

For many years Wesley rode horseback from place to place. As he grew older and became one of the best-known public figures in England, he rode in a carriage of varnished wood with painted yellow wheels. It is said that often some fifty horsemen would escort the lumbering vehicle from Hatfield into the City. He was stricken ill while preaching in the open air at Leatherhead and died at his London home next to the chapel on 2 March 1791. Both the chapel and the house are now objects of pilgrimage for Methodists and other Christians from around the world. ▶ Classical London M House on City Road, K-17 Chapel on City Road, K-17 Statue outside chapel, K-17 Tomb and monument at rear of chapel, K-17 Medallion, Westminster Abbey, C-10 Bronze replica of journal, outside London Museum, K-4 Plaque marking site of conversion, outside London Museum, K-4 Plaque commemorating conversion of Wesley brothers on gate of Postman's Park (Aldersgate Street side) Portraits, National Portrait Gallery, H-9

Wesley, Susanna (1669-1742) The famous mother of John and Charles was born in a still-standing house at the end of Spital Yard off Spital Square (marked by a plaque). Her father, the Rev. Samuel Annesley, was a Nonconformist minister ejected from his living at St Giles, Cripplegate in 1662. She gave up Nonconformity in 1689 and married Samuel Wesley, an ordained deacon and then priest in the Church of England. She combined intelligence with a disciplined piety and a loving Christian character, and she undertook the early education of each of her children at home. In her last years she lived with John at the Foundry Chapel. An impressive tombstone marks her grave in Bunhill Fields Burying Ground. It is said that her influence on John and Charles had much to do with the character of early Methodism. ▶ Classical London M Memorial tombstone, Bunhill Fields, K-1 Birth house, M-20

Wesley's Chapel The only Nonconformist chapel left standing in London from before the repeal of the Test and Corporation Acts is John Wesley's Chapel on City Road. Despite several expansions and reconstructions, this is essentially the same building in character and appearance that Wesley himself knew. Its story goes back some forty years before the foundation stone was laid, to 1739. This was just a year after he had begun his open-air ministry. But even then he realized that he needed a headquarters in London for his growing movement.

Wesley's first building was an old foundry located in the Moorfields, which had been ruined by an explosion. It was purchased for £115 and cost another £800 to make useable. There was a chapel which could seat about 1,500, a smaller meeting room, a school room, a book room, and up above was a set of rooms where Wesley lived with his mother. Here, in the wintertime, he preached Sunday evenings and weekday mornings at 5 a.m. And here he founded a free school, a free medical dispensary and a refuge for women and children.

The Moorfields were at this time still open, swampy ground, used for sports and ice skating and infested with robbers at night. The road from Moorgate led north through this area, and a bit further out on the west side was Bunhill Fields. The swamp across the road from the burying grounds had been filled in with earth excavated during the rebuilding of St Paul's Cathedral, and there were windmills nearby used in grinding flour for bread. Here, in 1777, Wesley rented an acre of ground for the site of his new chapel.

On 21 April 1777, John Wesley pushed his way through a huge crowd to lay the cornerstone of the new chapel. Then he stood on the stone and preached from Numbers 23:23, 'According to this time it shall be said: What hath God wrought?' The work took about eighteen months, with various delays caused by shortage of funds, stolen tools, and so on. The first public worship meeting was held on All Saints Day, 1778. Most of the money for the chapel came from small gifts but there were a few large ones as well. The pillars used to support the gallery were masts from warships donated by King George III.

In 1879 the chapel was damaged by fire but was restored in the original style. Then, in 1891, 100 years after Wesley's death, a major renovation was undertaken, with contributions from Methodists in many countries. King George's masts were replaced with marble pillars; stained glass windows and the present oak pews were installed; and the foundations were strengthened with concrete.

During World War II the bombing in the area of City Road levelled buildings in all directions, but miraculously Wesley's Chapel and his nearby house came through intact. However, by 1972 the chapel was condemned as unsafe for public use. An international fund-raising campaign brought nearly a million pounds from Methodists in twenty-four countries. On All Saints Day, 1978, the restored building was reopened in the presence of Queen Elizabeth and the Duke of Edinburgh. Today, Wesley's Chapel, with the founder's grave at the back and an impressive statue of him in the forecourt, is open to visitors daily (apply at Wesley's House). It is a shrine, not only of Methodism, but of the entire Nonconformist heritage in London.

▶ Classical London **M** Map location, K-17

Westminster Abbey Westminster Abbey is one of the world's most famous churches, certainly the best known in the English-speaking world. Whole books have been written about it, and indeed the wisest thing for a first-time visitor to do is go into the Abbey Bookshop and buy an illustrated guide. However, these few paragraphs will serve as a general introduction.

Back in very early Saxon times, when monastic communities were springing up all over Europe, a group of Benedictine monks settled on a tract of land surrounded by the waters of the Thames at high tide and known as the Isle of Thorns. Though the monastery was known at the time of Dunstan (960), no traces of it have ever been found. The most important fact is that this was the site chosen by the pious Saxon King Edward (1042-66) for his new palace. Edward had been brought up partly in the royal court of Normandy and was a good friend of Duke

William, later known as 'the Conqueror'. When Edward decided to rebuild the monastery abbey which would serve as his final resting place, it was logical that he would employ the new Norman style of construction. Edward the Confessor's church, then, became the first Norman building in England (and the largest in either England or Normandy). Nothing now remains of this church above ground, though its foundations have been discovered and scholars have determined that it occupied roughly the same area as the present Abbey.

Edward the Confessor was buried before the high altar of his newly finished church in 1066, and thus he began a tradition that was to last until George II was laid to rest in Westminster Abbey in 1760, nearly 700 years later. In all, thirty-two sovereigns or their consorts are interred here, though only seventeen have monuments. The last monument to be erected was that of Queen Elizabeth I. Considerably before 1760 some monarchs and their consorts (Henry VIII, Jane Seymour and Charles I) were buried in St George's Chapel, Windsor Castle, and most have since been buried there as well.

On Christmas Day, 1066, the same year that Edward the Confessor was buried in the Abbey, William the Conqueror was crowned here as William I of England. That has been an unbroken tradition (excepting only Edward V and Edward VIII) to the present day. In 1296 the great king Edward I captured the ancient Scottish coronation stone at Scone and brought it to England. A year later he had a special coronation chair made, with a place for the Stone of Scone underneath the seat. This was used for the coronation of Edward II in 1327, and at every coronation since, and has rested in the Abbey continuously except for short periods during the Commonwealth and World War II. The Stone of Scone disappeared for a short time after a break-in on Christmas Eve, 1950, but was found in Scotland a few weeks later.

As we know from Chaucer, the Middle Ages were a time when English men and women of every class 'longen to goon on pilgrimages'. The pilgrims sought the shrines of martyrs such as that of King Edmund in Gloucester Cathedral. Soon after Edward's death, they began to throng to Westminster. In the thirteenth century King Henry III, when still a boy, was present at Canterbury Cathedral when the body of Thomas a Becket was placed in a new tomb, soon to become one of the most famous shrines in all Christendom. Henry was proud of his Anglo-Saxon ancestry and was devoted to the veneration of Edward the Confessor. Some years later he decided to build a new tomb for the remains of Edward behind the high altar and to rebuild the church itself. The work was started at the east end in 1245, under the direction of the architect Master Henry of Reyns, and by 1269 had been rebuilt in the new Gothic style as far west as the choir. On 13 October of that year the body of the Confessor was placed in a magnificent gold shrine resting on a Purbeck marble and mosaic base. Though sadly defaced, it remains today one of the great treasures of English history.

Work on the nave was commenced in 1475, during the reign of Richard II, but for various reasons it took over 150 years before it was entirely completed. Fortunately Henry Yevele, Richard II's mason and a great architect, determined that the nave should be a unity with the rest of the building by carrying on the original plan of Henry III. Henry IV, Richard's successor, neglected Westminster Abbey and gave liberally to Canterbury, planning to be himself interred near Becket's shrine. However, by a strange irony he was praying at the shrine of the Confessor when death by a stroke overtook him. The next king, the famous warrior Henry V (immortalized by Shakespeare as Prince Hal), continued the work on the nave, and during his time the great west window and the vaulting were completed.

It was in January 1503 that work commenced on a chapel that was to become one of the most perfect examples in all England of the perpendicular style of Gothic architecture. The first of the Tudor monarchs, Henry VII, had decided to erect a shrine for the remains of Henry VI, but this was destined to be his own monument. From the beautiful carved stalls to the glorious stained glass to the exquisite fan vaulting high above all, this was a magnificent piece of work. And it remains so today, despite the loss of most of the original glass.

The Reformation caught up with Westminster Abbey on 14 January 1540, when the monastery was dissolved under Henry VIII. Before long many of its moveable treasures were sold off and scattered, and much which was not moveable was defaced. Because of its important place in England's history the building itself, including Henry VII's chapel, was fortunately spared. A further disaster, however, occurred during the Civil War, when in 1643 a committee was appointed to demolish 'monuments of superstition and idolatry'. It was at ths time that the glass in Henry VII's Chapel was destroyed, together with other priceless works of art.

Two other interesting developments during Reformation times were the founding of the famous Westminster School and the end of the right of sanctuary for debtors. The former got its start when Henry VIII founded the College of St Peter, Westminster. A grammar school which had operated on the precincts for some 200 years was incorporated into the new College, and under Queen Mary the sons of many prominent people in the court were sent there. Over the years Westminster has taken its place beside Eton and Winchester as one of England's great educational institutions. The right of sanctuary for debtors at Westminster had been granted by Edward the Confessor. While within the precincts, the fugitive was safe from his adversaries so long as he took an oath to behave himself properly, wear no weapons and not go out of bounds. This right was finally abolished by Parliament in 1623.

A third great tradition involving Westminster Abbey (following coronations and royal burials) got its start at the Dissolution. From being the church of a monastery and the burial place of kings, Westminster Abbey became a national possession where commoners, too, could be laid to rest. At first these included courtiers and wealthy individuals of no particular distinction. But gradually it became an established policy for the nation's heroes either to lie in Westminster Abbey after death or to be commemorated there. Further, there has been a tendency for great persons of a particular calling to be grouped around a key figure—statesmen around Chatham, poets around Chaucer, musicians around Purcell, scholars around Casaubon, scientists around Newton, and so on. Of special interest from the perspective of Christian history are the grave of David Livingstone in the centre of the nave, the monument of the seventh earl of Shaftesbury near the west door, a tablet to William Tyndale and medallions to John Wesley, Charles Wesley and Isaac Watts in the south choir aisle.

The two imposing west towers of Westminster Abbey were built in 1738-39 by John James, successor to Nicholas Hawksmoor, who in turn was a successor to Christopher Wren. Wren was appointed Architect to the Abbey in 1698. It was his idea to have a central tower with a spire, but for one reason or another neither he nor Hawksmoor was able to complete this plan. But Wren and Hawksmoor did recast the exterior of the Abbey and fill the north and west windows with glass executed by Joshua Price. The medieval choir stalls were replaced in 1775, a sad loss, and other unfortunate changes made during the late eighteenth and early nineteenth centuries. However in 1849 Sir Gilbert Scott was appointed architect, and he was the first to use scientific means to preserve the Abbey. Since his day the value of this great London monument has been amply recognized. It stands now not only as London's number one tourist attraction but as a living reminder that England's history is inseparable from the Christian faith. ▶ Medieval London   **M** Map location, C-10

Westminster Cathedral This imposing Byzantine-style structure facing Victoria Street at the back of a small pedestrian piazza is the mother church of the diocese of Westminster. It is also the Metropolitan Church of all England and Wales; its archbishop is the ranking Roman Catholic prelate in the country. It was built just at the end of the Victorian era and the beginning of the twentieth century (1895-1903) specifically for this purpose. Cardinal Wiseman, the first archbishop of Westminster elected in 1850, had no church at all that could serve permanently as his cathedral.

The church measures 360-feet deep and 156-feet wide, and the cross atop its bell tower reaches a height of 284 feet. It is constructed of brick but ingeniously retains the impression of Byzantine ornateness. A great arch stretches over the main doorway, under which is a mosaic representing Christ our Lord holding an open book on which is written (in Latin): 'I am the gate: if any one enters by Me he shall be saved - John 10:9'. Mary and Joseph stand on either side, and kneeling are St Peter and St Edward the Confessor. Above the arch is an inscription large enough to be read at some distance (also in Latin): 'Lord Jesus, King and Redeemer, save us by Thy blood'.

The visitor entering Westminster Cathedral steps into a vestibule (narthex) from which an unobstructed view can be gained of the awesome 342-foot nave and, beyond, the sanctuary with its high altar and towering baldachino. Along the aisles and in the transepts are twelve chapels where mass is offered. Above are three towering domes, and from the main arch hangs a great thirty-foot rood. The eight, dark green columns that support the galleries were cut from the same quarry that supplied the marble for Santa Sophia in Istanbul. The chapels abound with works of religious art; the Chapel of the Holy Souls is said to display in completed form what the entire cathedral will some day be like. Of particular interest is the Chapel of St George and the English Martyrs, where Thomas More and John Fisher are represented in the altarpiece. ▶ Victorian London **M** Map location, B-6

Westminster Chapel Westminster Chapel is the best example of Victorian church architecture in Central London (as opposed to the Neo-Gothic style popular at the time, of which there are several fine examples). Like the Metropolitan Tabernacle and City Temple, it eloquently demonstrates the huge growth in popularity of the Nonconformist bodies during the nineteenth century. Originally a Congregational chapel (but now an Evangelical Free church), it was built in 1865 to seat 2,500 people. Even today two great galleries rise up on three sides, and the pulpit looks down from a lofty height, fashioned so the preacher could make himself heard to large crowds before public-address systems were invented.

This grand old chapel, located on Buckingham Gate not far from the palace, has been a focus of Bible-centered preaching from the beginning. Three of its ministers, in fact, have been internationally famous preachers and writers: Dr G. Campbell Morgan, 1904 to 1917 and 1933 to 1945; Dr John Henry Jowett, from 1918 to 1922; Dr Martin Lloyd-Jones from 1939 to 1977. It still draws a large crowd on Sunday mornings (though the second balcony is unused), and numerous activities are held during the week. ▶ Victorian London **M** Map location, B-7

Westminster Hall and St Mary Undercroft Westminster Hall forms a part of the present Houses of Parliament, and it is the building seen most prominently from Westminster Abbey across the way. It is the most ancient part of the Parliament buildings, having been first built by William II in 1097, and the present hall by Richard II in 1394-1402. From the thirteenth century until 1882 the chief English law courts sat here, at first in the hall itself and later in separate buildings.

It is now normally empty except when used for the lying-in-state of monarchs and eminent statesmen (among the latter Winston Churchill in 1965). It is a great architectural treasure, one of the largest and finest medieval timber-roofed buildings in Europe.

Here in Westminster Hall Sir Thomas More was condemned to death in 1535, Guy Fawkes in 1603 and Charles I in 1649. Here, in 1653, Oliver Cromwell was installed as Lord Protector. Beneath is St Stephen's Crypt, now known as St Mary Undercroft. Its beautiful medieval groined vaulting and ancient bosses have been restored and the crypt richly redecorated. While not open to the public it is still occasionally used for christenings and marriages in the families of members of Parliament. ▶ Medieval London **M** Map location, C-11

Whitefield, George (1714-70)

George Whitefield was a student at Pembroke College, Oxford, when he came into contact with the 'Holy Club' and subsequently experienced spiritual conversion. He was ordained and soon gained the reputation of being a gifted preacher. After a short period of service in London he accepted an invitation from the Wesleys to go to Georgia in 1737. On a visit home that same year he preached for the first time in the open air at Bristol, a practice which he continued for the remainder of his life. During this visit he also laid the foundations for the famous Kingswood School near Bristol. He then returned to Georgia until 1741.

Whitefield was an itinerant evangelist on a par with John Wesley in effectiveness, and (it is said) more eloquent in style. He often preached some twenty sermons a week, and travelled vast distances under hazardous conditions, including seven journeys across the Atlantic to America. In consequence of his association with Calvinistic divines in New England, including the famous Jonathan Edwards, he became convinced of their view of salvation (that the sovereign God pre-ordains man's salvation) as opposed to Wesley's Arminian view (that God's salvation is available to all men on the basis of free choice). While this divergence in viewpoint made no difference whatever in the quality or effectiveness of Whitefield's preaching, it separated him from the Wesleys. In 1743, in association with the Countess of Huntington, he founded the Calvinistic Methodist Society.

Like John Wesley, Whitefield tended to make his home in London and to return there after his frequent journeys. He first preached in the area of Islington, and over the years he filled the pulpits of many churches in Central London, in particular St Helen's.

His first tabernacle was in the Moorfields just north of Wesley's Foundry on a road called Windmill Hill (now Tabernacle Street). Later when he became better known Whitefield built a larger tabernacle on Tottenham Court Road which attracted great crowds, including certain of the important and famous as Lord Chesterfield, David Hume, Horace Walpole, David Garrick and the Prince of

Wales. Critics called it 'Whitefield's Soul Trap'. But he was ever mindful of the plight of the working classes and of orphans, widows, prisoners and others in need. A fitting tribute was written by the poet William Cowper:

> He followed Paul—his zeal a kindred flame,
> His apostolic charity the same.

▶ Classical London   M Whitefield Memorial Church (on site of Tabernacle), F-5   Portraits, National Portrait Gallery, H-9

Whitehall Banqueting House   One of the earliest Renaissance-style buildings in London (by Inigo Jones) and part of the uncompleted royal palace on Whitehall, it was also the scene of the execution of King Charles I. A bust of Charles I over the door commemorates the event. Located across from the Horseguards.   ▶ Stuart & Commonwealth London   M Map location, C-12

Whittington, Richard 'Dick' (died 1423)   Famous lord mayor and philanthropist of medieval London about whom various legends have come down to us.   ▶ Medieval London   M Memorial window (modern), St Michael Paternoster Royal, L-13

Wilberforce, William (1759-1833)   Wilberforce is best known for his role in the abolition of slavery, though he was involved throughout his life in numerous causes to further the gospel of Christ and the betterment of mankind. Among his goals were the improvement of manners and morals in English society and the evangelization of the upper classes, as Wesley had the working classes. He was active in the foundation of the Church Missionary Society and the British and Foreign Bible Society. Though a very little man, his eloquence in public speaking was legendary. James Boswell records that on hearing him 'the shrimp grew and grew and became a whale'.

After an education that included boarding schools and Cambridge University, Wilberforce became a Christian at age twenty-five through reading the New Testament with a former instructor, Isaac Milner, while on a tour through Europe. He had entered politics in 1780 at age twenty-one by being elected a member of Parliament for Hull. In 1784 he was elected for Yorkshire, a powerful seat that he held for twenty-three years. He associated himself with the Clapham Sect, and through friendship with John Newton and Thomas Clarkson of that group and the prime minister, William Pitt the Younger, he became involved in the campaign to abolish slavery. This was to occupy him for the rest of his life; the complete abolition of slavery did not occur until 1833, the year of his death.

In 1797 Wilberforce published his one great book, *Practical View of the Prevailing Religious System of Professed Christians in the Higher and Middle Classes in this Country Contrasted with Real Christianity*. For forty years it was a bestseller. As David Edwards says in *Christian England*, ' "Real Christianity" was to Wilberforce a straightforwardly biblical religion, to be accepted as the guide and rule of all human life. God's love for him was the essence; and the morality he urged was always loving conduct. So this *Practical View* had an influence both wide and deep in the classes to which it was addressed. Edmund Burke spent the last two days of his life reading it.'

Wilberforce and his fellow campaigners were often close to despair, and he himself was always in frail health. But no doubt he carried John Wesley's words to him in his heart. In the last letter of his life the great evangelist had written, 'Unless God has raised you up for this very thing, you will be worn out by the opposition of men and devils. But if God be for you, who can be against you? Are all of them together stronger than God?' In the end, not only did Wilberforce and his companions win a great moral victory, but their achievement opened the opportunity for evangelical missions to penetrate Africa and India. ▶ Classical London **M** Plaque on residence, 44 Cadogan Place, Chelsea, A-10 Portraits, National Portrait Gallery, H-9

The bells of St Mary-le-Bow called Dick Whittington back to London.

Williams, Charles (1886-1945) Williams, who for most of his career was
employed by the Oxford University Press in London (he moved with
the Press to Oxford in 1940), is now generally thought of as one of the
circle of Christian literary figures associated with C.S.Lewis and
J.R.R.Tolkien. His works include religious drama (including *Thomas
Cranmer of Canterbury*, 1936), poetry, criticism, theology (such as *He
Came Down from Heaven*, 1937), and a series of seven novels, which
he called 'metaphysical thrillers'. The last of these, *All Hallows' Eve*
(1945), is set in wartime London, and is probably the most eerie and
bizarre of them all. Yet it, too, develops the theme of Christ-like
redemption. Critics feel that Williams will be remembered longest for
his Arthurian poem, *Taliesin through Logres* (1938), and its sequel,
Region of the Summer Stars (1944). But a number of his books are still
in print, including all of the novels, and his popularity, though not as
great as that of Lewis or Tolkien, continues to grow. ▶ Twentieth-
century London

Williams, Dr, Theological Library In the latter part of the seventeenth
century Williams, a Welshman and notable preacher though without
formal education, became pastor of the Presbyterian chapel in Hand
Alley, London. After the death of Richard Baxter he was recognized
as the Presbyterian leader in the city. Through the money acquired by
marrying two well-to-do wives (at different times) he founded a
theological library that today consists of over 110,000 volumes. The
library, located on Gordon Square near the University of London, is
open to qualified research scholars. **M** Map location, G-7

Williams, George (1821-1905) George Williams began his career as a
draper's apprentice, and was converted through reading a book by the
American evangelist Charles Finney. He joined a draper's firm in
London and rose to be a partner. Williams was deeply interested in
the wellbeing and spiritual welfare of his fellow employees, and he was
an advocate of temperance and an opponent of tobacco and
gambling. In 1844 twelve young men, all but one fellow employees,
met in Williams's rooms to form the Young Men's Christian
Association. The goal was to win other young men to faith in Christ.

Lord Shaftesbury accepted the presidency of the Y.M.C.A. in
1851, which he held until his death in 1886. Williams himself then
became president for the rest of his life. He worked tirelessly to
develop the Y.M.C.A., which spread throughout the British Empire
and the United States. A world alliance was formed in Paris in 1855.
In 1894, upon the golden jubilee of the London 'Y', Williams was
knighted by Queen Victoria. Besides his work with the Y.M.C.A., he
was an active participant in the British and Foreign Bible Society, the
Church Missionary Society and several other Christian
organizations. ▶ Victorian London **M** Portrait, Central YMCA,
Tottenham Court Road at Great Russell Street, F-6 Portrait, National
Portrait Gallery, H-9 Medallion, crypt of St Paul's, L-15

Winslow, Edward (1595-1655) Winslow became a member of John Robinson's Separatist congregation in Leiden, Holland, while making a tour of the Continent. He subsequently became one of the 'Pilgrim Fathers' who sailed on the Mayflower to Massachusetts in 1520. He made the colonists' first treaty with the Indians and was the first to be mar- ried at Plymouth (to a widow, after his wife died during the first winter). He was a member of the governor's council and governor of Plymouth Colony in the years 1633, 1636 and 1644.

Business for the colony brought Winslow back to England several times. On one of these visits he was imprisoned by Archbishop Laud on the charge that he had taught in the church as a layman. He published a book on missionary efforts in Massachusetts, the *Glorious Progress of the Gospel among the Indians in New England*, and in 1649 was instrumental in getting Parliament to create the Society for the Propagation of the Gospel in New England, London's first missionary society. ▶ Stuart & Commonwealth London ▯ Named in Pilgrim Fathers Memorial, St Bride's Church, J-12

Wolsey, Thomas (c.1474-1530) We noted in the story of Thomas Becket how the English kings often used churchmen as counsellors and administrators. The reason for this was that in medieval times higher education was limited almost exclusively to men going into holy orders. So it was natural that the sovereign would find talented men among this class to whom he could entrust diplomacy and statesmanship. Much of Henry VII's success, for example, was due to the wisdom and skill of Cardinal Morton, archbishop of Canterbury, who was his chief advisor for most of his reign.

And so it was with Henry VIII for his first eighteen years on the throne. He chose a bold, articulate churchman named Thomas Wolsey, who in time was so relied upon by the king that he was the practical head of the government. In gratitude, Henry appointed him lord chancellor, archbishop of York, cardinal and papal legate. But when Wolsey failed, after much effort, to get the pope's approval for a divorce from Catherine, Henry removed him from office, took over his properties including his new palace of Hampton Court (which Wolsey voluntarily signed over to the king in the hope of appeasing him), and finally had him charged with treason. Mercifully, Wolsey died before being brought to trial. ▶ Reformation London ▯ Portrait, National Portrait Gallery, H-9 Hampton Court Palace, N-2

Wren, Christopher (1632-1723) The ashes of the City were not yet cool from the Great Fire of 1666 when plans for rebuilding were commenced. An Oxford professor named Dr Christopher Wren, skilled in mathematics, astronomy and model-making, was appointed by Charles II as Surveyor General. Wren, together with the bishop of London and the archbishop of Canterbury, made up the committee for reconstructing the City's churches.

Wren designed fifty-one of the churches himself, and others were designed by his surveyors. In each church he emphasized the font, the altar and the pulpit, underscoring the three essential functions of baptism, communion and preaching of the Word of God. In the seventeenth century the preaching of sound doctrine was considered of first importance, a result of the impact of the Reformation. The churches otherwise show wide variety, though understandably all are built of brick and stone and not of wood.

Wren's masterpiece was the great domed St Paul's Cathedral, and he carefully designed the exteriors of other churches so as to highlight the effect of St Paul's on the skyline. Even today, though there are taller modern buildings in London, St Paul's still dominates London's landscape. ▶ Restoration London **M** Portrait, National Portrait Gallery, H-9 Memorial on tomb, crypt of St Paul's, L-15

Wren Churches Sir Christopher Wren was primarily responsible for the sweeping introduction of neo-classical or English Renaissance church

St Paul's Cathedral, the masterpiece of the churches rebuilt by Wren after the Great Fire, is London's earliest Christian foundation.

buildings into London after the Great Fire of 1666. In place of the great spire of St Paul's there arose a stupendous dome; all over London, instead of the forest of medieval church towers that existed before the fire, an amazing variety of tiered steeples supported by arches and columns graced the skyline.

The Wren churches are unique to London. No city in the world—even Florence in Italy—has such a wealth of architectural treasures conceived by the genius of and constructed within the lifetime of one man. They are, moreover, the flowering of the Renaissance in England, originals, each different and unique in its own right. Yet each bears the marks of its maker and (for the most part) conforms to the neo-classical principles which Wren brought to perfection.

In all, Wren and his assistants were responsible for fifty-four new churches, fifty-one of them within Old London, plus St Paul's Cathedral. Let us now look at what has happened to them, and which of them have been spared for us to enjoy today:

In 1781 St Christopher-le-Stocks, Wren's only namesake and one of the first built, was destroyed in the Gordon Riots.

Fourteen were demolished in the course of London's modern development prior to World War I.

Three were totally destroyed in the blitz and one, St Mary Aldermanbury, was re-erected at Fulton, Missouri.

Five remain only as towers, or ruins within public gardens.

Fourteen which were damaged in the bombing have been restored and are once again in use. They are:

St Andrew, Holborn	St Lawrence, Jewry
St. Andrew-by-the-Wardrobe	St Mary Abchurch
St Anne & St Agnes	St Mary-le-Bow
St Bride, Fleet St	St Michael Paternoster Royal
St Clement Danes, Strand	St Nicholas, Cole Abbey
St James, Garlickhythe	St Stephen, Walbrook
St James, Piccadilly	St Vedast, Foster Lane

Ten received only minor damage or none at all. They are:

St Benet's Welsh Church	St Martin, Ludgate
St Clement, Eastcheap	St Mary Aldermary
St Magnus, London Bridge	St Mary-at-Hill
St Margaret Lothbury	St Michael, Cornhill
St Margaret Pattens	St Peter, Cornhill

In separate catagories are St Paul's Cathedral (L-15) and St Sepulchre, Holborn (J-19). St Sepulchre might be considered a Wren church that received only slight damage, but there is some question as to whether Wren was actually involved in the reconstruction after the Great Fire. Also much of the earlier structure remains. St Paul's, on the other hand, is something more than a church building. Although the east end and north transept of St Paul's received direct hits, the

west end and dome of this, one of the world's great Christian monuments and a symbol of the indomitable spirit of the people of London during the bombing, were miraculously preserved.
▶ Restoration London

Wyclif, John (or Wycliffe) (c.1320-84) John Wyclif was master of Balliol College at Oxford and a brilliant theologian and lecturer. His studies of the Scriptures led him to the conviction that priests and friars ought to live in poverty and that the state ought to seize the property of churchmen who lived immoral lives. He also questioned the secular power of the pope. While bitterly opposed by the clergy, his views gained wide acceptance. For a time he was given the support and protection of John of Gaunt, the duke of Lancaster, who acted as king while Richard II was still a minor.

In 1377 Wyclif was called to answer for his teachings before Bishop Courtenay at St Paul's Cathedral. The duke of Lancaster accompanied Wyclif to this meeting and engaged Courtenay in a heated argument. Before Wyclif had a chance to speak, the meeting broke up in confusion. Later that year, however, the pope condemned Wyclif's writings and in March 1378 Wyclif appeared before the archbishop at Lambeth Palace and was ordered to stop spreading his views. Only his influence at the royal court saved him from more severe punishment.

Wyclif's teachings grew even more radical after his hearing at Lambeth Palace. He argued that if the Bible was the only authority in matters of faith, 'all Christians and lay lords in particular, ought to know Holy Writ and to defend it'. He held that if the pope insists on maintaining unscriptural doctrines 'he is very antichrist', and that the doctrine of transubstantiation was philosophical nonsense not deducible from Scripture. He was forced, along with a number of others who sided with him, to leave Oxford in 1382.

Wyclif was an amazingly prolific writer, and he continued his work from 1382 to 1384 at his parish church in Lutterworth. He died of a stroke in December 1384 while conducting mass and was buried in the churchyard. In 1428 his remains were exhumed and burnt by papal order. A monument to Wyclif may be seen today in the crypt of St Paul's Cathedral.

The first Bible in Middle English associated with Wyclif's name was the work mainly of Nicholas of Hereford, though others including Wyclif himself may have been involved. It was a literal version from the Latin Vulgate intended for use by the clergy, and it appeared in 1384—the year of Wyclif's death. Several years later a revision was produced by John Purvey, Wyclif's secretary, which was more idiomatic and intended for the general reader. In 1408 the Constitutions of Oxford forbade the production or use of vernacular Scriptures except with official sanction, but Wycliffite Bibles were circulated and read secretly all throughout the fifteenth century.
▶ Medieval London   **M** Monument, crypt of St Paul's, L-15

Zinzendorf, Nicholas (1700-60) Nicholas Ludwig, Count von Zinzendorf, was the founder of the Moravian Brethren or Moravian Church. His family background and early life in Germany was within the Pietist movement, but his Christian experience broadened through contact with other branches of the church. In 1722 he established a Christian community for Bohemian refugees, called Herrnhut, on his estate at Berthelsdorf. It still exists in East Germany. The Community sent out numerous foreign missionaries, and he himself travelled widely preaching and establishing Moravian congregations. Sometime after 1736 he began a congregation in London and for five years did pastoral work there, 1749-50, 1751-55.

PART
2

LONDON
— FROM —
AGE TO AGE

BRITISH LONDON

(before AD43)

In the beginning of the Christian era—that is, when Jesus Christ was born in Roman Judea and Caesar Augustus ruled the Empire—the Latin civilization that had spread as far north as modern Belgium and France had barely penetrated the British Isles. Julius Caesar had twice made exploratory raids, but Britain was still a remote and mysterious island across the misty sea.

Where the Thames wends its way through the present metropolis of London there were in the times of Jesus vast forests on either sides with a margin of beach and large patches of swamp. Because of the river and the transportation it afforded, there was a settlement here and probably had been since people first occupied this island. It would have been evidenced by some sort of ford or ferry approximately on the site of London Bridge, crude timber docks on the north side. On the slope where Cannon Street Station is now located would have been a British village surrounded by a circular earthenwork fortification. The name of this village was probably something like 'Londinion', meaning 'wild' or 'bold', perhaps derived from the personal name 'Londinos'. From this (by way of the Romans) came the modern name of London.

These Britons were Celts, a group of tribes loosely linked by language, religion and culture that dominated Northern Europe for some seven centuries before the Romans came. They cultivated the soil, kept domesticated animals, wove cloth, made pottery, and mined for tin and iron. With the iron they invented chain armour and were the first to shoe horses, give shape to handsaws, files and other tools we use today, develop seamless rims for chariot wheels, and pioneer the iron ploughshare. Wielding beautifully crafted carbon-steel swords and clad in their chain mail, the wild and reckless British charioteers struck terror into the ranks of their enemies, whom they often challenged to single combat.

The religion of this British tribe was Druidism, a superstitious worship of the fairies and elves who lived in trees, springs and other natural places. The oak and the mistletoe were especially sacred. Formal religious ceremonies were led by a class of priests called Druids. In times of crisis they practised human sacrifice.

Remains of circular Celtic fortresses, villages and so on exist in fairly large numbers here and there in the British Isles, but no traces at all are left in London. However, the Romano-British collection in the British Museum and the British exhibit in the Museum of London include various Celtic artifacts and weapons, some of them dredged from the Thames, dating from the first century or before. This constitutes our scant knowledge of those first Londoners.

ROMAN LONDON
(43-449)

In AD43, about the time when persecution was driving the Christians of Jerusalem to Phoenicia, Cyprus and Antioch, a full-scale Roman invasion of southeast Britain took place, led by the Emperor Claudius himself. Soon Claudius' lieutenant and the first governor of Roman Britain, Aulus Plautius, arrived on the site of London, the first historical event of the city to be recorded. A significant fact has come down to us regarding this governor's wife, Pomponia Graecina. The description of her life and conduct by Roman historian Tacitus has led scholars to suspect that she was a Christian.

The Romans, who called the settlement 'Londinium', built their own docks, public buildings and villas on the north bank of the river on the same piece of high ground formerly occupied by the British fort. A diorama in the London Museum also shows a bridge across the Thames. Eventually the settlement spread over a tract roughly equivalent to one square mile. Around the year 360, walls were constructed which later became the foundations of the walls of medieval London. Even today the City proper is circumscribed by this boundary. Traces of the old Roman walls may be seen near the Tower of London, in Cannon Street and elsewhere, and excavations for new buildings still unearth Roman foundations.

The Romans brought Latin civilization with them, including their system of law and their pantheistic religion with the emperor as the head cult figure. Many discoveries have been made in London of the remains of altars, dedicated to Jupiter and other Greco-Roman gods, and also of heroic statues of the emperors, including Claudius. Unofficial religions apparently flourished as well; in 1954 the remains of a temple of Mithras were discovered near Queen Victoria Street. Late in the Roman era Christian worship probably took place in house-chapels, in surroundings that symbolized the Saviour by subtle artistry. The famous Lullingstone Pavement in the British Museum's Romano-British Collection is an example of this. But in the crypt of St Bride's church just outside the walls there is evidence of a Roman building that just may have been a Christian church.

The main source of our scanty knowledge about Christianity in Britain in Roman times is from *The History of the English Church and People*, written in 731 by Bede, a monk from Jarrow in Northumbria. We also have the works of a Christian Briton, Gildas, from the sixth century. Unfortunately there is little about London itself. We learn that in AD58 the Roman governor, Suetonius Plautinus, mounted an all-out attack on the western lands and effectively destroyed Druidism on Anglesey Island, its last stronghold. In AD60 Londinium was nearly wiped out by a fierce attack from the Iceni tribe led by Queen Boudica (or Boadicea). Her heroic statue (nineteenth century) is near the west end of Westminster Bridge. This uprising was suppressed by Suetonius Plautinus also. According to Gildas, it was shortly after this, in AD63, that Christianity was first introduced to Britain

The first bearers of the gospel to Britain were not Romans, but Greek traders — many more first-century Greeks than Romans were Christian and Greek ships made frequent visits to Roman Britain. (Legends of Simon Zelotes or one of the other apostles having preached in Britain have no historic foundation, however.) Apparently the Romanized Britons became Christians in substantial numbers, and also many of the occupying Roman troops. It should be borne in mind that the great missionary to the Irish, Patrick, was from a Romano-British Christian family. When the fierce persecution under Emperor Diocletian reached Britain in 303 we have the record of the first martyr, St Alban, who suffered for sheltering a Christian minister. Bede tells us that when the persecution subsided 'faithful Christians... came into the open and rebuilt the ruined churches'. So very probably numerous churches, with their clergy, existed by the beginning of the fourth century.

Constantine the Great, who in 313 issued the famous Edict of Milan granting religious liberty throughout the empire, was born in Britain. He was proclaimed caesar by the garrison at York on the death of his father in 306. Helena, his mother, became a devout Christian and spent the rest of her life doing works of charity. After 313 various councils of church leaders were held in Europe and Asia. In the Acts of the Council of Arles held in 314, the name of a bishop of London, Restitutus, is on record for the first time in history.

For further information about Roman London, see the following subjects:

AXON
ONDON

(9-1066)

year 407 is important in English
ory because by this date the
wing turmoil in Roman
ernment and the increasing
aught of invading tribespeople
where in Europe required the
drawal of the Roman legions from
ain. In 410 the Romanized Britons
e advised by the Emperor
orius to take their own measures
protection against barbarian raids;
lso recognized their
ependence. By 410 the British
ple had lived under the Romans
over 350 years and under a
ernment tolerant of Christianity
early 100. The faith of the British
ch was known to Continental
ers such as St Martin of Tours, St
y, Bishop of Poitiers and even
t Jerome in Palestine who had
British pilgrims. But the Britons
e woefully unprepared for the
ster that would soon overtake
n once the professional armies
e removed.
ccording to Gildas, King Vortigen
ent first invited the Saxon
iors from their homeland at the
th of the Rhine as mercenaries, to
ace the Roman legions. For a few
s there was uneasy peace, with an
sional raid from across the seas
om Scotland. Then in 449 the
turned into a massive flood of
aric peoples that rolled over and
pletely engulfed the Romanized
ns. The Britons fought back
ely, and a few heroic leaders like

Vortimer of Kent and the legendary
King Arthur in South Wales held
their ground, but only briefly. The war
went on for 130 years, and during
that darkest of Dark Ages most of the
physical structures of Romano-British
civilization — buildings, furniture,
books, artwork and so on — including
churches and their contents, were
utterly destroyed.

And what about the defeated
Britons? Many fled to Wales, where
Christianity lived on. Great numbers
were brutally slain, but some were
kept as slaves. A few places like St
Albans that had Christian significance
seem to have survived, and even
a very few church buildings. But very
little of the British language or of the
concepts of the Christian faith seems
to have been passed along to the
Anglo-Saxons. The hatred between
the two races was so deep that the
Welsh refused to make contact with
the invaders even to evangelize them.

It is difficult for historians to
reconstruct what happened to
London during the fifth and sixth
centuries. The invaders kept no
records, and neither Bede nor the
Anglo-Saxon Chronicle of the ninth
century mention London. Because of
its swampy location, undesirable for
agriculture, it is probable that the
first waves of barbarians were not
attracted to the district where
London lies. They had a superstitious
fear of cities, and after destroying
them and massacring the inhabitants
left the ruins alone while they
themselves dwelt in log huts in the
farmlands and woods. Some historians
think London was never attacked,
but that the inhabitants, cut off from
all means of survival, simply fled or
perished.

At the end of the sixth century,

however, Christianity returned to Saxon England, and with it the recorded history of London. It reappears as a small commercial settlement and chief city of the East Saxons, one of several small kingdoms into which England had been divided. In 597 a group of missionaries sent by Pope Gregory the Great had landed in Kent. Bertha, wife of King Ethelbert, was a princess from Gaul (France) and a Christian, and the king with a large group of nobles accepted baptism. A church was established at Canterbury, eventually to become the seat of England's archbishop. Augustine, the first archbishop, ordained one of his priests, Mellitus, as bishop of the East Saxons. The king of the East Saxons, Sabert, was a nephew of Ethelbert and a true Christian. Again, many of the people professed to believe and Ethelbert built them a wooden structure on Ludgate Hill where the great domed cathedral stands today. While the present St Paul's is less than 300 years old, it should be borne in mind that it is the earliest Christian foundation in London.

The Saxons and Angles had brought with them to England their Teutonic religion that was more like a warrior's mythology than anything deeply mystical. Woden, god of war, and Thor, god of the storm, were of chief importance, and their names have survived in our weekdays — Wednesday (Woden's day) and Thursday (Thor's day). As Trevelyan has written, 'The old Saxon and Danish faith was a religion of barbarism with no elements in itself of further progress, and the spontaneous conversion of its adherents to Christianity seemed a confession of this fact.'

But unfortunately paganism was

deeply rooted in the hearts of the people of London, and when Sabe died Mellitus was driven out. Som years later (653) Sabert's descend Kind Sigebert, was brought to faith in Christ through friendly convers with Oswy, the Christian king of Northumbria. Bede tells us that it was through the labours of Sigebe and a priest named Cedd sent to him from Northumbria (and later ordained bishop of the East Saxo that London was reclaimed for C

Over the years that followed t return of Christianity the city gre and prospered as a commercial centre. It also became a place of pilgrimage following the death an canonization of the celebrated Bi Erkenwald, fourth successor of Mellitus, whose shrine greatly enriched St Paul's. Control of Lor passed from the kings of Kent to the kings of Mercia in the midland and the Mercian King Offa is said to have built a chapel in the city, which later became the church o St Alban's, Wood Street (destroy the bombing).

But the prosperity of London it an attractive prize, and in the D Viking raids of the ninth century, it was attacked in the year 842, resulting in a 'great slaughter'. In t winter of 871-72 it was occupied by the Danes until recaptured by West Saxon King Alfred in 886. Alf strengthened the old Roman wall of the city and redesigned the str in the medieval pattern that still to some extent today. Over the hundred years or so a number o Saxon churches were founded w its precincts. Our knowledge of t unfortunately, is not very comple the Saxons were not skilled reco keepers. We do know that seve

...anding today in the oldest part ...f the city were established in Saxon ...mes. Some of these bear the names ...f Saxon saints, as follows: St Alphage, ...t Botolph, St Dunstan, St Edmund, ...t Ethelburga and St Ethelreda. But ...nly two of today's city churches have ...hysical remains from Saxon times: ...t Bride's and All Hallows, Barking.

When Alfred recaptured London a ...umber of Danes who had married ...axon wives remained behind to ...ecome citizens. Alfred settled these ...the area between the Ludgate and ...e village of Charing (the present day ...rafalgar Square). At the east end of ...is area a church was built for their ...e, the predecessor of St Clement ...anes, in the Strand.

Towards the end of the tenth ...entury the Danes once again tried to ...ke London, and attacked the city ...om the river on a number of ...casions, but never again successfully. ...n one occasion the city was ...efended by a Christian Norwegian ...ng, Olaf, who according to legend ...lled down the wooden London ...idge to thwart the attackers. The ...urch of St Olave's, Hart Street, ...dedicated to him. Ironically, the ...anish king, Cnut (or Knut), who led ...e attack in 1016, was within a year ...cepted by the Londoners as king ...all England.

The crown of England (and ...ndon) passed to Harthacnut, Cnut's ...n, and when he died without an ...ir was offered to Edward, son of ...e former English king. Edward was a ...eply committed Christian, so much ...that he earned the nickname 'the ...nfessor' (or priest). He spent much ...his time in Normandy at the ...yal court there, as he and the ...orman ruler, Duke William, shared ...ommon Scandinavian ancestry. At

a place west of London where a Benedictine monastery was located Edward had a great new Norman-style church built — Westminster Abbey. It was finished in 1065, and a few months later became his burial place and London's most venerated shrine.

For further information on Saxon London, see the following subjects:

Alfred the Great
All Hallows, Barking
Augustine of Canterbury
Bede, the Venerable
Danes In London
Erkenwald
Lindisfarne Gospels
Mellitus
St Ethelburga, Bishopsgate

MEDIEVAL LONDON

(1066-1485)

Medieval London is what most people are thinking about when they refer to 'Old London' or 'London Town'. This is the London of our childhood imaginings, of Dick Wittington and his cat, of London Bridge falling down and "Oranges and lemons", say the bells of St Clemen's'. It is the London of turretted castles and cavernous cathedrals, of open markets and street cries and narrow lanes overhung by gabled houses, of towering city gates and massive walls and forests of spires.

Happily, a remnant of medieval London remains for us to see, despite fires, riots, plagues, enemy bombs and modern 'progress'. And of that remnant, a majority consists of buildings used for Christian purposes, because Christianity was what the Middle Ages was all about.

Technically, the term 'medieval' (from the Latin *medium aevum* meaning 'middle ages') refers to the thousand or so years from the fall of the Roman Empire in 476 to the beginning of the Protestant Reformation in 1517. 'The centre of life in this millennium was the church, so much so that the medieval world was a church-state. Emperors and kings received their privilege from the church, and feudal society descended accordingly with an endless round of homage between lords and vassals—all of them ultimately vassals of the church.'

London became a medieval city in appearance from 886 when King Alfred redesigned its streets to lead either to the cathedral or to the great central market. But in practice the city did not become a true part of this church-state until 1066. In this year William, the duke of Normandy, invaded England with the blessing of Pope Gregory VI. By his defeat of the Saxon Earl Harold at the Battle of Hastings he became 'The Conqueror'. William and his Norman knights brought to England the European feudal system and an alignment with the Christian culture of the Continent. These Normans radically changed the language, culture, politics, architecture and religious life of England, including London, forever.

Specifically, three great developments occurred in London at the Conquest. First, William took steps to guard against any uprising b 'the large and fierce population' by building two fortresses on the river, one east and one west of the City. The eastern one was the famous White Tower, the beginning of the Tower of London, destined to play such a significant role in the drama of the English Reformation 500 year later. Second, the Conqueror offere the citizens of London a charter, in the form of a letter, which read i part:

I inform you that I intend you to have all the rights in law you had i the days of King Edward, and eac child to be his father's heir after h father's day; and I will not allow ar man to do you wrong.

The third development (which actu started with Edward the Confessor

*Temple Church, built by the Crusader
 ~hts Templar.*

was that Westminster became firmly established as the seat of English government and a royal residence. The influence of various English sovereigns on the course of Christian history, not to mention that of Parliament, is a most important part of our story of Christian London.

Over the years the crude church buildings constructed by the Saxons were replaced by superior structures, higher, roomier and lighter inside due to more and larger windows. Beginning with Norman architecture, an improved version of earlier Roman construction, church buildings in London became loftier, more ornate, more refined from the Conquest to the late fifteenth century, culminating in the exquisite Chapel of Henry VII in Westminster Abbey. London led in sheer massiveness of Gothic structures as well: Old St Paul's was the largest cathedral in Europe.

For three centuries London became the home of ever more monastic houses. First there was the Benedictine Abbey of St Peter established in the tenth century on the 'Isle of Thorns', the forerunner of Westminster Abbey. Another pre-Conquest community, St Martin-le-Grand, was attached to an earlier royal palace in the City itself, located roughly where the Central Post Office stands today. By 1180 William Fitz-Stephen reports thirteen monastic churches, two Crusader orders which occupied large properties, traces of which still exist. The streets of the City were thronged by shaven-headed monks and friars in black, white and gray, and the gorgeous robes of their abbots and priors could often be seen in processions. In great palaces along the Thames and in other prominent parts of London lived the powerful bishops, who had seats in the House of Lords and a voice in governing all of England, seldom visiting their respective sees in the country districts.

The fourteenth century saw the first important reaction to the wea and luxury of the church and its fai to teach the truth of Holy Writ. Th peasants under Wat Tyler invaded London in 1381, killed the archbish of Canterbury and destroyed the estates of wealthy churchmen. John Wyclif wrote voluminously of cleri abuses and was twice called to London to answer for his attacks. His friendship with John of Gaunt, uncle of the boy-king Richard II, sa him from punishment, but in the fifteenth century many who dared read the English Bible produced by his followers suffered the supreme penalty at Smithfield.

Thus medieval London was a cit dominated by the Roman Catholic Church. Like other great cities of Europe, ecclesiastical buildings in so ways were to London of the Midc Ages what the modern office build is to the London of today. The pealing of numerous bells filled the from dawn to curfew, and inside the churches and chapels, amid clc of incense, the saying of mass wen on continuously. Christian holy day dominated the calendar; all special events were in one way or anothe sanctified (or tolerated) by the chu

This way of life continued virtua unchanged for nearly 500 years. T end—or at least the beginning of end—came on the intellectual leve with the 'New Learning' during the reign of Henry VII. On the physica level it occurred abruptly in 1536 the momentous decision of Henry VIII to dissolve the monasteries.

For further information on
Medieval London see the following
subjects:

Albert Memorial Chapel, Windsor
All Hallows, Barking
Becket, Thomas
Caxton, William, & the Invention of
  Printing
Charing Cross
Chaucer, Geoffrey, and *The
  Canterbury Tales*
Crosby, John
Crosby Hall
Crusades
Eleanor, Queen
Ely Chapel
Fitz-Stephens, William
Henry II
Hospitals
Jerusalem Chamber
Jews
John of Gaunt
Knights
Lambeth Palace
Langton, Stephen
Lollard Movement
London Bridge
Magna Carta
Medieval Church Buildings in
  London
Nunneries in London
Old St Paul's
Oldcastle, John
Pageantry in Medieval London
Peasant's Revolt
Rahere
Relics
St Bartholomew the Great,
  Smithfield
St Ethelburga-the-Virgin
St George's Chapel, Windsor
St Helen, Bishopsgate
St John's, Clerkenwell
St John's Gate
St John the Evangelist, Tower
St Olave, Hart Street

St Sepulchre
Sanctuary
Sawtrey, William
Southwark Cathedral
Temple Church
Tower of London
Tyler, Wat
Walls and Gates of Old London
Westminster Abbey
Westminster Hall
Whittington, Richard
Wyclif, John

RENAISSANCE LONDON

(1485-1536)

The Renaissance (from a French word meaning 're-birth') was an intellectual and artistic movement which had a profound, lasting impact on European culture in the fourteenth, fifteenth and sixteenth centuries. It began in Italy with Petrarch (died 1374) and involved some of the greatest and most gifted men of all time: Giovanni Boccaccio, Lorenzo Valla, Leon Battista Alberta, Leonardo da Vinci, Raphael, Machiavelli, Michelangelo and Cellini to name a few. Essentially the Renaissance centred around a study of the form and content of the ancient Greek and Roman classics. Its result was to change the focus of culture from God and the world to man and his relation to the present world.

In the north of Europe, however, the Renaissance attracted scholars who were more interested in the Greek New Testament and the great Christian classics than in the pagan texts. Their study led to a conviction that the medieval Roman Catholic Church had strayed far from the New Testament simplicity taught by the apostles and practised in the early church. Thus the great Erasmus of Rotterdam and those who were influenced by him were keen to apply their studies to reform in the church, and they became known as 'Christian Humanists'.

The period of peace and prosperity that came to England after the Wars of the Roses and during the reign of Henry VII from 1465 to 1527 encouraged certain English scholars to look further into Christian Humanism. Three such scholars who studied the classics in Europe and then returned to teach at Oxford were Grocyn, Linacre and Colet. John Colet (1466-1519), son of a lord mayor of London, was an outstanding Christian as well as a classicist. In 1497 he delivered a series of lectures on the original Greek text of the apostle Paul's epistles. He advocated clerical reform and was himself appointed dean of St Paul's Cathedral in 1505. His good friend Erasmus of Rotterdam, under Colet's influence, produced the first printed edition of the Greek New Testament, the so-called *Textus Receptus*, in 1516. This played an enormously important part in the Bible-translation work of Tyndale and others, which in turn helped, more than any other single factor, to bring the Reformation to England.

As for any visible effects of the Renaissance on Christian London, there were none in architecture until the seventeenth century. The first London church in which some Renaissance principles were incorporated into the design was St Katharine Cree, rebuilt 1628-30. Late in the century Inigo Jones employed the new design in the Queen's Chapel at St James and in St Paul's, Covent Garden. However, artists such as Hans Holbein introduced Renaissance painting to London early in the sixteenth century, as is seen in the magnificent portrait of Henry VIII in the National Gallery of Rome. By the end of the fifteenth century in England a wide variety of arts and crafts such as woodcarving and metalwork were showing the influence of Humanism. Numerous examples may be seen in the Victoria and Albert Museum.

For further information on Renaissance London, see the following:

REFORMATION LONDON
(1536-58)

The great upheaval of the Reformation occurred in London and throughout England during a span of twenty-two years. It started with the dissolution of the monasteries in 1536 and closed with the death of Mary I and the accession of Elizabeth I in 1558. During this period England went through a painful and often violent transition from Roman Catholicism as the state religion to the moderate Protestantism of the Church of England.

In many ways London was still a medieval city even after the Reformation ended and, indeed, for another century or more. Walls surrounded the city as they had for hundreds of years. Old London Bridge, built up with houses and shops, was still the only crossing over the Thames. The great 493-foot spire of Old St Paul's could still be seen for miles away. The Tower of London, with its moat and turrets and contingent of beefeaters and soldiers, still guarded the eastern approach of the river; and the steeples and towers of over a hundred parish churches were still crowded together within its one square mile.

But in 1536 came the beginning of sweeping changes. All the monastic houses, great and small, some of which had been a part of Christian London for 500 years, were now being closed and the properties either put to other uses or pulled down. The interiors of many of the churches were being altered as well, with the images disappearing, the stained glass and religious pictures being removed or whitewashed over, and everything generally being made much more plain and simple. In addition, a few miles up the Thames near the village of Hampton, there was a gorgeous new royal residence built by Cardinal Wolsey but handed over to Henry VIII. This was to be home for five of Henry's brides, and the scene of the undoing of three of them.

The changes brought about by the English Reformation seem to fall into the following steps, as Edward Cheyney has described them. The church was subordinated to the state, and was also separated from the authority of the pope, the king being made its supreme head on earth. Monasteries and monastic orders were abolished. The Bible and the church liturgy were changed to English. Ceremonies of the church were simplified, and long-accepted Roman Catholic doctrines were discarded and replaced by doctrines more in line with the Bible.

The first two of these steps were accomplished by the 'Reformation Parliament' in co-operation with Henry VIII. The third was masterminded by Thomas Cromwell, Henry's chief advisor, whom he appointed vicar-general for ecclesiastical affairs after the death of Wolsey. The translation of the Bible into English and its use in the churches was partly brought about by Henry VIII as well, but the genius of William Tyndale, Miles Coverdale and others in achieving a superior translation was also a major factor. The king was no Protestant, and he had no idea of changing the doctrines or ceremonies of the old church. The remaining

changes occurred during the short reign of the boy-king Edward VI when there was a rapid swing of the pendulum toward Protestantism. The chief lasting Christian contribution during Edward's reign was made by Archbishop Thomas Cranmer, who produced the initial version of the Book of Common Prayer.

To understand what happened in London and the rest of England during the Reformation it is necessary not only to see what was accomplished during these twenty-two years but also to look from two other perspectives. First, one has to go back in time and consider all the pre-Reformation factors at work: the Wars of the Roses, John Wyclif and the Lollards, the Renaissance or 'New Learning', the *Textus Receptus*, and finally the courageous men and women who braved the rack and the stake during the early part of Henry VIII's reign to spread Luther's ideas in England. Second, it is very important to see that the most significant results of the Reformation took place over a century or more *beyond* the actual twenty-nine years of the Reformation period, when the people of London and England through the impact of the Bible became Christians personally.

For further information on Reformation London see the following subjects:

ELIZABETHAN LONDON

(1558-1603)

During the reign of Elizabeth London was not only the home of numerous literary giants, among them William Shakespeare himself. In her days also lived John Stow, the worthy chronicler of that ancient metropolis. His *Survey* describes London in minute detail and shows us a medieval metropolis undergoing substantial change, wrought mainly by the dissolution of the monasteries. Many of these establishments lay in ruins or had disappeared altogether, and in some cases beautiful Elizabethan structures were built on the sites. The Charterhouse is a notable example. The increase in wealth of the upper classes was reflected in elaborate tombs and memorials within the churches, some remaining to our own time. However, while some buildings were repaired during the Elizabethan period, no new churches were built in London during her reign.

Yet the Elizabethan era was a most significant time in London's and all of England's history for Christianity. As the Norman invasion of William the Conqueror in 1066 had brought spiritual and temporal unity with the Roman Catholic Church in the rest of Europe, so Elizabeth's reign, which completed the work begun during Henry VIII's time, brought unity to the English church by creating a new and independent body, neither Roman Catholic nor altogether Protestant.

Elizabeth was born from a marriage forbidden by the pope, and

227

she had reason to fear for her life during the reign of her Catholic half-sister, Mary. She wanted no part of papal domination in her realm. Her chief advisor, Lord Burleigh, and her archbishop of Canterbury, Matthew Parker, were both Protestants. But she also loved established order and was above everything else devoted to England, so the forms and doctrines of the European Calvinists were not attractive to her either. Thus, acting boldly in the capacity of absolute ruler established by Henry VIII, she chose for all her people a 'middle way'.

The settlement of the critical religious question, which occurred at Elizabeth's first parliament two months after her succession in 1558, is called the 'Elizabethan Compromise'. Although it was violated for much of the century following her reign, it resulted in the unique and flexible body that is the Church of England. By two important laws, the 'Act of Supremacy' and the 'Act of Uniformity', church government went back to the episcopal system arrived at under Henry VIII, all acts against control by the pope—repealed under Mary—were reinstated, the order and ceremonies of the church were to be the same as under Edward VI, and the mass was abolished and replaced by the Book of Common Prayer. Later the doctrines of the church were officially set forth in what are known as the 'Thirty-nine Articles'.

Not only was the official religious position settled peaceably in Elizabeth's day, but also during her time the Reformation began to make a widespread difference in the lives of the general populace. A notable sign of this was the tremendous popularity of John Foxe's *Actes and Monuments*,

which chronicled the sufferings of those who had dared to make the Bible their supreme religious authority during the days of Henry VIII and Mary. As Trevelyan has written:

> When she [Elizabeth] came to the throne, the bulk of the people halted between a number of opinions, and the anti-Catholic party still consisted of anti-clericals as much as of Protestants. When she died, the majority of the English regarded themselves as ardent Protestants, and a great number of them were living religious lives based on Bible and Prayer Book.

Finally, we look back to Elizabethan London for the roots of two great movements, both related to the history of Christianity and also interrelated with one another. First was the flowering of the English language, brought to a peak of classical perfection through the genius of William Shakespeare and a host of gifted contemporaries. Out of such rich soil grew the Authorized (or 'King James') version of the English Bible which is unrivalled—except by Shakespeare—in its contribution to both the style and the imagery of everyday English ever since.

The other movement which arose in Elizabethan London (despite the canny queen's rigourous attempts to suppress it) was Puritanism (mainly Presbyterians, but also Congregationalists and later Baptists). The Puritans (the special English name for Protestants) became a major political, as well as religious, force, and succeeded in reducing the power of the monarchy and in making Parliament and Parliamentary law supreme in English government. The

Puritans made England a Bible-reading nation, produced several great Christian classics and laid the foundation for modern church organization. As Trevelyan suggests, they were the true children of the Reformation.

STUART & COMMONWEALTH LONDON

(1603-6)

During the fifty-seven years between the accession of the Stuart king, James I, to the throne of England and that of his grandson Charles II, there were few changes in the external appearance of London and its many churches. Only one church building was put up in the old city. Inside the churches, however, it was another story. Much of the medieval ornateness that had escaped during the Reformation was defaced or destroyed by Puritan reactionaries during the Commonwealth period, including the stained glass in the Chapel of Edward VII. And between the years 1603 and 1660 London and all of England was shaken by religious events of tremendous import.

On the positive side, it was a period when religion was taken seriously by more people in England than even during the Reformation of the previous century. Several of the great Protestant denominations gained public recognition at this time, notably the Baptists, Congregationalists, Presbyterians and Quakers, and by mid-century there were Nonconformist congregations all over London. The Presbyterians, in fact, nearly succeeded in making Presbyterianism the national religion. But it was also a dark period in England's history. Established precedents, individual rights, property and human lives all fell victim to the tragedy of irreconcilable religious differences leading eventually to the violence of civil war. And when the Commonwealth experiment finally came to an end in 1660 with the re-establishment of the monarchy it was only to plunge the nation into a new dark age of intolerance.

As in the century before, the English sovereigns played the primary role in determining what form of worship and church government would be endorsed by the state. But whereas the Tudor monarchs, Mary excepted, managed to gain the approval of the majority of their subjects, the Stuarts met with increasing resistance. The reason for this seems to be that, as has been pointed out, the Reformation with its emphasis upon an open Bible made a widespread impact upon the common man during the Elizabethan age, and by 1603 a vast number of English men and women were Christians in

the personal sense. Now not only did the clergy and university professors struggle with such issues as whether all churches should follow one set form of service, but merchants, craftsmen and small landowners did so as well.

On the other hand, much of the blame seems to lie with the kings

Oliver Cromwell, the great hero of the English Revolution.

themselves. Had James I and Charles I been men of insight into human nature and able to recognize that they, despite their power, needed the consent of their subjects to rule successfully, harmony might have been achieved without tearing the country asunder. As it was, however, both of these rulers were convinced that God had ordained them to hold all the power of government in their own hands, and England had to endure a religious war dividing not only the nation, but villages and households. Fortunately, London was at least spared the physical aspects of war as she was the stronghold of Parliament and proof against Royalist attack.

Briefly summarized, the years between 1603 and 1660 seem to fall into two main periods, which in turn can each be divided into two periods. The first covers the reign of James I from 1603 to 1625, and then that of Charles I from 1625 to the beginning of the civil war in 1642. Generally this period can be thought of historically as the rise of the Puritans (or Protestants, primarily Presbyterians) and the revolt of Parliament against the monarchy.

The second period includes the civil war and the captivity of Charles I until his execution in 1649, which led to the Commonwealth experiment from 1649 to 1660. This ended with the death of Cromwell in 1658 and the election of a new Parliament which in turn restored the monarchy. Generally this period can be viewed as England's experiment with a theocracy, or rule by religious forces, and with a dictatorship in which one man, a devoutly religious man, held the nation together by his personal power and charisma.

For further information on Stuart & Commonwealth London, see the following subjects:

Andrewes, Launcelot
Charles I
Charterhouse
Civil War & the Execution of the King
Cromwell, Oliver, & the Commonwealth
Donne, John
Fawkes, Guy, & the Gunpowder Plot
Hampton Court Conference
Helwys, Thomas
James I
King James Version of the Bible
Laud, William
Mayflower Barn
Pilgrim Fathers
Queen's Chapel, St James Palace
St Katharine Cree
St Paul's, Covent Garden
Solemn League & Covenant
Walton, Izaak
Whitehall Banqueting House

RESTORATION LONDON

(1660-1714)

The 'Restoration' in English history refers to the return of Charles II to the throne of England in 1660, an event greeted with thanksgiving to God by devout royalists, like John Evelyn, and with anxiety and fear by all the former supporters of Cromwell. What we have designated the Restoration 'period' is actually the fifty-four years *following* the Restoration, when the last four Stuart monarchs ruled England. It falls roughly into two parts.

The first part takes in the reigns of Charles II and James II, from 1660 to 1688. This is sometimes called the 'penal' period for Nonconformists and Catholics. Great numbers of Nonconformist ministers were defrocked and jailed, and Catholic priests who ministered secretly were punished even more severely. The Great Plague in London occurred in 1665, followed the next year by the Great Fire and the destruction of most of the church buildings in Old London. The monarchs were inconsistent in their religious policies, though Charles II attempted to encourage freedom of conscience. James II was an avowed Roman Catholic and was eventually forced to flee the country. Both lived lives of open immorality.

The second part comprises the reigns of William III, Mary II and Queen Anne, from 1688 to 1714. William and his wife, Mary, the daughter of James II, were the first monarchs elected by Parliament. Both a Toleration Act and a Bill of Rights were passed shortly after they came to the throne. Anne, the younger sister of Mary, was the last of the Stuarts. She was a staunch supporter of the 'high church'. Her reign was marked by a weakening of the power of the monarchy and the rise of the modern two-party political system. At the end of her reign it became a law that the sovereign be a member of the Church of England.

The event that most affected the outward appearance of Christian London was the Great Fire of 1666. Over eighty church buildings were lost, including the famous cathedral of Old St Paul's. The colossal task of rebuilding these places of worship fell mainly to a single man of genius, Sir Christopher Wren, and occupied several decades. In fact, the last stone was not put into place in the new St Paul's until 1710.

The struggle for religious freedom went against the Nonconformists at the Savoy Conference held in 1661, and soon numerous laws were passed which were intended to create a single state church. However, these were resisted by courageous men of God such as Richard Baxter, and many Nonconformist churches kept their identity despite severe suffering for their clergy. Two of the greatest Christian literary works of all time were written between 1660 and 1689, *Pilgrim's Progress* by John Bunyan and *Paradise Lost* by John Milton. Joseph Addison, one of England's most famous essayists and Christian statesmen, was prominent in London after 1689. It was a period of deep piety when the Bible was the supreme rule of life for a large segment of the population of London and all of England. Ironically, its decline seemed to be hastened by the achievement of toleration.

For further information on Restoration London, see the following subjects:

CLASSICAL LONDON

(1714-1837)

The dates given for 'Classical London' start with the reigns of a new dynasty of monarchs, the House of Hanover, and end with the accession of Victoria, whose reign was an entire age in itself. The term 'Classical' refers to a style of architecture that was used for most churches in London built during this period (actually starting with Inigo Jones in the early seventeenth century). That is, they adhered to principles of structure originated by the ancient Greeks which were re-introduced into Western Europe during the Renaissance. After the Great Fire Sir Christopher Wren and his assistants filled Old London with Renaissance-style church buildings. But even if the fire had not occurred, it is quite likely that London would have followed the lead of other European cities where Classical (strictly speaking, 'neo' or 'new'-Classical) architecture was very much in vogue by the early eighteenth century.

As the Great Plague had reduced the population of London to around 600,000, new churches in addition to those destroyed and replaced were not needed during most of the seventeenth century. But by the early 1700s London began to expand outside the walls of the old City. In particular, the area of Central London which today we call the 'West End' developed most rapidly in the eighteenth century. From very early times traffic had flowed from Ludgate along Fleet Street and the country road that is now the Strand to Westminster, the site of royal palaces and the seat of government. Also from Cheapside, the City's marketplace, steady traffic streamed out of Newgate and along the highways of Holborn and Oxford Street to Tyburn, now Marble Arch, and thence to the West and Northwest. Soon the rural aspect of places such as Soho, Piccadilly and Bloomsbury began to fade as houses and parks grew, and these became fashionable suburban districts. The churches that were built to serve the growing population in these new estates were generally in the Classical style.

In the eighteenth century the religious power struggle between the sovereign and Parliament was over. George, the German Elector of Hanover who became George I of England, was a Protestant, as have been all the kings and queens since. George III, the most popular monarch since Elizabeth, was, in fact, a sincere and humble Christian. Even today, the English monarch plays an extremely important part in upholding the nation's commitment to Christianity and the Bible (officially, at least), and the coronation as well as royal weddings and funerals are always deeply religious events. A few attempts were made by James II and his descendants to rally support for a return of the Stuarts and Catholicism, chiefly in Ireland and Scotland. But these 'Jacobite' uprisings failed tragically and ended following the defeat of 'Bonnie Prince Charlie', James II's grandson, in 1745.

Ironically, the religious fervour of the seventeenth century, which by the time of the Commonwealth affected the personal lives of vast numbers of Londoners, had become subject to a reactionary movement by the eighteenth. After the Act of Toleration, people gradually became apathetic in religious matters, and many became cynical. Following on the heels of the new scientific views of Lord Bacon, Isaac Newton, John Locke, Descartes, Galileo and others, a belief grew up that the universe was governed by 'natural law'. God came to be regarded as an absentee deity who had set the universe in motion and then left it to run by itself. Faith in the divinity of Jesus Christ and the doctrines of the Thirty-nine Articles, the Westminster Confession and other creeds were rejected as 'unreasonable'. This fashionable new gospel was called Deism, and London became a centre for its espousal.

Thus the 'Age of Reason' illuminated London with brilliant minds such as Alexander Pope and Lord Chesterfield. The thriving wool industry at home and military success abroad brought wealth and security to England as a whole. The society of the eighteenth century seemed to have solved the problems of the past and come of age as an ideal civilization. If reason were the key that would unlock all truth, the nation could expect only to grow more and more Utopian. But the realities of shocking poverty and wage slavery in the wake of the new machine age, of epidemic drunkenness, flourishing social vices and political corruption at every level (powerfully satirized by the engravings of William Hogarth) shattered the dream. Who knows but that it might have turned into the 'Age of Revolution' (as in France) had not London and England experienced religious revival.

Revival came in the late 1730s with the open-air preaching of George Whitefield and John Wesley. Thousands of 'societies' sprang up all over England helping men and women from all classes, but especially the common people, to give up drunkenness and other vices and follow Jesus. Everywhere the language of the Bible was sung in the beautiful hymns of Isaac Watts and Charles Wesley. In London both Whitefield and Wesley established chapels which doubled as outreach centres for social services. Nonconformist chapels increased in the City, including several large buildings constructed for this purpose towards the end of the eighteenth century. Popular figures such as the Countess of Huntingdon and the Rev. Rowland Hill used unusual methods such as parlour Bible studies for wealthy matrons, Sunday schools and even vaccination to communicate the love of God. By the early nineteenth century the first pioneers had gone to remote parts of the earth from newly formed missionary societies, John Newton had inspired William Wilberforce to fight against slavery, and the Clapham Sect had carried the principles of the Christian gospel into the highest echelons of government.

For further information on Classical London, see the following subjects:

VICTORIAN LONDON

(1837-1901)

In 1837 eighteen-year-old Victoria, granddaughter of George III, became the monarch destined to the longest reign in English history. During her tenure England became fully industrialized, bringing great new wealth as well as great new social problems to the nation. This was evident nowhere so dramatically as in London; even today one sees in the suburbs the interminable rows of identical Victorian tenements as well as the spacious five-storey Victorian townhouses. The City sprawled on for miles, following the paths cut by the railways from half a dozen great new terminal stations. Seven new bridges spanned the Thames. And thirteen Wren churches were either sold or demolished to accommodate commercial development in the City.

The building of new churches in the Victorian era took place mainly in the suburbs beyond Central London. By 1878 there were about eighty churches in the City of London proper and over 1,000 in Greater London. A number of these edifices were constructed under the Church Building Act of 1818 in which Parliament set aside one million pounds for this purpose as an expression of thanksgiving for the defeat of Napoleon at Waterloo. The Church of England itself also raised money for many new places of worship.

But the great growth in population was also accompanied by a corresponding growth of Nonconformists. Older bodies such as the Baptists, Methodists and Congregationalists tended to become 'respectable', with buildings that looked like those of the established church and, in some cases, very large memberships. Westminster Chapel is a good example of a handsome Victorian Nonconformist church still standing in London. The Catholics, too, put up some imposing buildings, such as the Brompton Oratory, in later Victorian times. Newer and more radical Nonconformist groups appeared, such as the Christian Brethren and the Salvation Army. These tended to meet in nondescript chapels, upper rooms, rented halls and storefronts, leaving a great spiritual heritage but few visible traces to posterity.

Around the beginning of the nineteenth century there began a new movement in church architecture which became known as the 'Gothic Revival'. The result was a tendency to drop the Classical model and return once more to the grand medieval style of pointed arches, carved stone pinnacles and flying buttresses. The first such building in London was St Luke's, Chelsea, designed by James Savage and consecrated in 1824. Later in the century the movement was much influenced by the architect A.W.N. Pugin, who designed the Houses of Parliament, and the essayist John Ruskin; Pugin believed that Gothic was a truly Christian architecture. Under the influence of the Oxford Movement, there was an attempt to turn back the clock on the interior of churches to pre-Reformation ornateness. Clear windows were replaced by Victorian stained glass, elaborate screens and other 'religious' furnishings were added, and sometimes dark panelling was installed. This 'Victorianization' has in recent times been much lamented by authorities concerned with church preservation, and in some cases the Victorian alterations have been removed. Neo-Gothic churches, however, are still very much in evidence in London.

On the spiritual side, the great evangelical revival which had swept the nation in the days of the Wesleys and George Whitefield had lost its vigour by the beginning of Victoria's reign. However, a large evangelical (or 'low church') wing grew up in the established church and was by far the most powerful party by mid-century. There was also a strong 'high church' or Anglo-Catholic section and also a smaller but very influential 'broad church' or liberal-scientific presence, which gained much by the theories of Charles Darwin. The Nonconformist bodies, representing approximately half of the churchgoing population, made their influence felt in London through popular gospel preachers such as Charles Spurgeon. In 1873 the famous American evangelist D.L.Moody and singer-composer Ira Sankey paid their first visit to England, touching off a second nationwide revival. Their campaign in London, lasting four months, attracted an unprecedented two-and-a-half million people!

Victorian London saw Christians becoming active in reform movements of all sorts designed to alleviate suffering, reduce poverty and provide education for the masses. These included men of considerable wealth and political influence such as the Seventh Earl of Shaftesbury, who fought to establish labour laws protecting women and children, missionaries like John Thomas Barnardo, who in 1867 began his celebrated home for street children in East London, and radical preachers like William Booth and his equally vocal wife, Ruth, who reached out with the gospel, bread and clothing to men and women in the gutters of the City. It also included one of the greatest novelists of all time, Charles Dickens, who used his pen to expose the social evils of the Victorian class system.

During Victoria's reign the British Empire reached around the world. By the time of her Diamond Jubilee in 1897, celebrated with a great service outside St Paul's Cathedral and festivities throughout the Empire, the sun literally never set on the Union Jack. Victoria and her consort, Prince Albert (who died in 1861), were themselves devout Christians, and Christianity was part of the 'Victorian' way of life, at least on the surface.

But Britain's strategic worldwide economic and political power, while much abused, also opened a tremendous opportunity for missionary enterprises. Victorian London was the headquarters of several large missionary organizations such as the Church Missionary Society, the London Missionary Society, the Baptist Missionary Society, the General Methodist Society and the China Inland Mission. These sent thousands of candidates around the world (often to be opposed by British commercial interests abroad). The gospel of Christ was thus spread throughout the British Empire much as it had been throughout the Roman Empire in the days of the apostles. In 1873 one of the nation's highest honours was paid to a member of

John Henry Newman had a great and lasting influence on the Church of England.

the London Missionary Society, David Livingstone, whose body was brought from Africa and laid to rest beneath a stirring memorial in the nave of Westminster Abbey.

For further information on Victorian London, see the following subjects:

All Saints, Margaret Street
Barnardo, John Thomas
Booth, William
Brethren, The
Brompton Oratory
Carlile, Wilson
Catholic Apostolic Church
China Inland Mission
City Temple
Dickens, Charles
Faber, Frederick William
Farrar, R.W.
Gladstone, William
Gordon, Charles George
Hughes, Hugh Price

TWENTIETH-CENTURY LONDON

(1901 to the Present)

The death of Queen Victoria in 1901 was, symbolically at least, the beginning of the end of the greatest age of peace and prosperity in the long history of Britain. In stark contrast, the first half of the twentieth century was dominated by two wars whose magnitude exceeded any previous armed conflict in the annals of the human race. In the World War I modern weapons such as tanks, poison gas and submarines were used extensively for the first time. Bombing from the air using aeroplanes and dirigibles was another first, and London came under attack on several occasions. While 174 buildings were destroyed and 617 badly damaged, fortunately no historical churches were included (a curious exception being the gate house of St Bartholomew the Great, whose facade was blown off in a dirigible raid, revealing a beautiful half-timbered structure underneath).

World War II, however, was another story. The Luftwaffe was one of Hitler's major weapons, with the purpose of bringing Britain to her knees in the shortest possible time. From August 1940 to August 1941 between 45,000 and 50,000 bombs were dropped, killing 10,000 people in London and injuring some 17,000 others. By March 1945, 29,890 had died, 50,497 had been injured and 12,000 buildings had been destroyed,

239

according to London Museum figures.

The first attack on the City took place on 24 August 1940, during which the church of St Giles, Cripplegate was hit. On December 29 a concentrated attack with incendiary bombs badly damaged St Lawrence, Jewry, together with the Guildhall next to it. On 16 April 1941, what the Germans claimed was the greatest air raid of all time took place. A number of City churches suffered extensive damage, and Chelsea Old Church was demolished. Another terrible attack on May 10 caused irreparable destruction to several more churches, and the deanery of Westminster Abbey was burned out. The hideous flying bombs, which first fell on 13 June 1944, did most of their damage in the suburbs, but a direct hit was made on the Guards Chapel in Westminster during a Sunday morning service and many were killed. The very last rocket destroyed Whitefield's Tabernacle on Tottenham Court Road.

After VE Day in May 1945, the massive work of restoration was begun. Some edifices of inestimable historic value, such as St Mildred's, Bread Street, and the Dutch Church of the Austin Friars, were a total loss. In most of these cases the ruins had to be removed. In a few instances, St Dunstan's-in-the-East, for example, the tower and ruins were incorporated into a public garden. Sometimes the tower alone has been left standing, as in the case of St Mary Somerset on Upper Thames Street. Other churches were badly wrecked, but the structures were still sound and some of the original features remained. A number in this category were faithfully restored, and today visitors are often unaware that they

are not seeing the complete original. In fact, some of the restoration work removed undesirable additions so that the interiors look more like the original architects intended them to look. The work of restoration was slow and costly, but great credit is due to the City of London, to the church authorities, and to the members and friends of London churches in preserving as far as possible this priceless religious and historical heritage.

Thus, since World War II there has been a new appreciation of London's churches on architectural and historical grounds. Because many of the congregations of old parish churches in the inner city had all but disappeared, a plan was put forth in 1952 called the City of London Guild Churches Act, which became law in 1954. This Act preserved many of the churches by freeing them from parochial responsibilities and constituting them 'guild churches', with concern only for weekday congregations and for special forms of religious work. Still others, St Andrew Undershaft and St Peter's, Vere Street, for example, have been designated Chapels of Ease to assist the work of active parish churches in the area. Today there are thirty-nine historical churches standing in the City of London, most of them beautifully preserved, and several times this number in Greater London.

Spiritually, the Christian church in London, as elsewhere, has passed through various stages as it has reacted to the mind-boggling metamorphosis from Victoria's world to our own. At the end of the nineteenth century and on into the Edwardian era, the influence of scientific developments led the more liberal preachers to emphasize human progress and the humanity of Christ at the expense of the gospel. This was countered by a strong conservative reaction, which stressed the infallibility of the Bible. Another reaction, which arose with Karl Barth in Switzerland shortly after World War I, became known as the New (or Neo) Orthodoxy. It saw great importance in spiritual conversion, while accepting some of the literary and scientific criticism of the Bible from the liberal side.

An important twentieth-century movement to affect London, especially since World War II, has been the attempt by the World Council of Churches to achieve unity among all Christian bodies. Known as the Ecumenical Movement, it is still exerting a growing influence. In the past decade or two 'liberation theology', which views the goal of the gospel as freeing the poor and disadvantaged from exploitation, has also gained a following among the clergy. The emergence of congregations stressing the gifts of the Spirit such as healing and 'speaking in tongues', both in the established church and in house groups, is another significant aspect of Christianity in and around London. As in the nineteenth century, the evangelicals outnumber all the other branches of Christianity in the City, and in some cases their churches are growing in the face of decline elsewhere.

Since the 1950s, however, English society has become increasingly secularized. The *UK Christian Handbook* for 1985/86 (published by MARC Europe), which gives statistics on every conceivable aspect of the church in the United Kingdom, indicates an average church membership of 16 per cent for the whole country (the 1987-88 handbook revises the figure to 15 per cent). Average church attendance in the United Kingdom is 11 per cent (and probably much lower in London). But this same handbook catalogues an astounding spectrum of Christian activity—bookshops and publishing houses, arts and theatre groups, missionary societies, charitable and relief organizations, radio and TV producers and so on— which indicates that Christianity is very much alive in London. The following conclusion by Peter Brierley, European Director, MARC, fits well our overview of the history of Christian London in the twentieth century:

The picture is far from cheerful, yet there is cause for hope. The trends are not all downwards; and we must not allow ourselves to be mesmerized by falling rolls. The original rise of the Christian Church, itself not to be explained by extrapolation of trends or sociological analysis, should remind us that we have to do with a King who is Lord of history, and only the side with the ultimate truth can be sure of having the last laugh. 'Love-laughter, which sounds loudly as heaven's gates swing open and dies away as they shut.'

For further information on 20th-century London, see the following subjects:

Chesterton, G.K.
Dutch Church, Austin Friars
Eliot, T.S.
Graham, Billy
Meyer, F.B.
New English Bible
Sayers, Dorothy Leigh
Sheppard, Dick

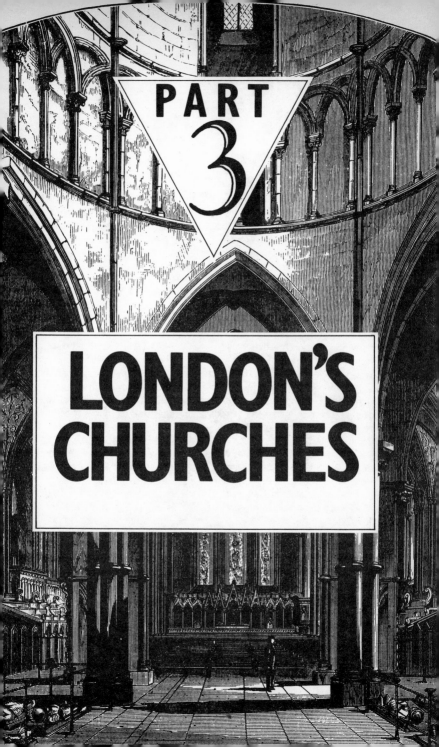

PART 3

LONDON'S CHURCHES

Architecture of London Churches

For the first three centuries of Christianity, until after the Edict of Milan granting toleration in 313, there were no Christian church buildings as such. In Roman-occupied Britain, the few Christian remains existing from the fourth century or so indicate that the church probably met in homes or in chapels that were part of the Roman villas. The first church *building* in London that we know about was St Paul's on Ludgate Hill, erected during Saxon times in 604.

Many Saxon churches eventually were founded following St Paul's between the years 604 and 1066, but none remain today. Only a few traces are left at All Hallows, Barking and St Bride's. The reason is that the Saxons were crude builders and possessed only rudimentary engineering skills. Many buildings were made of wood and had only a limited life span. The ones built of stone were smaller imitations of Roman basilicas, with thick stone walls and dark interiors. After the Norman Conquest they would have been replaced by the larger and better-built Norman structures. And even if some survived they would have perished in the great fire that levelled London in the year 1135.

On the other hand, London possesses a wealth of historic churches and chapels dating from the eleventh century onward. Some knowledge of the visible features of the different styles of architecture will help to make your visits to these venerable monuments more interesting.

Medieval church architecture

The ancient churches of London have undergone more than their share of alterations and additions over the years, but it is possible for the careful observer to identify in them the several styles of church architecture that prevailed from the eleventh to the fifteenth century. In general terms, the age of a medieval ecclesiastical building in England can be determined by its architecture, as follows:

1066-1200 - Norman
1200-1300 - Early English
1300-1400 - Decorated
1400-1500 - Perpendicular

The Normans were considerably more skilled in building than the Saxons, and thus some of their structures have survived in London, notably in the Chapel of St John the Evangelist in the Tower of London (1078), St Bartholomew the Great, Smithfield (1123), and the Temple Church (1185, 1240). Norman architecture, a branch of the Romanesque style which flourished all over Europe in the eleventh and twelfth centuries, is based on principles derived from the Romans. It can be recognized by thick walls, very large round pillars, round-topped arches, squat towers and a generally massive appearance. Norman doorways are round arches above, supported by as many as six pillars set in the thickness of the wall. Another feature of Norman churches is the high stone vaulting which they invented to support the heavy stone ceilings. These were extensions of the system of low vaulting used as the foundation.

The major style of architecture to be seen in the great cathedrals and countless churches throughout Europe is Gothic, which prevailed for some 300 years. The term indicates a distinctly European or Germanic style, as opposed to the Classic style of the Romans and Greeks. In England the Gothic churches are further divided into three styles that followed one another, known as Early English, Decorated and Perpendicular. The hallmark of the Gothic style is the pointed arch. This new shape completely changed methods of building, because its strength allowed structures to be taller without being heavier. The pointed arch together with another new development, the flying (or extended) buttress, made massive walls and thick columns unnecessary. Higher ceilings and slender columns gave the naves of Gothic churches a light and airy feeling, tending to draw the attention upward. Several Gothic arches were often combined to create the beautiful lancet windows which are so typical of medieval buildings.

Westminster Abbey (1269) is the finest example of Early English to be found in London. Its cloisters are particularly exquisite and very rare in England, as most such monastic structures were destroyed during the Reformation. The choir and Lady Chapel of St Saviour's in Southwark (1207) are also Early English.

In the fourteenth century, church builders began to add decoration to the simple style of Early English. They used more ribs above the vaults, and where the ribs crossed they attached beautiful stone centrepieces,

or bosses. When these were painted bright colours they created a very rich appearance. A new kind of curve, the Ogee, was first used in the Decorated period, and this was applied with magnificent effect in the stone tracery of windows. Glorious stained glass was also a product of the Decorated period. Ely Chapel (early fourteenth century) is one of the rare examples of Decorated remaining in London.

The last period of Gothic church architecture, occurring mainly during the fifteenth century, brought this style to perfection. It is called Perpendicular, the name suggesting an emphasis on height. On the outside this effect was created by yet another new kind of arch, called the four-centred arch. This is a broad, blunted version of the pointed Gothic arch, and enabled builders to make the windows much larger. In fact, in some cases (King's College Chapel in Cambridge, for example) the walls appear to be almost all glass in between the buttresses.

On the inside of Perpendicular churches, the impression given is of glass from floor to ceiling, making the interior appear wonderfully light and the ceiling immensely high. This effect is increased by the use of fan vaulting, another feature of the Perpendicular style. Stone work between the ribs above the vault is delicately carved to look like folded cloth. The best example of this style in London is to be seen in Henry VII's Chapel, Westminster Abbey (1503). Its characteristics may be observed, however, in All Hallows' Barking, St Helen's and even some later churches as St Sepulchre's and St Andrew Undershaft.

Renaissance church architecture

Not much church building went on between the late fifteenth and early seventeenth centuries. But from the 1620s to the early nineteenth century the churches built in London were, with few exceptions, imitations of the classical style, inspired by the Renaissance. That is, they were designed by architects who used ancient Roman or even Greek buildings as models but then suited these models to their own individualistic creations. Actually, it was more a two- or even three-step process—the English architects adapted classical models invented by Italian, French and Dutch architects, who earlier had borrowed them from the ancient Romans and Greeks. And the most original of the English classical churches were imitated by other English (and American) architects. For example, the 'father' of numerous American Colonial-style buildings is probably James Gibbs, the designer of St Martin-in-the-Fields.

In Italy and Europe this revival of building styles from the pre-Christian era took place first from around 1420 to 1490. This period has become generally known as the Renaissance or 'New Birth'. The architects of this early period in Italy created some large buildings, such as the great Duomo in Florence by Brunelleschi, but they were particularly interested in doing highly individualistic things with ancient forms— enriched mouldings, carved friezes, inlays of marble, panels of glazed terra cotta, carved doors... The outsides of Renaissance buildings from this period are often flat, depending for effect upon the distribution and adornment of the openings, mouldings and cornices.

The second period of the Italian and European Renaissance, from about 1490 to 1560, is sometimes called the Formally Classical period. The visible characteristic of a Formally Classical building is what is called 'the orders'. Basically, an 'order' is made up of a shaft or column often tapered and fluted, a capital or 'cap' on top of the column, and a three-tiered structure called an entablature making up the roof which the column and its capital support. The Formally Classical building has rows of these 'orders' which together form the front (or which may surround it entirely as in the case of the Parthenon in Athens). Influences from all of the styles of the Renaissance may be found in London's churches.

In England the Renaissance in architecture was introduced first by Inigo Jones, who as royal surveyor was commissioned under Charles I to prepare designs for a new palace at Whitehall. The Banqueting Hall, finished in 1622, was the only part of the new palace completed. It is considered his masterpiece and is Jones's adaptation of the style of Andrea Palladio whose work he most admired. He also built the Queen's Chapel at St James Palace (1623) and St Paul's Church, Covent Garden (1633). The latter building is in the Formally Classical style, the first of many churches of this design in London.

However, London's greatest Renaissance architect was Christopher Wren, who, given the unique opportunity after the Great Fire, filled the City with his own original designs. Wren churches, including the magnificent St Paul's Cathedral, have given London a unique 'hallmark' different from any other city of the world. Wren was followed by several other gifted designers, in particular James Gibbs and Nicholas Hawksmoor, whose buildings are London landmarks known the world over.

Gothic Revival

By the beginning of the nineteenth century, architecture had lost its reliance on classical principles of proportion going back to the ancient Greeks and Romans and instead 'rested on the twin functions of association and visual effect'. In other words, the architects wanted buildings to *suggest* or be associated in people's minds with classical Greek temples and the like, but they felt free to dispense with the rules of proportion used by the Greeks. John Nash, for example, was guided entirely by 'visual effectiveness' when he designed the circular portico of All Souls, Langham Place, so as to create a pivot for two unaligned streets.

However, under pressure from critics who questioned such permissiveness, architects gradually began once again to pay more attention to principles. This led to a serious consideration of the meaning and proper use of styles of architecture. A.W.N. Pugin (1812-52) 'made it his business to understand Gothic design thoroughly'. Significantly, he grew to love the Christian world-view that produced it and was received into the Roman Catholic Church in 1835. He strove to convert the Christian church of his day to the true use of the Gothic style.

The Gothic Revival in church architecture, still to be seen in a number of churches throughout London, emerged partly as a result of the moralistic purpose advocated by Pugin—that of honestly reproducing church buildings as close to the originals as possible. And the originals were, in total, expressions in stone and wood and glass of Christianity and the Bible. It was also encouraged by the essayist John Ruskin, who argued (in *The Stones of Venice*) that, because Christianity recognized the individual value of every soul, the Gothic style with all its individualistic workmanship is the most admirable of styles. 'The finer the nature, the more flaws it will show.'

A third important contributor to the growth of the Gothic Revival, especially in church furnishings and decoration, was the Oxford Movement. Edward Bouverie Pusey, when asked by a correspondent to define 'Puseyism' (a synonym for the Oxford Movement, of which Pusey was perhaps the most articulate leader), listed six points, of which one was 'Regard for the visible part of devotion, such as the decoration of the house of God, which adds insensibly on the mind'. The Oxford Movement exerted a strong influence on the church of the Victorian era to recapture, through the skill of architects such as Herbert Butterfield, the mystery and lavish beauty of church decoration of the medieval period. All Saints, Margaret Street, is the best example in London today of this 'mystery and lavish beauty'.

Saints Named in London Church Dedications

All Saints Dedicated to all the saints. **'All Hallows'** means the same thing.

St Andrew Andrew was a disciple of John the Baptist who, along with his brother Simon Peter, became an early follower of Jesus. Andrew and Simon were fishing, and Jesus called them with the words, 'Follow me and I will make you fishers of men' (see Matthew 4:18-22). He is said to have suffered martyrdom on an X-shaped cross, which became his symbol.

St Alban Alban was born in Roman times, in AD305. Britain's first martyr, he was beheaded for helping a priest escape who was fleeing from persecution.

St Alphage This Saxon saint was bishop of Winchester and later archbishop of Canterbury. He was held for ransom by the Danes and ultimately murdered in 1012. His church still stands at Greenwich.

St Anne St Anne, or Anna, was the aged prophetess serving in the temple who recognized the infant Jesus as the Messiah (see Luke 2:36-38).

St Agnes She was a girl of thirteen who died for her Christian faith in Rome, circa 250. She is one of the youngest martyrs on record.

St Bartholomew St Bartholomew was one of the twelve apostles. According to tradition, he was martyred in India.

St Benet, or St Benedict St Benedict (c. 480-547) was founder of the Benedictine order of monks, author of the Benedictine Rule and in general the father of monasticism in Western Europe.

St Botolph Botolph, or Botulf, studied in Germany and became a Benedictine monk. He founded a monastery at Ikanho, near the present town of Boston, in 654 and died in 680. Somehow Botolph became known as the protector of travellers, a kind of English St Christopher. Churches were dedicated to him at four of London's gates so that those commencing a journey could stop and pray. Three of these churches remain.

St Bride This is a nickname for St Bridget (c. 453-523), an Irish saint nearly as famous as Patrick or Columba. She founded a model monastic community that inspired countless others. Bridget was said to be generous to a fault, giving away not only her own possessions but those of the other members of her family. In reference to this the American writer Phyllis McGinley penned a humorous poem that ends with the lines:

> Who had the patience of a saint
> From evidence presented here?
> St Bridget? Or her near and dear?

St Clement Clement of Rome was a presbyter in the church at Rome in the late first century and the author of 1 Clement, one of the earliest letters of the Christian church in existence outside the New Testament. It was, in fact, read for a time in the early churches as an apostolic letter.

St Cyprian The son of wealthy and cultured pagan parents in Carthage who became a prominent master of rhetoric and probably a lawyer before his conversion in 246. He dedicated himself to poverty, celibacy and the Scriptures, became bishop of Carthage, but because of his strict views was embroiled in numerous controversies. Eventually he was banished and beheaded in 258.

St Dunstan Dunstan was made abbot of Glastonbury in 943 and applied the reforming principles of the Cluniac order to institute stricter rules. He was archbishop of Canterbury 960-88 and was the greatest church statesman of pre-Conquest England. He strove to raise the moral life of the secular clergy, fostered the learning of handicrafts and encouraged the translation of the Gospels into Anglo-Saxon.

St Edmund Late in the ninth century large bands of Danish Vikings drew together in a united body and ravaged the entire eastern regions of England. The *Anglo-Saxon Chronicle* says that in East Anglia 'King Edmund fought against them, but the Danes got the victory and slew the king and subdued all the land and destroyed all the churches they came to'. This occurred in the year 870.

St Ethelburga-the-Virgin Ethelburga was the sister of Erkenwald, bishop of London whose shrine in Old St Paul's attracted thousands of pilgrims. She was the first abbess of the famous convent at Barking in the seventh century. Bede tells the story of her great fortitude during a plague that carried away many of the monks and nuns, and how her own death was foretold in a vision.

St Etheldreda Etheldreda was the daughter of a Saxon ruler named Anna, king of the West Angles. She was born in Suffolk about the year

630 and eventually became abbess of the convent of Ely. She died in 679. Until the Reformation her shrine could be seen in Ely Cathedral. Her nickname was 'St Audrey', and cheap goods sold at a fair held on her saint's day gave rise to the word 'tawdry.'

ESt Helen or Helena St Helen was the mother of Constantine the Great, the first Christian ruler of the Roman Empire. She resided in what is now Trier in Germany and made a pilgrimage to Palestine, founding the Church of the Nativity in Bethlehem. She is said to have discovered a piece of the true cross.

St James There are three Jameses prominent in the New Testament, two of them among the original twelve apostles and the other, James the brother of Jesus and leader of the church in Jerusalem, later recognized as an apostle. However, dedications to St James are usually understood to mean James the Great, the son of Zebedee and brother of the apostle John. He is the patron saint of Spain, where his bones are said to be enshrined at St James Compostela. In medieval times (and even in our own day) this was an extremely popular destination for pilgrimages.

St Katherine St Katherine (or Catherine) was a Roman lady who, in the year 307, professed Christ at a sacrificial feast proclaimed by the Emperor Maximilius. She was condemned to be tortured on a toothed wheel, but the wheel broke at her touch and she was instead put to death with a sword. Her emblem is the 'Katherine-Wheel.' Being of royal blood, she eventually was adopted as the patron saint of English queens. The 'Cree' in St Katherine Cree is derived from 'Christ' or 'Christ Church'.

St Lawrence (Laurence, Laurentius) He was one of seven deacons at Rome during the time of the Emperor Valerian. According to tradition, Lawrence was commanded by the Roman praetor to deliver up the church's treasure. He assembled the poor who were under his charge and said, '*These* are the treasures of the church'. For this he suffered martyrdom by being roasted alive on a gridiron, now his symbol (to be seen on the weathervane).

St Magnus There was a St Magnus who was the Norwegian earl of the Orkneys in the twelfth century. He was murdered by his cousin in 1116 and buried in Kirkwall Cathedral, canonized in 1135. But if the Church of St Magnus, Martyr, was dedicated in the eleventh century or before, there must have been an earlier St Magnus who is now unknown.

St Margaret Margaret of Antioch probably was a martyr under Diocletian in 303. References are made by the early church writers Ambrose and John Chrysostom of a Margaret who, being threatened with rape, jumped to her death off a building and thus preserved her chastity. She was the subject of a medieval cult and was one of the 'voices' heard by Joan of Arc.

St Martin This is St Martin of Tours (c.385-400), pioneer of monasticism in Gaul, missionary and instructor of missionaries. Martin, son of a pagan Roman soldier, was attracted to Christianity at an early age. His father enlisted him in the army at age fifteen. At age eighteen, on the way to Amiens in freezing weather, he divided his cloak with a beggar. Later he had a vision of Christ wearing the divided cloak. He began monastic life with Hilary at Poitiers, founded several communities and, in later life, was made bishop of Tours by popular acclaim.

St Mary or St Mary the Virgin Dedicated to the mother of Jesus.

St Michael the Archangel Michael, leader of the heavenly hosts against the forces of evil. He is mentioned in the Bible in Daniel 10, Jude 9 and Revelation 12:7.

St Nicholas Probably because of his alleged generosity, Nicholas is one of the most popular patron saints of all time. He especially favours seamen and travellers, and there are over 300 churches dedicated to him in Britain, mostly near the coast. He was also believed to bring gifts to children on December 6, his feast day. The original Nicholas was bishop of Myra in Asia Minor in the fourth century.

St Olave Olav Haroldson was a Norwegian who in 1014 assisted the Saxon king Ethelred the Unready in a defence of London against the Danes. His oarsmen put cables around the piers and pulled down the old wooden London Bridge to prevent the enemy from invading from the south. Later, as king of Norway, he was killed in battle by the nobles, who resisted his attempt to make them Christians by force.

St Peter Peter was the apostle to the Gentiles and, according to Roman Catholic tradition, was the first bishop of Rome. He was thought to have been crucified near Rome during the persecution by Nero in AD64.

St Saviour Dedicated to our Lord.

St Stephen Stephen was a deacon in the church formed in Jerusalem at Pentecost. He was stoned to death by Greek-speaking Jews after a fiery speech, becoming the first Christian martyr (see Acts 7:54-60).

St Vedast Vedast was a priest in Gaul, now modern France. In the year 496 he baptized Clovis, the pagan king of the Franks (Germans) with three thousand of the warriors. He became bishop of Arras in 499. Only one other church in England bears his name.

St Mary Aldermary, unusually, was rebuilt by Wren in Gothic style.

American Associations in London Churches

The following London churches have associations of particular interest to Americans:

All Hallows, Barking President John Quincey Adams married here, 1797.

St Bride's Pilgrim Fathers memorial reredos; altar and monument commemorating Edward Winslow, founder of the Society For the Propagation of the Gospel in New England; memorial to Virginia Dare, first English child to be born in America.

St Clement Danes American Shrine to the 19,000 airmen killed in World War II.

St Ethelburga's, Bishopsgate Memorial windows to Henry Hudson.

St Margaret's, Westminster John Greenleaf Whittier, American poet, quoted in memorial window to John Milton; monument to Capt. Peter Parker, naval hero killed in a battle against the Americans; memorial to Sir Walter Raleigh, who made early voyages to America, named the territory 'Virginia' after Queen Elizabeth, and introduced potatoes and tobacco to England.

St Sepulchre Monument to Capt. John Smith enumerating his exploits, including his rescue by Pocahontas; also windows commemorating his voyage to Virginia in 1607. See also statue of Captain John Smith in courtyard at the right of St Mary-le-Bow.

Southwark Cathedral Memorial chapel to John Harvard, founder of Harvard University.

Christian Bookshops in Central London

Catholic Truth Society, Westminster Cathedral Piazza, 25 Ashley Place, London SW1, tel. 834-1363

Christian Literature Crusade, 26-30 Holborn Viaduct, EC1, 583-4835

Church House Bookshop, 31 Great Smith Street, London SW1, 222-9011

Friends Book Centre, Friends House, Euston Road, London NW1, 387-3601

London Institute for Contemporary Christianity, St Peter's Church, Vere Street, London W1, 629-3615

Mowbrays, 28 Margaret Street, London W1, 580-2812

Salvationist Publishing & Supplies Ltd., 117/121 Judd Street, Kings Cross, London WC1, 387-1656

Scripture Union Bookshop, 5 Wigmore Street, London W1, 493-1851

St Pauls Multi Media Bookshop
199 Kensington High St
London W8 6BA.
M - Sat. 9.30 - 5.30
071 937 9591
↔ Kensington High St.

SPCK Bookshop with Chas. Higham Secondhand Religious Books, Holy Trinity Church, Marylebone Road, London NW1, 387-5282 ↔ Great Portland Street
(M - Th 9 - 5.30) (F 9.00 - 5.00)

Tavistock Bookshop, 86 Tavistock Place, London WC1, 837-7661

The Well, 2 Eccleston Place, London SW1, 730-7303

Westminster Abbey Bookshop, 20 Deans Yard, London SW1, 222-5565

In addition to the above, a number of the churches listed in this book operate bookstalls selling books, pamphlets, postcards, slides and so on related to the particular church, as well as Bibles and other religious literature.

Calendar of Official Christian Events in London

6 January	Royal Epiphany offering in the Chapel Royal, St James
26 January	Australia Day. Service at St Clement Danes
30 January	Decoration of Charles I's statue, Trafalgar Square and commemoration service at St Mary-le-Strand
6 February	New Zealand Day. Service at St Lawrence Jewry
1 March	St David's Day. Leeks given to Welsh Guards at Windsor, attended by the Duke of Edinburgh
17 March	St Patrick's Day. Shamrocks distributed to the Irish Guards
Late March	'Oranges and Lemons' Service at St Clement Danes
Ash Wednesday	Stationers' Company attend service at St Paul's
Tuesday in Holy Week	Bach's 'Passion Music' at St Paul's
Maundy Thursday	Royal Maundy money distributed in Westminster Abbey
Good Friday	Holiday. Widow's dole at St Bartholomew's
Easter Monday	Easter procession at Westminster Abbey
Wednesday after Easter	'Spital Sermon' at St Mary Woolnoth
6 March	Stow Memorial Service at St Andrew's Undershaft
23 March	St George's Day. Services at St George's Chapel, Windsor. Shakespeare's Birthday Service at Southwark Cathedral
25 March	Anzac Day. Service at Westminster Abbey
30 May (approx.)	Pepys Memorial Service at St Olave's, Hart Street
15 September	Battle of Britain Day. Fly-past about midday, thanksgiving service at Westminster Abbey at 3 p.m. following Sunday
21 September	Boys of Christ's Hospital attend service at St Sepulchre's
Late September	Mayor and Corporation attend service at St Lawrence Jewry
1 October (approx.)	Law courts open. Services at St Margaret's, Westminster and Westminster Cathedral
16 October	'Lion Sermon' at St Katharine Cree
Second Sunday in October	Harvest of the Sea Thanksgiving at St Mary-at-Hill, attended by fishmongers and London dignitaries
21 October	Trafalgar Day celebrated; service at St Paul's and parade to Trafalgar Square to commemorate Nelson's victory
5 November	Guy Fawkes night; bonfires and fireworks commemorate the 'gunpowder plot'
11 November	Armistice Day. Service at Cenotaph at 11 a.m. on nearest Sunday (Remembrance Sunday).
22 November	St Cecilia's Day. Musical service at St Sepulchre, Holborn
30 November	St Andrew's Day
1st Tuesday in Advent	Handel's 'Messiah' at St Paul's Cathedral
25 December	Christmas Day
26-28 December	Carol service and procession at Westminster Abbey

Times of Opening

British Library and British Museum
Open Mon to Sat 10-5; Sun 2.30-6

Hampton Court Palace
April to September: Open Mon to Sat 9.30-6; Sun 11-6
October to March: Open Mon to Sat 9.30-5; Sun 2-5
Closed 24,25,26 Dec and 1 Jan

Jewish Museum
Open Tue to Thur (and Fri in summer) 10-4; Sun (and Fri in winter) 10-12.45
Closed Mondays, bank holidays and Jewish holidays

Museum of London
Open Tue to Sat 10-6; Sun 2-5
Closed Mondays, 24,25,26 Dec and 1 Jan

National Gallery
Open Mon to Sat 10-6; Sun 2-5
Closed Good Friday, May Day, 24,25,26 Dec and 1 Jan

National Portrait Gallery
Open Mon to Fri 10-5; Sun 2-6
Closed 24,25,26 Dec, 1 Jan, Good Friday, 2 May

St Paul's Cathedral
Open 7.30-6 (summer); 7.30-5 (winter)

Tate Gallery
Open Mon to Sat 10-5.50; Sun 2-5.5 *Closed* Good Friday, May Day, 24,25,26 Dec and 1 Jan

Tower of London
Open Mon to Sat 9.30-5; Sun 2-5
Closed Good Friday, 23-26 and 31 Dec, 1 Jan

Victoria & Albert Museum
Open Mon to Thur and Sat 10-5.50; Sun 2.30-5.5 *Closed* Fridays; 24,25,26 Dec, 1 Jan and 2 May

Westminster Abbey
Open Mon to Fri 9-4; Sat 9-2, 3.45-5; Sundays and great festivals open to those who are attending services